The Influence of East Europe and the Soviet West on the USSR

edited by
Roman Szporluk

Published in Cooperation with the
University of Michigan Center for
Russian and East European Studies

The Praeger Special Studies program—
utilizing the most modern and efficient book
production techniques and a selective
worldwide distribution network—makes
available to the academic, government, and
business communities significant, timely
research in U.S. and international economic, social, and political development.

F.

3

The Influence of East Europe and the Soviet West on the USSR

PRAEGER SPECIAL STUDIES IN INTERNATIONAL POLITICS AND GOVERNMENT

Praeger Publishers   New York   Washington   London

Library of Congress Cataloging in Publication Data
Main entry under title:

The Influence of East Europe and the Soviet west on the USSR.

   (Praeger special studies in international politics and
government)
   Based on revised and updated papers presented at a
conference on the influence of Eastern Europe and western
areas of the USSR on Soviet society, sponsored by the Center
for Russian and East European Studies, University of
Michigan, May, 1970.
   "Published in cooperation with the University of Michigan
Center for Russian and East European Studies."
   Includes index.
   1. Russia--Civilization--East European influences--
Addresses, essays, lectures.   2. Russia--Civilization--
Baltic influences--Addresses, essays, lectures.
I. Szporluk, Roman.
DK276.I48   301.29'47   75-3752
ISBN 0-275-07500-1

Lℯ

PRAEGER PUBLISHERS
111 Fourth Avenue, New York, N.Y. 10003, U.S.A.

Published in the United States of America in 1975
by Praeger Publishers, Inc.

Printed in the United States of America

ACKNOWLEDGMENTS

This book consists of studies originally prepared for the Conference on the Influence of East Europe and Western Areas of the USSR on Soviet Society, organized in May 1970 by the Center for Russian and East European Studies of the University of Michigan. In all cases but one they have been substantially revised and/or updated for this edition.

The purpose of the conference was to define the influence on the Soviet Union of the communist-ruled states of East Europe and the areas of the USSR that were incorporated during or after World War II and to determine the extent of this influence. It was hoped that the conference might indicate what further research on this subject was needed and stimulate such research. Thanks are due to all conference participants, in particular to discussants of individual papers: Professors Morris Bornstein, Walter D. Connor, Melvin Croan, Max Hayward, the late Henry L. Roberts, Robert S. Sullivant, and Rein Taagapera. For technical reasons it has proved impossible, unfortunately, to include their contributions here.

The individual authors wish to express appreciation to the following persons for their assistance:

Yaroslav Bilinsky to Professors Volodymyr Bandera and Vsevolod Holubnychy for their kind help with economic and other aspects; to Denys Kwitkowsky for supplying important materials on northern Bukovina; and to the staff of the Prolog Research Corporation of New York City.

Deming Brown to Professors Ladislav Matejka and David Welsh for their extremely helpful advice on Czechoslovak and Polish literature, respectively.

Zvi Y. Gitelman to Judy Donald and Patricia Kolb for their research assistance, as well as to Professors Melvin Croan, Steven M. Goldstein, and William Zimmerman for their valuable comments.

V. Stanley Vardys to Dr. Jaan Pennar, the late Professor Juris Veidemanis, Dr. Rein Taagepera, Dr. Herbert Valdsaar, Professors Ivar Ivask and Astrid Ivask, the late Professor Zeonas Ivinskis of the University of Bonn in Germany, for their helpful comments and suggestions; and to Kate Ewing, who put together the chart on the Baltic production profile and helped in other ways.

On behalf of all contributors to this volume, the editor wishes to thank the Center for Russian and East European Studies, University of Michigan, and Professors Morris Bornstein and Alfred G. Meyer for making possible the conference in which this book originated, and to Professor William Zimmerman, Center Director, for his support of the project at a later stage. The editor is grateful to Anita Grinvalds and Ann Pollack for editing and typing individual chapters, and to Steven L. Guthier for help in preparing the entire manuscript for publication, and for compiling the index.

CONTENTS

LIST OF TABLES

LIST OF FIGURES

INTRODUCTION
Roman Szporluk

After the October Revolution of 1917 Russia was the only country in the world (save Outer Mongolia) to proclaim itself a dictatorship of the proletariat and builder of a new social, economic, and political system. It was only after World War II, however, that the "capitalist encirclement" of the Soviet Union was broken: In East Europe, Poland, Czechoslovakia, Hungary, Romania, Bulgaria, Yugoslavia, Albania, and East Germany "entered the road of socialist construction." In the process they imitated the Soviet example of socialism, but also to varying degrees they deliberately tried to differentiate themselves from the Soviet Union. The Soviet influence on the socialist states of East Europe has often been noted; yet one should not assume, even granted the Soviet Union's superior power, size, and worldwide role, that the existence of a socialist Eastern Europe for over 25 years has had no influence on the Soviet Union. The participants in this conference felt that an assessment should be made of the influences East Europe might have had on the USSR, and that, whatever their findings would be, these would add something to our understanding of the Soviet Union.

There are several reasons to expect socialist states established in East Europe after World War II to have exercised an influence on the Soviet Union. First, socialism as conceived by Marx and Lenin is an international system that in principle rejects national narrowness, isolationism, xenophobia. Accordingly, one might assume a priori that any socialist state would be willing and ready to learn of the experiences of others and to adopt them whenever appropriate. Since East European states, in particular Czechoslovakia, Poland, and East Germany, were starting from a higher level of development in 1945 than Russia had achieved in 1917, it was reasonable to anticipate that their own progress toward socialism might result in developments interesting to the Soviets. A variety of economic, political, and cultural traditions, institutions, and ideas provided by the inclusion of East and Central European nations into the socialist orbit prima facie should have been a factor stimulating receptivity to new socialist experimentation in the Soviet Union itself. (Needless to say, for the same reasons it could have been postulated that individual East European countries would be learning from the USSR and sharing experiences with each other.) Victory in the war, having secured for the Soviet Union not only peace but a powerful position in Europe, presumably should have removed any suspicion that openness to external influence would be a threat to the regime.

1

There also were reasons for expecting that the Soviet Union, which had undergone its Stalinist revolution in the 1930s, would be resistant to change, especially foreign-inspired change. As it happened, the Soviet Union after the war adopted the view that it had nothing to learn from its junior partners in the socialist bloc, and that they were to be the recipient of its lessons. According to the official ideology of Stalinism, the people's democracies were an inferior form of socialism and they were expected to become more and more like the Soviet proto- type as they progressed. Logically, they eventually would qualify for admission to the Soviet Union as component republics. In fact this did not happen, and the Soviet Union and the bloc at large underwent a profound transformation after the death of Stalin. The recognition of the socialist nature of Tito's Yugoslavia by the post-Stalinist Soviet leadership had profound and long-ranging theoretical implications in relativizing the historical position of the USSR in the family of social- ist states. Since the socialist states of East Europe have survived as independent states (formally at least) and have been recognized as legitimate socialist states, their very existence has subverted the position of the Soviet Union as the one prototype of the socialist future of mankind. Did this process of international relativization or theo- retical "downgrading" of the Soviet Union make itself felt within the USSR itself, and if so in what way?

EAST EUROPE'S IMPACT ON THE USSR

Professors Zvi Gitelman (University of Michigan), Leon Smolinski (Boston College), Zygmunt Bauman (Tel Aviv and Leeds), and Deming Brown (University of Michigan) have examined, in areas of their respective special expertise—politics, economics, sociology, and literature—whether the Soviet Union has been influenced by its fellow socialist states, in what way, and to what degree.

Gitelman examines the diffusion of political innovation from East Europe to the USSR under conditions specific to the Soviet-East Euro- pean relationship. Under Stalin the nature of the relationship was imperial. Eastern Europe was completely subordinated politically to the Soviet Union. In the post-Stalin era, when relations of subordi- nation ceased, new institutions, organizations, and political ties began to evolve, and the relations between the Soviet Union and Eastern Europe became consensual and then, in part, cooperative. In Gitel- man's view, the Soviet-East European relationship is still in the process of self-definition and for this reason no stable process of the diffusion of political influence has so far been established. His study seeks to formulate some general conclusions about the

mechanism of the diffusion, to identify the rules of the game of innovation diffusion, and to examine three case studies of innovation
diffusion in Yugoslavia, Czechoslovakia, and Hungary. These studies
show how difficult the East European political situation is; innovation
must be made in a highly uncertain atmosphere, and the USSR's treatment of Czechoslovak and Hungarian political innovations illustrates
the dilemma of partial political autonomy.

Smolinski argues that it might have been beneficial for the Soviet
Union after World War II to have allowed the East European socialist
countries to adopt the Soviet models selectively and to modify them
according to local conditions and needs. Such a selective adaptation
might have helped to introduce correctives in the Soviet economy as
well. Moreover, this approach might have made the socialist system
more attractive and acceptable to the "uncommitted" countries in
search of better methods of economic development. Had this approach
been adopted, East European influence on the USSR could have been
very strong. However, the Soviet government did not take this view
because it believed that Eastern Europe was destined to pass along
the same road that Russia had traveled, with only minor adjustments
as to tempo.

After Stalin's death, Smolinski says, it was plausible to expect
that Soviet theorists and practicing economists would become willing
to learn from East Europeans. For a considerable time, however,
there were very few contacts between East European and Soviet economists. Gradually, the situation improved. Economists began to
attend joint conferences and some Polish works were put out in Russian
translations. Polish-language literature, including the periodical
press, began to reach the Soviet Union, and other channels of potential
influence such as the Comecon commissions and individual contacts
were used. On the whole, though, the effect of these contacts seems
to have been small.

The two most important long-term departures from the Soviet
model—the retention of individual peasant farming in Poland and
Yugoslavia, and the establishment of workers' councils in Yugoslavia—
had no influence on the Soviet Union, despite the interest initially
displayed by Khrushchev in Yugoslav worker self-government. Conceivably, the Soviets' decision to disband their machine tractor
stations may have been influenced by the previous analogous decision
implemented in Poland. Smolinski believes that East European influences upon the development of Soviet mathematical economics, as
well as applications in planning, also have been small. It appears that
Soviet scholars were completely ignorant of the important work done
by Yugoslavs in this area beginning in the 1950s. The Soviets have
acknowledged some influence on the part of economists from Poland
and Hungary.

In the field of economic policy and reform, while it is true that some measures first taken in East European countries have later been followed in the USSR, the chronology in itself does not allow us to attribute the Soviet actions to East European influence.

Smolinski believes that one development, the establishment of sovetskie firmy by merger of several establishments producing the same kind of products, was influenced by the Polish and Czechoslovak example; interestingly enough, the first such Soviet firm was organized in the West Ukrainian city of Lvov (Ukrainian form: Lviv), and won official approval only after an interval of several years.

Future East European influence may be felt in a negative way, Smolinski thinks, because Soviet planners may be inspired by the East European example to avoid making certain choices, because they either are unsuccessful or have undesirable political effects. While it is hard enough to give East Europeans credit for inspiring action by the Soviets, it will be even harder to attribute influence to the actions the Soviets decide against. The Czechoslovak experience, where economic reform was combined with a major political departure from the Soviet model, may have had a strongly inhibiting effect on the Soviet desire to imitate East Europe. In the future, Smolinski concludes, East European influences on Soviet economic thought and policies will become more dependent on Soviet domestic developments.

The influence of East European sociology on Soviet science is discussed by Zygmunt Bauman. He limits his discussion to Polish sociology, for he feels that of all East European countries only Poland had a strong independent sociology that was not seriously weakened during Stalin's regime. Poland, according to Bauman, had three original sociological schools and a strong humanist tradition. Polish sociology was most important in fulfilling a legitimizing function for the emerging Soviet social science after 1953; if a Western social science could be used in a socialist country like Poland, then why not in the Soviet Union?

The "old guard" ideologists in the Soviet Union strongly disapproved of sociology. Earlier, the party had distinguished between "historical materialism" as a revolutionary social theory and the bourgeois "pseudo-science" of sociology. Some sociological studies were attempted in the 1920s, but the political situation in the 1930s brought sociological research to a halt. After Stalin's death, however, younger scientists in the USSR supported the methods of Polish sociologists and fought against the old guard to establish social studies in the USSR. The more modern, Western, empirical sociology, for one thing, offered the younger sociologists a chance for upward mobility at a time when purges had ended. Soviet sociology developed very rapidly, and in fact became more advanced than Polish sociology in its mathematical sophistication. Soviet sociology took up problems of management rather than investigative studies of a humanist or socially reformist nature, such as those done earlier in Poland.

Thus Polish sociology did influence Soviet sociology, but the latter borrowed its methods for different purposes. Bauman further seems to imply that Polish sociology (like Western sociology) is becoming more managerial and moving away from its humanist traditions. It may be that Polish and East European sociology will now be more strongly influenced by the Soviets than vice versa.

In discussing Czechoslovak and Polish influences on Soviet literary life, Deming Brown compares the development of literature in Czechoslovakia, Poland, and the USSR since the death of Stalin. During the period of Stalinist control, literary influences went from east to west and the party line was followed on such matters as censorship, policy of the writers' unions, and policy of academic institutions. In Poland and Czechoslovakia, however, the period of Stalinist control had been much shorter than in the USSR (from 1948-49) and literature had not been so corrupted. After 1954 there was a parallel development in all three countries toward more liberalization, less censorship, and more Westernization. In the USSR, for example, there was a rehabilitation of some early twentieth century Russian and Soviet literature, a wider range of permitted literary topics, more translation of Western literature, and a reexamination of historical problems. The development of Polish and Czechoslovak literature had been freer than that of the USSR, and these literatures have been more like Western literatures in esthetic experimentation and psychological and philosophical concerns. Brown concludes, however, that while it is hard to define and measure literary influence, there seems to have been little noticeable Czech or Polish influence on literature in the USSR. The parallel developments in these literatures have other general historical and cultural explanations. Although Soviety liberal writers admired the liberal public stance of Polish and Czechoslovak writers, for example, there is little evidence that their admiration had any direct literary influence.

One of the most interesting problems Brown raises is the influence of Czechoslovak and Polish literatures on non-Russian literatures in the USSR (Estonia, Latvia, Ukraine). Polish, Czech, and Slovak literatures have been translated into Soviet minority languages no less than into Russian, and some Polish and Czech authors have been translated only into Estonian or Ukrainian and not Russian. There has, then, been a selective policy of translation in all literatures of the USSR, but it was less selective in the Baltic and other Western regions of the USSR than in Russia. It may well be that Czech and Polish literatures have influenced the non-Russian Soviet literatures more than the Russian.

THE ROLE OF THE SOVIET WEST

The influence of the areas of the USSR annexed during or after World War II is the other principal theme of this volume. The postwar USSR differs from that of the prewar years, and not only by its vastly expanded international position. The Soviet Union also came out of the war significantly changed in its geographic boundaries and population. It acquired from Finland in 1940, and again in 1944, an area that was incorporated into the Karelian republic (since 1956 an autonomous republic within the Russian Republic). In 1940 three independent states, Estonia, Latvia, and Lithuania, became Soviet. In 1939 the USSR occupied half the territory of Poland. After a period of German occupation (1941-44), it was recovered by the Soviet Union in 1944, with some modifications in favor of Poland (Bialystok and Przemysl). Moldavia—that is, the Romanian province of Bessarabia and a part of Bukovina—was occupied by the USSR in 1940. Finally, by virtue of a Soviet-Czechoslovak treaty, Subcarpathian Ruthenia (Transcarpathian Ukraine) was ceded by Czechoslovakia in 1945.

Some of these areas had belonged to the Russian Empire until World War I; others had never belonged to Russia. In any case, the distinction soon lost meaning because the formerly tsarist provinces that were separated at the end of World War I did not share in the first 20 years of the Soviet regime. For this reason a communist Soviet regime introduced in Lvov in 1939 or in Riga in 1940 was equally alien or equally autochthonous (depending on one's view), even though before 1918 the former city was under Austria while the latter was under Russia. The incorporation of the Baltic states, Western Ukraine, and Moldavia brought into the domestic life of the Soviet Union new people with their own languages, traditions, and problems. Obviously, in a most direct and most important way the Soviet political system, culture, and society exerted an enormous influence on these areas after they became Soviet. Was there a reciprocal influence by these newly Sovietized areas on the Soviet system as it worked in these areas and/or in the rest of the Soviet Union?

The introduction of communist power in the Baltic states and the parts of Poland, Czechoslovakia, and Romania that were incorporated into the USSR is a historical variant of communist takeover that was carried out in ways different from both the "classical" Russian case and the "people's democratic" model. The Sovietization of these areas was properly launched only after 1944. For some reason, both Soviet and non-Soviet scholars have abstained from analyzing and comparing the two parallel processes of "socialist construction" after World War II in East Europe: the East European path properly so called and the other path, which one might call "West Soviet" or "the other" East European.

And yet the student of comparative communism, no less than a historian, should find it instructive to observe what happened in the Western areas of the USSR. In most cases there had existed a close similarity if not identity in the social and economic structure of the Soviet areas and the nearby regions of Poland, Czechoslovakia, or Romania. The West Ukrainian (and ex-Polish) oblasti of Lvov, Ternopol (Ukrainian: Ternopil), and Stanislav (Ukrainian: Stanyslaviv) shared with the regions of Rzeszow and Krakow, in People's Poland, centuries of uninterrupted historical experience preceding the outbreak of war of 1939. The former, however, claimed to have completed building socialism by 1950 or so, while the named Polish provinces, like Poland as a whole, were still building socialism in the 1970s. This happened despite the fact that they "entered the path of socialism" virtually at the same time. (Like West Ukraine, certain districts of present-day Poland, specifically Bialystok and Przemysl, were Soviet in 1939-41, but it has not occurred to anyone to see them for this reason as in any way more advanced than the rest of Poland, which became socialist in 1944.)

The same question may be asked about the fate of the ex-Romanian lands now under the Soviets as compared with the independent Romanian republic, or about Lithuania and Belorussia (which, like the Ukraine, include ex-Polish areas) in comparison with Poland.

It is a merit of the studies of Professors Yaroslav Bilinsky (Delaware), V. Stanley Vardys (Oklahoma), and Stephen Fischer-Galati (Colorado) that they remind us of this "third" road to socialism and thus broaden the material base on which generalizations concerning transition to communism in Europe should be made. The communist regimes installed beyond the Soviet borders imitated and were inspired by Soviet ideas and institutions, but their personnel was recruited from among the local residents—except for the Soviet military and security experts in some countries and/or a contingent of former emigres, long resident in Moscow. The building of socialism in the western areas of the Soviet Union, by contrast, represented the introduction of an imported sociopolitical model that was carried out by a party, state, military, and cultural/ideological apparatus sent there from the East.

Vardys examines the influence or, as he prefers to put it, the role of the republics of Estonia, Latvia, and Lithuania in the development of Soviet society and culture since their reincorporation into the USSR in 1944. (Soviet rule had first been established in 1940, but in 1941-44 the area was under German occupation.) A brief historical review of Balto-Russian relations in the period preceding the establishment of the Soviet regime in Russia concludes with the observation that the Balts had little impact on either imperial policies or Russia's cultural outlook; however, Vardys makes the important point that the

Germans of the Baltic area, both by themselves and as transmitters
of ideas, values, and attitudes originating further west, did exercise
an important influence in prerevolutionary Russia.

Insofar as the contemporary situation is concerned, Vardys
argues that the Balt influence in Soviet politics is weak. Few Balts
have advanced to posts in the central machinery of the state, and those
who did either have been given honorific titles or were identified
through their careers with the interests of Moscow rather than those
of the region they ostensibly represent.

The role of the Baltic region in the economy of the Soviet Union
has been much more significant. Unlike West Ukraine or Moldavia,
this region belongs to the most developed part of the USSR, both in
industry and in agriculture. The three Baltic states, especially
Estonia and Latvia, have high living standards; one consequence is
the immigration to the area from other, less prosperous parts of the
USSR.

Vardys devotes a major part of this study to the role of the Balts
in Soviet cultural and social life, noting that for many Soviet citizens
from the other republics the Baltic area represents "the West." He
believes that this impression is largely correct and refers to the role
of the Balts in the arts, sports, and cultural fashions. The Baltic area
remains more open to influences from Scandinavia and Western Europe.

In order to determine the extent of Baltic influence in "Western-
izing" Soviet society, Vardys suggests that it is necessary first to
examine what interaction exists between the local populations and
Russian and other immigrants who have been attracted to the Baltic
area by its economic progress. Latvians, Estonians, and Lithuanians,
he notes, do mix with Russians and, insofar as can be ascertained,
they tend to exercise a certain cultural influence on the newcomers.
A factor to be borne in mind while considering cultural crossinfluences, Vardys points out, is the tradition of political antagonism
between Russians and the local nationalities. This tradition of conflict
is lacking in relations between the Balts and non-Russian Soviet
nationalities; and in this connection Vardys notes that the Estonians
seem to have been exercising a certain influence on the culture of
the smaller Ugro-Finnic peoples of the Soviet North. Vardys concludes
that, as in the past, so in the foreseeable future, the Baltic republics
will be most effective in the USSR in the broadly defined cultural area;
their political import will remain minimal.

Bilinsky addresses the question of what is happening in contemporary Ukraine: How successfully have West Ukrainians become integrated with East Ukrainians who for centuries have lived in a different
political and cultural milieu? He places his question within a broader
framework—the formation of a general Soviet identity incorporating
all ethnic groups of the USSR, large and small. First, Bilinsky surveys

informal social, literary, and political contacts, noting cases when natives of West Ukraine have earned recognition in literature and the arts in East Ukraine as well. He also shows that among Ukrainian dissenters of recent years there has been a disproportionately high ratio of West Ukrainians, or persons who at some point worked or studied in the West. Economically, West Ukraine has been an underdeveloped, predominantly agrarian region; under the Soviet regime the change does not appear to have been sweeping enough to create jobs outside of agriculture for all who seek them. Bilinsky examines all available evidence concerning the direction of outmigration of local population: Do migrants move predominantly to the Eastern provinces of the Ukraine or to other Soviet republics? The data appear too scarce to allow anything but a very general estimate that a majority of migrants settle within the Ukraine. On the other hand, there has been considerable migration of Russians and East Ukrainians to West Ukraine, and these immigrants constitute the bulk of the leading industrial and managerial personnel. Bilinsky concludes that the influence of West Ukraine on the Ukrainian republic has been small at best in the economic sphere due to the region's significantly lower overall level of development. According to Bilinsky, West Ukrainian influence appears to have been greater in the educational and scientific area, especially in view of the role that Lvov, the most important city in the area, has traditionally played as a cultural center. However, for a variety of reasons the potential impact of West Ukrainians in the universities and scientific institutions of the Ukraine is smaller than might be anticipated. Bilinsky's conclusions point toward the marked role of West Ukrainians in the dissent movement, and as a factor in slowing down the assimilation of Ukrainians to Soviet—or Russian— nationality. Bilinsky does not exclude the possibility that West Ukrainians may play a decisive role in helping to reverse the assimilationist trend. He leaves the question open, however, as one that requires time and more research.

If in regard to its generally low level of development Moldavia resembles West Ukraine, its position within the USSR is peculiar; unlike the people of any other Soviet republic, the Moldavians may well be considered part of an external nationality, Romanian, rather than a nationality in themselves. Fischer-Galati outlines the history of this region, which became part of the Russian Empire in 1812, with the expulsion of Ottoman rule. Moldavia, or Bessarabia, as it was known until its reincorporation by the USSR in 1940, remained an unresolved source of conflict between Romania and the Soviet Union until it was finally ceded by Romania after World War II. However, the resurgence of Romanian nationalism under Gheorgiu-Dej and his successor Ceausescu has inevitably been accompanied by a new sensitivity to the question of Moldavia, its identity, and its role in

Soviet-Romanian relations. Although the Soviet government does not
need to fear that Romania will attempt to detach Moldavia, as it did
in 1918, the Soviet government remains sensitive to the potential
threat of Romanian nationalism in the region and appears to have
blocked contacts between Romania and Moldavia to a degree unparal-
lelled in relations between Soviet border regions and the states on
which they border.

The conference for which these essays were originally prepared
arrived at a general consensus that East Europe and western areas
of the USSR have had an impact on the Soviet system, even though
individual scholars differed as to the precise nature of that influence.

Some thought that these areas had a stabilizing, conservatizing
effect on the Soviet system by making internal change potentially
more dangerous, capable of producing consequences that would detri-
mentally affect the Soviet Union's international position.

Others, perhaps taking a more detached, long-range view,
believed that the inclusion of new territories, and the establishment
of new states professing ideological communion with the USSR, produced a variety of channels conveying influences from the outside to
various segments of Soviet society, such as professional groups or
territorial nationalities.

More immediately and directly, some participants pointed out
that the extension of the USSR and the rise of the socialist camp transformed the ethnic scene in the USSR. These changes made the nationality question more pressing and sensitive than it would have been had
the Soviet Union remained confined within its pre-1939 borders.

The conference did not produce any other consensus except for
the view that the study of Soviet-East European relations should not
be limited to the impact of the USSR on East Europe; it is also necessary to examine the impact of East Europe, including the more
recently annexed territories, on the Soviet state and society.

1

THE DIFFUSION OF POLITICAL INNOVATION: FROM EAST EUROPE TO THE SOVIET UNION
Zvi Y. Gitelman

It is widely acknowledged that since the death of Josef Stalin the nature of the relationship between the USSR and the various states of Eastern Europe has undergone a profound and dramatic alteration. While that relationship is still in the process of definition by the protagonists themselves, it may be asserted safely that new forms of dependence and interdependence among the various elements in the Soviet-East European entity have been evolved. It is generally acknowledged that in the Stalinist era the diffusion of political innovation and the transmission of political messages proceeded overwhelmingly from the USSR to Eastern Europe.

Today the picture is a mixed one. On the one hand, the conventional wisdom seems to be that "It is realistic to assume . . . that no great change is possible in Eastern Europe without corresponding change in Russia itself."[1] On the other hand, East European political systems are often seen as change agents influencing the Soviet system, and generally in a "liberalizing" direction. "Eastern Europe itself has long been recognized as a kind of ideological antechamber to the USSR. What is permitted in Eastern Europe becomes politically available, so to speak, inside the Soviet Union."[2] Since East Europeans seem to have been more adventurous, imaginative, innovative, and heterodox than their Soviet counterparts in such fields as economics, sociology, psychology, politics, and literature, the East European "antechamber" has introduced "liberal" ideas, and in some cases, practices, into the Soviet system.

―――――――――

Reprinted from Comparative Politics Series, vol. 3, no. 01-027 (1972), by permission of the publisher, Sage Publications, Inc.

It is not the purpose of this essay to test competing hypotheses about the direction of innovation flow; its aim is merely to provide an anatomy of the innovation process and its effects. To the hypotheses about innovation flow, we must add the possibility that the interdependent relationship of the Soviet Union and Eastern Europe may also result in a less visible, but no less real, conservatizing effect on the USSR. The USSR is burdened with the necessity of providing political leadership and policy cues for the East European states, and it must reckon with the fact that just as what is politically permitted in Eastern Europe becomes available in the USSR, so that which is politically legitimate in the USSR will be politically available to Eastern Europe. For this reason, since the late 1950s, at least, major doctrinal pronouncements in the Soviet Union have been made "with at least one ear cocked toward possible bloc reactions and domestic echoes of bloc problems."[3] Thus, it may be that Eastern Europe acts as a depressant on liberal innovation in the Soviet Union

The potential Soviet innovator may reason that while a well-socialized and politically reliable Soviet citizenry can absorb significant policy and institutional innovations with no destabilizing consequences to the system, the less thoroughly socialized and less reliable populations of Eastern Europe might react in unpredictable and destabilizing ways to the introduction of such measures. The Soviet population, for which Stalinism had been a more intense and prolonged experience than for any other East European nation, was able to adjust to de-Stalinization in a more satisfactory way, from the point of view of the leadership, than the Polish and Hungarian populations, or even the Romanians and Czechoslovaks. Similarly, it may well have been the case that the Soviet Union was prepared to make economic and political overtures to West Germany in the 1960s, but it was constrained by fear that the expansion of relations between West Germany and some of the other socialist states would weaken the socialist alliance and have detrimental domestic political effects in Poland, Czechoslovakia, and perhaps some of the other socialist states as well.

Our judgment as to the general nature of the East European influence on the Soviet political system rests ultimately on our conception of the nature of the relationship of the USSR and Eastern Europe and on empirical investigation of influence flows between the entities. It would be very useful for heuristic purposes if we were able to characterize the USSR/Eastern Europe entity as analogous to a known entity or type of relationship. The latter could then serve as a model for the USSR/Eastern Europe, and we could study the process of innovation diffusion in the model in order to generate testable hypotheses about the same process in the entity we are analyzing. However, the USSR/Eastern Europe in the post-Stalin era seems to be a regional alliance of a very special—perhaps unique—type, and it is difficult to find a heuristically useful model for it. Therefore, we shall content ourselves with describing and analyzing some of the defining characteristics of this entity, as well as indicating the changes that have transformed the Soviet empire into the present entity.

It may be useful to regard USSR/Eastern Europe in the Stalinist era as an empire. According to Ghita Ionescu, an empire is characterized by three basic elements:

(1) a political center animated by a historical mission of expansion; (2) religious or ideological coercion used to weld it into a single coordinated or expanding unit; (3) a sense of final purpose justifying it and inspiring its officers, soldiers and officials to transcend their individual role in the particular phase of development in which they find themselves. In the case of Stalin's Russia the three elements can be clearly seen.[4]

The imperial nature of the Soviet-East European relationship was manifested in complete political subordination of Eastern Europe to the Soviet Union, the methods of deviance control employed by Stalin, the economic relationships between the Soviet Union and the East European countries, the position and role of Soviet "advisers" and diplomats, as well as police functionaries, in Eastern Europe, the patrimonial leadership system, the narrow range of permissible political behavior, and, in general, the conformity to and imitation of the Soviet model that was forced upon all satrapies. To be sure,

even in 1949-1953, years which are considered to have been the "golden age of unity," the influence of the objective specific conditions was apparent in the policy of the individual Communist and workers' parties, at least to some degree, although this fact was not part of the theory on the relations among the socialist states at that state of development.[5]

But despite variations from the norm, such as Poland's abstention from collectivization of agriculture, it can be fairly stated that the Soviet Union and Eastern Europe were involved in an essentially imperial relationship.

It was the Soviet leadership after Stalin that consciously set about to alter this relationship, and it was supported in this effort by some of Stalin's former satraps who were eager to change their roles from that of patrimonial satraps at least to feudal vassals able to generate and command significant power resources of their own. The Soviet leadership, and particularly Khrushchev, changed both the theory and practice of Soviet-East European relations. Whereas previously coercion had been the usual way of repressing strains and controlling deviation on any major issue, Soviet leaders now entered bargaining relationships with East European leaders, though the coercion option remained available for use in extreme cases. "To bargain with subordinates implies some lessening of differences of status,"[6] and it is clear that this change in behavior was symptomatic of a larger change in the nature of the Soviet-East European relationship as a whole. R. V. Burks has written of changes in three types of linkages between the Soviet Union and the East European states:

(1) whereas under Stalin, leaders in Eastern Europe were "appointed and removed by the Kremlin much in the fashion of party cadres in the Soviet Union proper . . . Moscow no longer appoints and Moscow no longer removes." (Although, one might add, Moscow retains influence and perhaps even veto power over major appointments.)

(2) Policy formulation and implementation, once the exclusive privilege of the Soviet Union, is now a national responsibility, though it is in the interest of East European states to "follow the Soviet lead in all matters which do not affect them directly" since "Accretions to Soviet power and prestige in the international area generally reflect favorably on the kindred Communist polities of Eastern Europe."

(3) Ideology has become more important as a cohesive force holding the USSR and Eastern Europe together.[7]

Along with the diminution of coercion and the increased importance of ideology as cohesive forces, organizational devices and formal institutions, such as Comecon and the Warsaw Pact, replaced the highly informal and personal ties connecting Stalin and the East European satraps. Furthermore, whereas in the Stalinist system all units of the empire were isolated from each other to a great degree, so that each unit would form dependent and firm ties only with the Soviet center itself, in the present stage all sorts of genuine lateral ties have been formed among the East European states. They are now linked to each other, as well as to the Soviet Union, by a variety of formal instruments and informal devices. Moreover, whereas subnational units, such as professional groups, had been isolated and sealed off from their counterparts in other countries during the Stalin era, today these ties exist and seem to be growing in intensity and number. Thus, in some senses there is a higher degree of integration in USSR/Eastern Europe today than there was in 1949-53. In fact, this integration creates a new type of political system, a "concentric" or "dual" one, whose characteristics and importance we shall explore later.

In somewhat more general terms, we can characterize the changes that have come about in the post-Stalin era as changes in the mix of prescriptive and restrictive messages emanating from the Soviet Union and transmitted to Eastern Europe, and as changes from consensual relations to some approximation of cooperative ones. The Soviet Union has ceased to issue, directly or by implication, detailed directives on domestic and foreign policy to its East European allies, but it continues to define the limits within which policy choices can be made, those limits having been broadened considerably since 1953. This shift from a prescriptive to a restrictive role is paralleled by a similar shift in the domestic activities of Soviet and East European governments, with the exception of Albania. Kenneth Jowitt has pointed out that the changing nature of relations among the socialist states of Europe can be understood as a change from consensual relations, as Irving Louis Horowitz defines them, to cooperative ones. Consensual relations involve

> shared perspectives, agreements on the rules of association
> and action, a common set of norms and values. [Cooperation]
> makes no demands on role uniformity but only upon proce-
> dural rules. Cooperation concerns the settlement of problems
> in terms which make possible the continuation of differences
> and even fundamental disagreements . . . . Consensus is
> agreement on the content of behavior, while cooperation
> necessitates agreement only on the form of behavior . . . .
> Cooperation concerns toleration of differences, while con-
> sensus demands abolition of these same differences.[8]

In brief, consensus relations demand conformity on means as well as ends, whereas in cooperative relations there is agreement on ends, and agreement to disagree on means. The fundamental difficulty in Soviet-East European relations is that while lip service is paid consistently to the shift from consensual to cooperative relations, very often counterdoctrines (such as the so-called "Brezhnev Doctrine") are enunciated that effectively vitiate the agreement to disagree on means, the rationale for these counterdoctrines often being that betrayal of goals, rather than pursuit of different means, has "objectively" taken place.[9] Certainly, the proclaimed change to the acceptance of "multiple paths to socialism" is frequently contradicted by inconsistencies and contradictions in behavior. The problem is that the Soviet Union has not committed itself decisively and consistently to cooperative relations with other socialist states. Since the nature of the relationship and the rules of the game are unsettled and sometimes unknown, the players must operate in an atmosphere of high uncertainty and risk. This makes life especially difficult for innovators and change agents, who cannot easily predict and anticipate Soviet reactions to their innovations.

If these are some of the ways the Soviet bloc has evolved, the question remains as to whether we can comprehend its nature sufficiently to discern consistent behavioral characteristics or to reason about it by analogy to a model. Most Soviet descriptions of USSR/Eastern Europe refer to it as a "socialist commonwealth" (sodruzhestvo), but since so much of Soviet writing on the subject does not separate the normative from the descriptive, treating what ought to be as what is, it is not very helpful for our purposes.[10] Western scholars emphasize the irregularity of intrabloc relations. "The old one-way relations have been replaced by an operational and loosely institutionalized sub-system harboring an atmosphere of mutual dependence and value-sharing."[11] Jan Triska argues that in the world communist movement, including its East European component,

> There is no single state rule-making or policy-articulating organ, although there are contenders for the role. Rule implementation, conflict containment, and decision enforcement are other weak points in the system. The party-states (as well as the system as a whole) depend for their common endeavor on agreement and persuasion, which oscillates from various degrees of assertion to tentative consultative or advisory assistance, depending on the particular actors involved.[12]

In sum, the Soviet-East European alliance system is still very much in the process of self-definition, of working out in theory and in practice the fundamental regularities of its operation. For this reason, we cannot speak of a stable process of the diffusion of political innovation within the entity but must content ourselves with observations on that process at work in several instances and try to formulate some generalizations about the process in the awareness that the nature of the process will change as the nature of the entity itself changes. We will therefore examine some general propositions about innovation diffusion, point out some of the unique characteristics of innovation diffusion in communist systems, and finally, examine two cases that illustrate the rules of the game of innovation diffusion.

AN INVENTORY OF GENERAL PROPOSITIONS
ON THE DIFFUSION OF INNOVATION

Some of the propositions about innovation diffusion have been selected from the literature on the subject in order to better understand the specifics of the process in USSR/Eastern Europe. This set of propositions does not purport to rank-order the most important findings about diffusion innovation, nor even to include them all. It is also not our purpose to test these propositions by the empirical materials. The propositions are designed merely as a checklist, useful for heightening our awareness of how the innovation diffusion process has been perceived and analyzed, and for illuminating the particular process we are studying.

There are many definitions of innovation which vary largely according to the context in which the innovation is studied. In his discussion of innovation in organizations, Lawrence Mohr defines innovation as "The successful introduction into an applied situation of means or ends that are new to that situation. Invention implies bringing something new into being; innovation implies bringing something new into use."[13] For our present purposes we will define innovation as the development and implementation of a program or policy that is institutionalized and generally acknowledged to have systemic significance.

In order to persist and develop, political systems must be attentive and responsive to their environments, including the extranational environments.

> Without openness to new information from their environment . . . self-steering organizations are apt to cease to steer themselves and to behave rather like mere projectiles entirely ruled and driven by their past . . . . Every self-governing system must . . . remake its own memories and inner structure as it acts. These inner changes may be small or large at any particular step, but their cumulative effect is apt to be considerable.[14]

There may be a variety of obstacles to this learning process. Karl Deutsch focuses on "will," implying the desire not to learn, and "power," implying the ability not to have to do so.

> Will and power may easily lead to . . . self-destructive learning, for they may imply the over-evaluation of the past against the present and future, the over-evaluation of experiences acquired in a limited environment against

the vastness of the universe around us; and the over-
evaluation of present expectations against all possibilities
of surprise, discovery, and change.[15]

Both the will and the power of the Soviet Union may impede its reception of inputs, including political innovations, from the East European
states, especially since for historical and ideological reasons the
Soviet Union perceives itself as a teacher and guide, rather than as
a student and disciple, of other socialist states.

It is crucial to our understanding of the Soviet reception of innovative proposals emanating from Eastern Europe to be aware of the
way in which the USSR establishes its criteria for selection and judgment of those proposals:

> The individual in a complex organization . . . does not deal
> directly with all the sources of information potentially avail-
> able to him, nor does he evaluate every conceivable policy
> option. In place of the debilitating confusion of reality he
> creates his own abstract, highly simplified world containing
> only a few major variables. In order to achieve this manage-
> able simplicity he adopts a set of decision rules or standard
> criteria for judgment which remain fairly stable over time
> and which guide him in choosing among sources of informa-
> tion and advice. A decision maker decides both where to
> look for cues and information and how to choose among
> alternatives according to his decision rules; these rules
> also embody the current goals and aspirations of his organ-
> ization, or the values which the organization is designed
> to advance and protect. Hence, if we wish to predict the
> decision maker's behavior, we should try to discover these
> rules of thumb . . . which shape his judgment. His choices
> could then be explained in terms of the alternatives he
> considers, his knowledge of each alternative, the sources
> of his knowledge, and the standard decision rules he applies
> in cases of this kind.[16]

If we may extrapolate from the individual in an organization to decision
makers in a political system, we can see the relevance and importance
of delineating the "rules of thumb" Soviet political decision makers
use when considering innovative political alternatives. We should be
able to predict with greater accuracy which innovative proposals
stand a better chance than others in gaining Soviet attention, and
which are more likely to be adopted, accepted, or tolerated. We shall
explore this subject in the third section of the essay. For the moment,
let us enumerate several propositions about the diffusion of innovation
of a less general and abstract nature.

1. "Several acculturation studies seem to show that the tangible aspects of any culture are more readily diffused than are purely ideo-logical or behavioral aspects."[17] Tangible objects are easier to demonstrate and copy than abstract ideas. Second, "The advantage or disadvantage of one thing over another is more obvious than the advantage or disadvantage of one institution over another because the potentialities of a thing are more closely related to its physical properties. . . . The real point here is that knives are judged by the same standards, whereas religious and marital customs are not."[18] It is probably easier for the Soviet Union to borrow purely technological innovations than it is to adopt new political ideas or institutions, even when they are proposed by kindred socialist states, though some technological innovations may have undesirable "spillover" effects into the political and social arenas.

2. Innovations should demonstrate: (a) relative advantage over the idea or institution superseded; (b) compatibility with existing values and past experiences of the potential adopter; (c) "divisibility . . . the degree to which an innovation may be tried on a limited basis."[19] These three requirements are especially important in regard to the Soviet Union. Soviet decision makers, perhaps to a greater degree than their Western counterparts, are conditioned to assume that they live in the best of all possible worlds, and in order to persuade them to adopt a political innovation, its relative advantages must be clearly demonstrated. Second, since the Soviet system is an explicitly ideological one and is very conscious of its values and historical experiences, compatibility with Marxist-Leninist ideology, as defined by Soviet leaders, is a sine qua non for any proposed innovation. The principle of divisibility, which holds that "New ideas that can be tried on the installment plan will generally be adopted more rapidly than innovations that are not divisible,"[20] is of great importance in the context of USSR/East Europe. The Soviet Union may be willing to experiment with economic reform, but it did so by gradually increasing the number of enterprises operating under the new system, rather than by introducing the reform across the board at a single time, as did the Czechoslovaks and Hungarians. The Soviet leadership would be more reluctant to introduce a sweeping party reform, since that kind of change might have a greater "spillover" effect into many areas of Soviet life than would controlled economic reform. One could also conceive of the possibility that the USSR might want to introduce a new type of relationship with one or two of its East European allies, while maintaining existing relationships with others. This kind of change would not be easily divisible, and so it may be that the necessity to introduce the change, say, from consensual to cooperative relations, to all inter-socialist relationships effectively prevents the USSR from introducing such changes in any of them.

3. The chances for adoption of an innovation are enhanced if that innovation has been successfully adopted in another similar setting. Jack Walker's study of the diffusion of innovation among American states led him to conclude that "the likelihood of a state adopting a new program is higher if other states have already adopted the idea. The likelihood becomes higher still if the innovation has been adopted by a state viewed by key decision makers as a point of legitimate comparison."[21] The Soviet Union would be more likely to adopt an innovation that had been tested successfully in an East European state, particularly one the USSR could view as being somewhat analogous to the USSR in important ways. Clearly, no East European state compares with the Soviet Union in size and world power, but it is likely that the USSR would be more interested in certain kinds of experiences in the more developed socialist countries than in the experiences of Albania, Romania, or Bulgaria.

4. Some commentators on innovation diffusion and communication postulate that "at least some parts of the receiving system must be in highly unstable equilibrium, so that the very small amount of energy carrying the signal will be sufficient to start off a much larger process of change."[22] In a study of innovation in organizations, James Q. Wilson argues that "many organizations will adopt no major innovation unless there is a 'crisis'—an extreme change in conditions for which there is no adequate, programmed response."[23] It is possible that internal instability may promote a search by Soviet political leaders for alternative modes of political or economic organization, and it is undoubtedly true that it is precisely in times of leadership instability and power struggle that innovative policies and programs are introduced. These become weapons in the leadership struggle. The system may be most open to the introduction of new programs and policies at times of leadership struggle. On the other hand, such a situation, while it promotes internally generated innovation, may retard the acceptance of externally generated proposals for change since there may also be a reluctance to ask for the aid of supposedly inferior units in resolving disputes in the superior unit. This question should be explored further by examining the use made of East European programs and policies in Soviet leadership disputes, or more generally, in times of instability in the Soviet system as a whole.

5. "A voluntary association with broad, diffuse goals (typically associated with relatively low salience) will adapt more readily to environmental changes than will organizations with narrow, precisely stated goals (typically associated with high salience)."[24] Relative to other political systems, the USSR has narrow, ideologically defined, precisely stated goals which have high salience both within and without the system. Since these goals are relatively specific and there is a high awareness of them, all innovations and changes must be

justified in terms of those goals. This imposes an additional burden upon the East European change agent, his Soviet linkage group or actor, and Soviet decision makers.

6. "A generalization supported by many studies is that impersonal information sources are most important at the awareness stage, and personal sources are most important at the evaluation stage in the adoption process."[25] Soviet decision makers may become aware of East European innovations through publications and other impersonal sources, but when decision makers must evaluate the innovations, personal relations among leaders in Eastern Europe and the USSR and personal persuasion become   important. One advantage that East German and Hungarian innovators may enjoy is that Ulbricht or Honecker and Kadar seem to have the confidence and respect of the Soviet Politburo. This was not true of either the Novotny or Dubcek leaderships in Czechoslovakia.

7. Another "psychological" variable involves the characteristics of the linkage groups which transmit innovation from one system to another. First, "A linkage group becomes much more susceptible to the inputs from abroad if its ties to the domestic system are weakened—if it is, for instance, a segregated or discriminated minority, or if it is an economic class or social class which is disadvantaged or alienated."[26] This might apply to national minority groups, such as Ukrainians or Jews in the USSR, and could also include economic reformers, political nonconformists, dissident intellectuals, and other "nonestablishment types." Of course, while these groups may be more receptive to assuming the role of linkage agent, they are less credible and trustworthy to the recipient of the innovative stimulus. If these groups could, in turn, persuade other, more powerful and prestigious groups to join with them in the attempt to convince the client to accept the innovation, they may be able to overcome their low status disadvantage. In other words, in diffusing innovations from East Europe to the Soviet Union it may often be necessary to reach two kinds of linkage groups: an initially receptive but low-status group which might, in turn, act as a linkage to a less receptive but more influential group.

8. A third psychological factor to be considered is "that cognitive dissonance between a message and a past attitude is resolved by cutting down the message and retaining the attitude, if there is strong social support for the attitude."[27] Deutsch has found that this outweighs "by a factor of four or five to one [the] bandwagon effect." Support for traditional attitudes may not only be found; it may be mobilized as well. An innovative proposal emanating from East Europe, or from within the Soviet system itself for that matter, will undoubtedly encounter strong resistance from "traditionalists" or conservatives, as well as from those who have a vested interest in maintaining the status quo.

9. The psychological characteristics of the client are as important as those of the change agent and the linkage group. Certain individuals are more open-minded and receptive to change than others. Especially in Soviet-type systems, where individual leaders wield so much power, this variable can play an important, perhaps even decisive, role in determining the kind of reception given an innovative proposal. Clearly, Khrushchev's penchant for innovation was far greater than that of his successors, who criticized him for being overly enamored of new, untested schemes.

10. Information about the innovation proposed should be readily available to the client. "We can predict that an anticipated change will be resisted to the degree that the client system possesses little or incorrect knowledge about the change, has relatively little trust in the source of the change, and has comparatively low influence in controlling the nature and direction of the change."[28] The client should be made to feel sure about the consequences of the change. The change effort should be perceived as being self-motivated and voluntary. Finally, the change program "must include emotional and value elements as well as cognitive (informational) elements for successful implementation. It is doubtful that relying solely on rational persuasion (expert power) is sufficient."[29] The Soviet Union demands that proposed innovations, whether they are proposed for adoption in the USSR or merely for implementation in East Europe, remain always under party control, and that their consequences be fully explored. Naturally, it is desirable that the innovations have some expressive value and appeal. It also appears to be of great importance to the USSR to be able to present the innovation as being, in some form or other, self-motivated and certainly taken as a voluntary step, not imposed by any outside forces or by objective circumstances. All changes in Soviet policy and institutions are presented as "creative developments" of traditional values and forms, undertaken as voluntarist initiatives by a progressive system which is responsive to the need for change.

11. Developing the idea of predictability of consequences further, it is important to note that there is an ineluctable element of spillover in the adoption of almost all innovations. Accepting one idea often means that supporting or complementing correlates must also be accepted.[30] Moreover,

Sometimes the changes brought about simply "fade out" because there are no carefully worked out procedures to ensure coordination with other interacting parts of the system. In other cases, the changes have "backfired" and have had to be terminated because of their conflict with interface units.[31]

The Soviet Union cannot accept some types of economic reform since they do not seem to coordinate in an acceptable or desirable manner with "other interacting parts of the system"—the Communist Party apparat, for example. The Leninist formulation of "He who says A must say B" is especially true in a Soviet-type system where the various interacting parts are highly integrated with, and dependent on, each other.

12. Several observers have pointed out the impediments to innovation diffusion and some of the strategies that a change agent can employ to overcome them. The anthropologist A. L. Kroeber points to three general checks on diffusion: lack of communication, resistance in recipient culture, and "displacement." The first is largely a technical problem, except in cases where technological and political impediments to communication are purposively constructed to protect the potential client from external ideas and influences. Stalin's attitude toward the Yugoslavs after 1948 and Soviet and East German measures taken to cut down the volume of communications emanating from Czechoslovakia in 1968 are familiar examples of this kind of behavior. Resistance, according to Kroeber, is usually due either to the presence of traits in the recipient system felt to be irreconcilable with the invading traits, or to "the presence of cultural habits functionally analogous to the new elements which results in a block. Coffee is unlikely to invade rapidly or successfully a nation addicted to tea drinking."[32] This suggests that there may be greater resistances to innovation diffusion among similar political systems—socialist ones, for example—because there are entrenched institutions which can easily interpret the innovative proposal as a threat to their own power, and because the innovation can more easily be regarded as superfluous—its equivalent is already present in the client system. If, on the other hand, the innovation is perceived as not functionally analogous to an existing institution, behavioral pattern, or value, it might be regarded as irreconcilable with or hostile to the existing defining characteristics of the system. One can envision at least four logical possibilities:

● If the innovation is functionally analogous to an element in the existing system, there is a high likelihood of resistance and rejection.
● If the innovation is not functionally analogous and is seen as conflicting with defining characteristics of the system, rejection is also likely.
● If innovation is neither functionally analogous nor seen as challenging to defining characteristics there is a greater chance for favorable consideration and adoption.
● If the innovation seems analogous to accompanying characteristics of the system, there is a possibility of adoption, but a strong

likelihood of resistance to adoption by the vested interests whose function is likely to be transformed or displaced by the innovative proposal.[33]

Karl Deutsch has explored a variety of ways in which a nation-state can reduce or stop the inflow of external inputs. It may count on the disappearance of the external source of inputs, reduce the linkage groups or institutions, cut off contact with the input source, make the domestic system more stable and hence more impervious to external inputs, or try to effect a change in the environment itself. The USSR has employed all these tactics against East European inputs at one time or another, not only to protect itself but also to prevent innovative inputs from flowing from one East European country to another. (Stalin was undoubtedly correct in assuming that innovations would more easily pass from one East European state to another than from them to the USSR. While this essay deals with innovation diffusion from East Europe to the USSR, the intra-East European diffusion of political innovation is probably more frequent and perhaps more successful.) Stalin cut off contact with Yugoslavia and reduced even potential linkage groups by the purges of so-called "Titoists," tried to shore up the domestic political system, and, in a way, counted on the disappearance or increasing irrelevance of the troublesome external threat. These tactics also have been used by Stalin's successors vis-a-vis Hungary in 1956 and Czechoslovakia in 1968. A less visible defense that the USSR has for resisting East European or any other inputs is the "objective" factor of size:

> It is possible that the domestic system may get the same results by its sheer size. A very large country, very pros-perous and with very strong holds upon its population, may be able to withstand even major impacts of foreign propa-ganda by tying its potential linkage groups so strongly to the domestic system that all foreign inputs become rela-tively insignificant. Similar effects can be obtained by multiplying and intensifying small group ties, even in a small country . . . . The ties of integration to the main system become so strong that any inputs from abroad to potential domestic groups remain quite ineffective.[34]

By interlocking the elites of all domestic groups with the Communist Party, and by assiduously cultivating a strong sense of "Soviet patri-otism," the Soviet system has effectively tied its potential linkage groups, with a few exceptions, to the domestic system.

AGENTS, CLIENTS, AND TACTICS OF
INNOVATION PROPOSAL

These, then, are some of the conditions and tactics which militate against the diffusion of innovation from one political system to another. What are the counterstrategies that can be employed by the change agent? If East Europeans consciously or unconsciously play the role of change agents, how can they overcome Soviet resistance to innovation? We have already noted the necessity for a change proposal to be assimilable into the prevailing value system of the recipient, the necessity to have the recipient perceive a need for change, the importance of anticipating the consequences of change, and the wisdom of appealing to strategically placed groups or opinion leaders in trying to reach the final decision makers. Everett Rogers adds:

> Change agents should be more concerned with improving their clients' competence in evaluating new ideas and less with simply promoting innovations per se . . . a long range program to change values may be a more appropriate strategy of attack for some change agents than just a "single innovation" approach to change.[35]

This is probably not a wise strategy to employ when dealing with a Communist system, one which has a profound commitment to a set of values which are not easily abandoned or revised. In fact, it might be best to convince the client that adoption of the innovation involves no change in values whatsoever. It is more advisable to calculate on the incremental erosion of present values and their transmutation over time than to attempt a frontal confrontation and critical assault on fundamental values. As Herbert Shepard points out, one way of innovating in a resisting organization is to conceal the innovation as much as possible.[36]

In a suggestive article on "nonconforming enclaves" in organizations, Ruth Leeds observes that such an enclave often presents its innovations as techniques designed to facilitate attainment of organizational goals, not as a means of changing the goals:

> The commitment inspiring the non-conformists is frequently viewed as higher than that possessed by others in the organization . . . likely to provoke conflict. The non-conforming enclave is further distinguished by an unorthodox atmosphere which permeates many aspects of its life.[37]

Yugoslavia in the early 1950s, Czechoslovakia in 1968, Albania since
the early 1960s, and other nonconforming East European states have
all presented themselves to the USSR and other socialist countries as
affirming the fundamental goals of Marxism-Leninism and as being
more seriously committed to the "transitive" goals of the Communist
ideal than the "orthodox" states which have been diverted to the pursuit of "reflexive" goals and have departed from the true path.[38]
Certainly, the defenders of orthodoxy have charged, and not without
reason, that the general atmosphere prevailing in the deviating states
is not in conformity with established practice and, what is essentially
Soviet, tradition. The deviant or innovative enclaves respond, of
course, that the defenders of orthodoxy have become so committed to
their reflexive goals that new proposals for transitive goal attainment
can only be regarded with suspicion by those vested interests (Djilas'
"new class") which respond to innovative proposals with "trained
incapacity."[39]

Leeds mentions four basic ways in which the organization can
deal with its nonconforming enclave: (1) condemnation; (2) avoidance;
(3) expulsion; (4) protest absorption. The first three tactics will work
only if the enclave is weak. Condemnation will widen the rift by
forcing a polarization of the issues (as has been the case in the USSR's
dealings with Yugoslavia, Czechoslovakia, Poland, Romania, as well
as China). Avoidance might allow the enclave to grow rather than die
out. Expulsion might be in effect a loss of resources (allies) which
could have been channeled to serve organizational goals. Expulsion
might also lead to the emergence of a rival structure—for example,
an alternate "Communist International." Finally, if protest absorption
is the strategy pursued, the nonconforming enclave may gain access
to key positions and heavily influence or control the entire structure.[40]

In the protest absorption process, the organization's leaders will
confront the necessity to balance the demands of the nonconforming
enclave against those of a "middle hierarchy" standing between the
leaders and the enclave. The occupants of the middle-level roles are
the ones most likely to exhibit trained incapacity and are most
directly threatened by the innovative proposals of the nonconforming
enclave. Soviet middle-level officials may be the most strenuous
opponents of innovations which would upset Soviet institutional arrangements and programs. Analogously, the role of Gomulka and Ulbricht
in pressing the Soviet leadership to halt the Czechoslovak experiment
may be understood as similar to middle-level officials trying to get
top-level decision makers to reject decisively innovations with
unacceptable implications for their own bailiwicks. If the middle-
level resistance is overridden by the top leadership, the enclave
gains some autonomy to pursue its innovation:

This is followed by several more rounds of obstruction by
the middle hierarchy, unorthodox communication to the top
by the non-conforming enclave, and a gradually increasing
grant of resources, autonomy, and legitimacy to the enclave
by the top hierarchy. With each round the enclave comes
closer to approximating a new legitimate subunit . . . . In
exchange for autonomy and legitimacy from the top hierarchy, the enclave must agree to accept certain stabilizers
. . . mechanisms to insure the loyalty of the new unit to the
organization and its conformity to organization regulations.[41]

These stabilizers include rules of conduct, a regular source of inputs,
and agreement to limit the innovative activity to a particular sphere.
As we shall see, all these have been operative in regard to the
Hungarian economic reform. The Czechoslovaks' hints about the
relevance of their innovations in all sorts of spheres and beyond their
borders helped kill their chances for acceptance by the Soviet Union
and its allies.
  "In large measure, the significance of protest absorption for the
organization as a whole depends upon the bearing which the enclave's
cause has on the core policies and practices of the organization."[42]
As we have stressed, the closer to the core of Communist doctrine
and practice the innovation is, the more resistance it is likely to
encounter by top-level decision makers, whether within an East European state or the USSR.
  Finally,

An organization which has had long experience with nonconformity, e.g., the Catholic Church, might institutionalize
the rounds of protest absorption . . . . If the adoption of
protest absorption as a conscious organizational policy is
carried out effectively, an organization will strengthen its
ability to cope with non-conformity and to implement
changes flowing upward from the bottom.[43]

The Stalinist experience of rejecting and repressing nonconformity,
rather than absorbing it, has slowed the learning process of the Soviet
leadership. The Soviet leadership is just beginning to explore different ways of dealing with nonconformity, almost by definition involved
in innovation, and it may be a long while before it develops a flexible
response to innovation and nonconformity arising from East Europe,
or from any other quarter.
  These, then, are some of the generalizations about innovation
diffusion commonly found in the literature on the subject, and an

attempt to suggest the utility and relevance of such generalizations for the study of the diffusion of political innovation from East Europe to the Soviet Union.

SOME PROPOSITIONS ON THE DIFFUSION OF POLITICAL INNOVATION FROM EAST EUROPE TO THE SOVIET UNION

It has been remarked that in the literature on innovation diffusion "The prevailing focus of attention is on the individual innovator . . . not on the organizational setting in which innovation takes place."[44] In this section we propose to examine some of the factors specific to Communist systems ("the organizational setting"), especially the USSR, which cause them to deal with political innovation and its diffusion in a distinctive and probably unique way. After describing some of the salient features of the diffusion process from East Europe to the USSR, we shall attempt to draw up some tentative rules of the game for the process, recognizing that the rules themselves are very much a matter of debate and are therefore not permanently fixed or universally agreed upon.

It has long been recognized that the Stalinist system, and particularly the "command economy," had a depressant effect on innovation, not only of a political nature but of a purely technological one as well:

> The immediate difficulty is that innovation, whether indigenous or borrowed, involves much labor and high risk, while the rewards that Stalinist central planning offers in return are inadequate to say the least . . . . A totalitarian command economy is specially designed to prevent automatic, self-perpetuating sub-system processes, technological or otherwise. It is a basic principle that everything of basic importance must be done from above.[45]

Students of the Stalinist system are familiar with the dilemma of the industrial manager who cannot afford to innovate because the introduction of new processes or machinery would interrupt production schedules and the manager would fail to meet quarterly quotas, a failure with perhaps fatal consequences.

After the death of Stalin the Soviet Union was forced to take new departures in the field of foreign policy as well as in the economy. In both sectors there have been dramatic, highly visible new developments which have pressured Soviet leaders to fundamental reassessments and revisions: The advent of the nuclear era led to a change in Soviet global perspectives, and the increasingly inefficient and nonproductive command economy led to experimentation and partial dismantling. There has been no domestic political equivalent of the atom bomb, and, in contrast to some of the East European states, no dramatic political breakdown or crisis has occurred in the Soviet Union. For this reason, among others, there is no great and consistent pressure for political innovation in the USSR, though the Khrushchev era was distinguished (his successors might say marred) by several interesting political experiments and innovations. Czechoslovakia, Poland, Hungary, and the German Democratic Republic (GDR) have been confronted with serious crises which have elicited responses attempting to establish regime authority on the basis of new political formulas.[46] The Soviet Union has faced difficult political problems since 1953, such as declining economic growth rates, nationality rebelliousness, intellectual dissent, failures in the international arena including the "space race," agricultural problems, and some generational problems, to single out a few of the most visible. The new kolkhoz charter, which essentially sanctioned the status quo, the failure to revise nationality policy, the uncertain role of the Communist Party, and the failure to proclaim a new constitution promised since 1963, point to a conservative choice to postpone systemic political changes, presumably in the belief that at the present stage system maintenance is more important than uncertain experiments designed to enhance systemic effectiveness. There is more slack in the Soviet system than in many of the East European ones because a longer and more effective socialization process, undoubted Soviet power and prestige resulting from impressive domestic and foreign achievements, and the isolation of the population from external influences have provided the USSR with a greater reservoir of legitimacy than most other socialist countries in Europe have. Finally, as mentioned earlier, the dramatically different size of the Soviet Union enables it to deal with potential external inputs in a very different way from that in which smaller systems handle these inputs. It can turn its potential linkage groups inward much more easily than can, say, the Polish or Hungarian regimes.

The most obvious element distinguishing the innovation diffusion process among Communist systems from that obtaining within an organization is Marxist-Leninist ideology. One effect of the ideological nexus binding the socialist states together is to exacerbate differences of opinion among them and make disputes harder to solve. "When opposing views or substantive issues are couched in doctrinal terms, each dispute in effect becomes two—one substantive and one ideological—and demands buttressed by claims of ideological purity do not lend themselves easily to compromise."[47] Brzezinski claims that ideological disputes are not easily resolved by compromise, as financial or border disputes would be:

Barring an outright split, the usual solutions tend to be more extreme: the agreement of one protagonist to become doctrinally silent, although not necessarily retracting his original views; or the doctrinal subordination of one to the other. A third solution, a mutual agreement to become silent, is not stable if one of the parties involved is the center, since a doctrinally oriented movement cannot remain doctrinally silent in the face of continually changing reality.[48]

Nish Jamgotch, who views ideology as the "irreducible unifying force" of the Communist bloc, argues that the very power of the Soviet Union as an "ideologically oriented great power . . . must ultimately depend on its political transplants abroad."[49] While this seems to press the case for the importance of ideology too far, there is no doubt that ideology is an important component of Soviet-East European relations and that innovative proposals, even of a seemingly nonideological character, are very often evaluated in ideological terms, with the tacit or overt admission that the ideological effects of every innovation constitute one of its most important consequences.

A second, related consideration is the claim that "In a monolithic alliance, if non-conforming behavior should be successful in one issue-area, there is a high probability that such behavior will 'spill over' into other issues areas."[50] It was the realization of this truth that prompted Stalin to take such elaborate prophylactic measures against Yugoslavia, and that explains much of the behavior of the Soviet Union, Poland, and the GDR in Czechoslovakia in 1968. But in at least one instance the alliance leaders opted for a different tactic of deviation control. Rather than cracking down directly on Romania, the Soviet leadership has calculated correctly that it could afford to allow the "Romanian deviation" because it would remain an isolated phenomenon, not successfully emulated in other socialist countries.[51] Here the tactic of partial isolation has been successfully used. The Romanian party leadership has demonstrated that it is capable of preventing the spillover of heresy from foreign policy to domestic affairs, and this goes a long way to explaining Soviet tolerance of the Romanian regime.

The doctrinal component of Communist relations also accentuates the usual relationship between deviance and innovation. Almost all innovators are ipso facto deviants since they depart from the prevailing norms. In Communist systems, departure from prevailing norms is assumed to be not merely deviant behavior proceeding from ignorance or lack of ability but calculated nonconformity based on nefarious motivation and values. The worker who performed poorly in the Stalinist system was not merely a laggard but a "wrecker."

The motives of the innovator are always probed deeply in order to discover the "real" reason for his advocacy of the innovation. This is reflected by the Communist rhetoric of "hiding behind leftist phrases," "concealing true motivations," being "unmasked," "posing as a friend of the labor movement," and the like. Especially in a system which has no place for political competition and where all legitimate alternatives are defined by the party alone, nonsanctioned suggestions for innovation immediately raise questions about motivation and antisystemic attitudes. Even when the innovator denies deviation and strives very hard to prove his orthodoxy in deeds as well as in words, he is likely to be told that he is "objectively" a traitor, since by departing from official norms and even indirectly challenging authority he "objectively plays into the hands of the enemies of socialism." "Innovators are forced into a combative position" because "their novelties enter a social organization most of whose establishments are going concerns" and their innovations "enter as competitors or deprecators of one or another."[52] This general truth is magnified several times in the context of Communist systems and alliances.

Turning now to some structural considerations, we hypothesize that the type of leadership situation in the Soviet Union may directly affect the fate of political innovations, whether ideological or institutional, emanating from East Europe. It has often been said of the present Soviet leadership that its general conservatism is partially explained by the fact that a coalition leadership cannot strike out in bold, new directions since it needs to gain consensus on major policy decisions, and consensus decisions tend to be agreements on the lowest common denominator. Radical policies and experimentation are potentially destabilizing and are therefore to be avoided. This means that innovations with system-destabilizing implications will not be entertained by a collective leadership. This is persuasive only if there is no one in the leadership who is looking precisely for a chance to destabilize the leadership itself. If a member of the coalition is seeking to enhance his own power at the expense of others, he may be very tempted to borrow and champion an innovation as a "new look" or better policy. Khrushchev's breakup of the post-Stalin leadership and his ascendancy to the role of single or foremost leader was achieved in exactly this way. Under the one-man leadership system the leader may adopt innovations since he feels secure enough to experiment with them; he may reject them if he feels that his position is so precarious that a disastrous experimental failure would seriously threaten or erode his power, and in some instances he may even be forced to adopt innovations in order to secure his position. Tito in 1950 and Khrushchev six years later used extensive institutional and ideological policy innovations as weapons with which to fight off external and internal enemies and as tools to build more secure power bases for themselves.

Psychological as well as structural characteristics of leadership are important in determining the fate of an innovation proposal. Especially in systems where power is so highly centralized in the hands of a relative few, their psychological characteristics, insofar as they affect their political decisions and preferences, must be taken into account. To put it simplistically, we suggest that certain personality types are more likely to be receptive to innovation than others. There is differentiation among Communist leaders along these dimensions, just as there is among others. Some leaders tend to have more open minds than others, in the sense that while they, too, are committed to an ideology, they hold to it within an open mind which retains the capacity for reconceptualizing the nature of problems and synthesizing the elements in a new way. Those with closed minds have only analytic capacities—they can break down problems and suggest specific solutions to component parts, but they cannot reintegrate the whole into a new synthesis. Without being so foolish as to attempt long-distance psychology, it is tempting to suggest that Antonin Novotny consistently exhibited the traits of a closed mind, whereas Alexander Dubcek, a man of very similar background, training, and experience, displayed traits of the open mind, at least in 1967-69.[53]

One element in the USSR's claim to primacy is the fact that it was the first and for many years the only socialist state in the world. Vernon Aspaturian comments that

> There is . . . something absolute and irrevocable about chronological primacy. It can be neither reversed by historical repagination nor erased by ideological deracination. As the first party-state, the Soviet Union will continue to be the inspiration, direct or indirect, of all future Communist states, just as it survives as the common genealogical ancestor of all existing party-states.[54]

The chronological primacy of the Soviet Union is a brick in the barrier against the penetration of East European innovations because the "Soviet model" serves as the standard by which all innovative proposals are judged. The undoubted long-term successes of the Soviet Union domestically and internationally buttress the conviction that the most efficacious political system in the social world is the Soviet one, and the proponents of that system look with skepticism at attempts to "improve" the model. Success itself may prevent further learning and development.[55] The "importance of being first" is sufficient compensation for any possible feelings of inferiority vis-a-vis the more "sophisticated" Poles, Czechoslovaks, or

Hungarians. The conviction that the USSR is the socialist state closest
to a Communist society implies that to borrow from less developed
socialist states does not make historical good sense.

There are generally two ways in which East European ideological
and institutional innovations make an impact on the Soviet political
system: as the bearers of otherwise unacceptable, nonsocialist
political ideas and mechanisms, and as inputs into debates among
interest groups in the USSR. Since the loosening of the alliance and
the dismantling of the empire, the role of East Europe as a relevant
factor in the domestic political process in the USSR has increased,
and the increasing legitimacy and stature of the East European states,
combined with the greater openness of the Soviet system, has made
it possible for the East Europeans to serve as "transmission belts"
for Western ideas. A prime example of this is the role of Polish
sociology in the transformation of Soviet sociology into a discipline
more closely approximating Western sociology.[56] Since empirical
sociology was legitimate and officially sanctioned in one socialist
country, it could be adopted by a second socialist country. What could
not be borrowed directly from the West could be adopted if it had a
socialist imprimatur.

In his study of national-international linkages, James Rosenau
delineates three basic types of linkage processes:

1. "Penetrative"—where members of one polity actually participate in the political process of another. "That is, they share with
those in the penetrated polity the authority to allocate its values."
2. "Reactive"—"The actors who initiate the output do not participate in the allocative activities of those who experience the input,
but the behavior of the latter is nevertheless a response to behavior
undertaken by the former."
3. "Emulative"—this corresponds to "The so-called 'diffusion'
or 'demonstration' effect whereby political activities in one country
are perceived and emulated in another."[57]

In the Stalinist era the Soviet-East European linkages were both
penetrative and emulative. At present, the penetrative linkage has
been reduced, though Soviet troops still remain in some East European
countries and, as is obviously the case in regard to Czechoslovakia,
they may have a decisive impact on internal developments. By and
large the "reactive" linkages that exist do not take precisely the
form that Rosenau outlines. The behavior of Soviet political actors
is not simply "a response to behavior undertaken by" East European
political actors, but also a calculated use of East European inputs,
among others, for internal Soviet purposes. Of course, the invasion
of Czechoslovakia was a "reactive" linkage in Rosenau's sense, but

FIGURE 1.1

Difference Between Linkages in the Stalin Period and Today

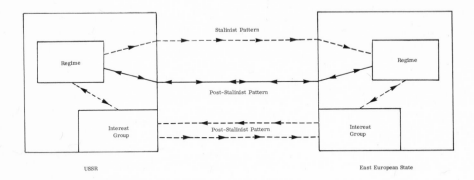

a more frequent "reactive linkage occurs when a Soviet interest group or individual actor uses East European inputs as a weapon in the domestic political struggle. The difference between linkages in the Stalin period and today may be observed in the simplified diagram in Figure 1.1. In the Stalinist era linkages were between regimes, and innovation was spread from the Soviet Union to the East European states. At present, interest groups in East Europe may generate innovative proposals and communicate them to sympathetic interest groups in the USSR who might then convey the message to the Soviet regime, which in turn can send on its evaluation of the innovative proposal directly to the relevant East European regime. There is still a great deal of regime-to-regime communication, of course, but now the flow in innovative proposals moves in both directions. In both polities there is also a two-way flow between interest groups and the regime.

This pattern is made possible by the existence of what we called earlier a concentric or dual political system, which may again be represented by an overly simplified diagram (see Figure 1.2). A Soviet political actor who finds that there are obstacles preventing him from communicating and exercising influence in his "home" system may try to communicate through the now more highly integrated "associated" systems. Soviet Ukrainian writers, unable to publish in Kiev, found outlets in Presov (Slovakia) and probably calculated that they would have a Soviet audience which read Ukrainian publications or listened to the Ukrainian radio in Presov. A Soviet political "liberal" might find it possible to publish in a Polish or Yugoslav journal but not in a Soviet journal, and some of his Soviet supporters—and opponents—may read that Polish or Yugoslav publication. For example, the Soviet Jewish scholar Yankl Kantor published articles on Jewish writers and politicians who fell victims to Stalin's purges not in Soviet publications but in the Warsaw Yiddish newspaper Folksshtime. Presumably, the China-Albania outlet would be used infrequently since only the most heterodox would find that channel appealing (the dissident Polish Communist Kazimierz Mijal, now residing in Tirana and broadcasting on Albania radio, is a quixotic

FIGURE 1.2

Concentric or Dual Political System

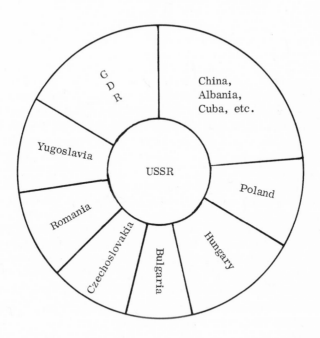

illustration of the latter case). The Yugoslav outlet, too, is an uncertain one, and its use would depend on the standing of Yugoslavia in the
alliance at any particular moment. The same would hold for nonruling,
especially West European, Communist parties.

There are many forums and mechanisms through which the various forms of communication may flow. For regime-to-regime communications there are the usual diplomatic and party channels, in
addition to the Warsaw Pact and Comecon structures. For interest
groups there are organizational delegations, tourism, contacts when
in a third country at the same time, and simply reading each other's
press and writing for it.

RULES OF THE GAME

Having outlined some of the possible channels of communication
of innovation, we turn now to a summary description of some of the
rules of the game which seem to govern the process of transmitting
an East European innovation to Soviet decision makers, either in an
effort to gain Soviet sanction to adopt and implement the innovation
within the East European country or, more ambitiously, in an attempt
to get the Soviet Union itself to adopt the innovation. While Soviet
adoption of an innovation will usually make that innovation available
and legitimate for East Europe, Soviet approval of an East European
innovation less frequently results in Soviet adoption of that innovation.
This seems to apply equally to ideas and institutions, though it is
more difficult to trace the diffusion of ideas and measure their impact.
Nevertheless, while the USSR has allowed East European countries to
drop the insistence on socialist realism as the only permissible
esthetic, it has clung to that doctrine within its own borders; while it
has tolerated multiple-candidate elections in Poland and Hungary, it
has not revised its own electoral practices accordingly. Thus East
European innovations may be accorded legitimacy, at least tacitly,
without themselves being adopted by the USSR. In fact, one would suspect that East Europeans are eager for the Soviet Union to adopt their
innovations simply because of the legitimacy it confers upon their
own ideas and actions, so that from the East European point of view
it matters little whether an innovation is merely approved or actually
adopted in the USSR.

Our problem is that there is no formal document or doctrine
setting out the rules of the game, and we must derive them from the
historical experience of the last 15 years or so. The rules are not
fixed and they are made, largely by the Soviet leadership, as situations arise. This makes the attempt to diffuse an innovation a

hazardous one, since the penalties for rejection and refusal of legitimacy may be severe. Nevertheless, we can attempt to draw up some
of the rules that seem to have emerged, especially in light of the
experiences of Yugoslavia, Poland, Hungary, and Czechoslovakia:

1. Perhaps the cardinal rule in innovation diffusion among socialist countries is that the innovator should never claim to be elaborating
an alternative, competitive "model" of socialism. The Yugoslav
"self-management system," the Chinese claims to have developed a
model of socialism suited to third world countries and to have solved
the problem of the transition from socialism to Communism, and the
Czechoslovak claims, however muted and tentative, to the development
of a form of socialism relevant to developed, industrialized countries,
are examples of unacceptable claims which make it likely that, rather
than adopting the systems being developed, the Soviet Union will deal
with them with rejection tactics. For reasons already discussed, it
is very difficult for the Soviet leadership to accept explicit doctrinal
claims which would call into question its own doctrinal and, indeed,
world-historical primacy. Even the Czechoslovak slogan of "socialism
with a human face" probably aroused uneasiness in the USSR because
it implied that there might be inhuman socialism, and not in Czechoslovakia alone. The ideological imperative of presenting a unified
front, the Soviet Union's self-image as the leader of the socialist
world, defining the general nature of socialist programs and institutions, and the recent history of the splits in the Communist movement partially as a result of competing claims to leadership in
innovation and development—all these make the Soviet Union wary
and ab initio unreceptive to grandiose claims which pretend to the
throne once occupied by the USSR alone.

2. A related unacceptable element in an innovative program is
the reduction of the role of the party. As we shall see, this was the
aspect of the Czechoslovak experiment that worried the Soviet leadership most, and for this reason the Hungarian regime is currently
emphasizing that its economic reform will in no way diminish the
role of the Communist Party in the political life of the country. The
problem is who decides whether the role of the party is being eroded
or not. Unfortunately for Tito in 1948, and for Dubcek 20 years later,
that decision ultimately rests in the hands of the Soviet leadership.
While Stalin's charges that the Yugoslav Communist Party was submerged in the national front and was a tool of the secret police—the
irony of the latter claim was not lost on the Yugoslavs—may have
been wholly specious, Soviet fears about the declining influence of
the Czechoslovak party seem more justified in view of the diminishing
membership of the party, the revival of the Socialist and People's
parties, the birth of new groups, such as Club 231 and the Club of

Committed Non-Party Members (KAN), and the fractionalization of the Communist Party of Czechoslovakia (CPCS). The party is the pivot of any Communist system, and any innovation which seriously affects its role and power is an innovation with serious implications for the very nature of the system.

3. Any innovative proposal which would directly or indirectly involve withdrawal of the innovating party from the Warsaw Pact and probably from Comecon would be unacceptable to the Soviet Union. The Czechoslovaks might have calculated that they have learned from the Hungarian experience in 1956 that withdrawal from the pact was intolerable, and for this reason they tried to emphasize their fidelity to the pact and its members. The problem for the Czechoslovak leadership was a dual one: to determine the 1968 rules of the game and to maintain sufficient control of the situation and of the population so that they could play by those rules.

4. Judging from the violent and sustained Soviet attacks on the literary and journalistic scene in Czechoslovakia in 1967-68, we can deduce that the abolition of party control of the mass media—that is, censorship—is an intolerable step. There is a logic to this rule: The higher integration and level of interchange among socialist countries would make it difficult and costly to keep an uncensored socialist publication out of a socialist system where censorship was still maintained. As it is, relatively less censored socialist publications, such as the Polish Polityka and the Yugoslav Politika, have been read with eagerness by Soviet citizens.

5. A more general and obvious prescription is that the proponents of innovation should seek to win the trust and confidence of highly placed Soviet politicians or interest group leaders. The innovators also should be careful in their choice of socialist allies, insofar as they have such a choice. The manifestations of support for the Dubcek regime which came from Romania and Yugoslavia in the summer of 1968 may have diminished, rather than enhanced, the legitimacy of the Czechoslovak innovators, for they raised the specter of Czechoslovak heterodoxy in foreign and domestic affairs, as well as of a renewed "Little Entente," this time acting as a nonconforming enclave within the Communist world. Innovators must also try to cultivate the support, or at least the benevolent neutrality, of the relevant middle hierarchy in the USSR, and perhaps in other socialist countries as well.

6. A corollary suggestion might be to avoid explicit, public approval in the West for the innovation or set of innovations. It is of course practically impossible to control the Western press from a socialist country, but there is no doubt that certain measures can be taken to reduce the chances that the innovative effort would be sensationalized in the West as a "loosening of the Soviet bloc," "revolt

against the Soviet master," "search for freedom," and the like.
Judging by the great play the Soviet media gave to Western reactions
to developments in Czechoslovakia from January to August 1968, this
is a sensitive point for Soviet leaders. Recent Hungarian attacks on
the Western media for sensationalizing changes in Hungary indicate
an awareness of this sensitivity.

7. A further corollary is to avoid criticism, especially public
criticism, of the USSR. One way of innovating in a resisting organization is to disguise the innovation. "Most organizations possess an
underworld of technique and technology some of which is simply used
to gain some freedom from the imposition of higher levels of authority, and some of which contributes to the achievement of corporate
goals."[58] The innovation could be represented as something other
than what it really is, something acceptable to the client. The Soviet
leadership seems ever alert to the danger of being fooled in this way,
but the tactic might be used successfully, particularly if the innovation
was not analogous to anything yet seen in the socialist repertoire.

8. Brzezinski enumerates three stratagems for a deviant member
of an alliance or organization:

● The deviant acts as if there were no distinction between his
and the center's doctrinal position. "This forces the center either to
tolerate the deviation, allowing it perhaps to spread, or to take the
first step in joining the issue, in effect launching a process or argument which it naturally would prefer to avoid. The skillful deviant
makes the choice difficult by his strategy of ambiguity—always implying the possibility of his returning to the position of doctrinal
subordination while gradually consolidating his position and probing
the international movement for other sources of support."
● The deviant can use the "asset of weakness" and plead inability
to enforce orthodoxy (Poland's failure to collectivize was based largely
on this tactic).
● The deviant can employ the "asset of fanaticism . . . being
more extreme than the center restrains the center by implying to it
that the deviant 'has his heart in the right place but is a little
extreme.'"[59]

It is worth repeating that the major difficulty with these—or any
other—rules of the game is that they are not fixed and are decided
pretty much ad hoc and unilaterally. It is as if one team in a basketball game decided as the game went along what constituted a legal
score, a foul, or any other infraction. The opposing team could only
hope to guess the next ruling or change of rules and would be at a
tremendous disadvantage in trying to develop a strategy or game
plan. Until the ground rules for behavior in USSR/East Europe are

laid down and agreed upon by most of the protagonists, this uncertainty will prevail.

THE DIFFUSION OF POLITICAL INNOVATION:
THREE CASE STUDIES

In this section we will examine some experiences, one still in progress, in the diffusion of political innovation from East Europe to the USSR. It is from the Czechoslovak and Hungarian experiences in recent years, as well as from the Soviet-Yugoslav rift of the 1950s, that we have derived our rules of the game, and by examining these cases we can observe the process in somewhat greater detail. In each case a brief profile of the defining characteristics will be drawn, and the Soviet reception accorded to the innovative proposals will be compared.

Yugoslavia

The dispute between the Soviet Union and the Yugoslav Communist Party had its origins in World War II but emerged in a public debate beginning in 1948. The origins and causes of the dispute have been well documented and need not detain us.[60]

It must be remembered that, far from developing a new system or model of socialism in 1948, the Yugoslavs' initial reaction to Stalin's charges was to try to prove their superorthodoxy by slavishly copying the Soviet pattern in collectivizing rapidly and announcing a ridiculously ambitious industrialization plan. But the Yugoslavs were making the mistake of taking Stalin's charges too literally:

> The Russians were not interested primarily in what the rulers of Yugoslavia were doing with their absolute power, whether they were pursuing a pro- or anti-Great Serbia policy, whether the Communist Party of Yugoslavia was run according to its statute or not. By 1948 the Russians' main if not only interest was to replace Tito and the elite surrounding him by their own men. [The ideological and political charges against the Yugoslavs] came as a superstructure; they represented a rationalization, probably sincere, of the original and most important belief that Tito was a traitor since, more because of his position than by his choice, he could not be a pliable instrument in the hands of Moscow.[61]

Nevertheless, the charges against Tito are relevant to our inquiry because they reflect some of the unacceptables to Stalin. The method of dealing with Tito and his comrades, putting him beyond the pale of the socialist camp, should be noted as typical of the preferred Stalinist tactic for dealing with deviation.

Since in Stalin's time the doctrine of multiple roads to socialism had not yet been legitimated, anyone who objectively developed a different formula for the attainment of socialism, or was judged to have done so, was forced to develop an alternative model if he wanted to continue calling himself a socialist; the only way to reconcile self-identification as a socialist with identification by others as a renegade or a capitalist tool was to develop a different variety of socialism. In a way, Stalin forced the Yugoslavs to develop a competing socialist system. This the Yugoslavs did, beginning in 1950 with the "self-management system," including the workers' councils, the abandonment of strict controls in the arts, the abandonment of collectivization, the acceptance of aid from the West, the evolution of an independent foreign policy, and the promulgation of the eventual withering away of the party, among other doctrinal and institutional innovations still in effect in Yugoslavia today.

Beginning in 1955 the Soviet leadership repudiated Stalin's treatment of the Yugoslavs, and since that time there has been an uneven pattern of reconciliation and estrangement between the Soviets and the Yugoslavs. It would be futile to try to trace every twist and turn in Soviet-Yugoslav relations since 1955. We shall only note some points relevant to Soviet reactions to Yugoslav political-economic innovations within Yugoslavia itself.

In the Belgrade declaration of 1955 Khrushchev stated flatly that "questions of internal organization, or difference in social systems and . . . different forms of Socialist development are solely the concern of the individual countries."[62] This was a repudiation of the universality of the Soviet model and, if it were to be understood as a genuine statement of general principle, meant that there was some vaguely defined leeway for socialist systems to experiment and innovate in their political forms. It was a proclamation of indifference to Yugoslav innovation, something midway between rejection and adoption. Very soon after, however, perhaps under the pressure of the Hungarian and Polish events of the fall of 1956, Pravda attacked the Yugoslavs for proffering and promoting their alternative model of socialism to others:

> Is it right to denigrate the Socialist system of other countries, and to praise one's own experience, publicizing it as universal and the best? One cannot help but see that more and more frequently in the Yugoslav press the idea is appearing that

the "Yugoslav road to socialism" is the most correct or
even the only possible road for nearly all the countries of
the world.

The same article commented favorably on the workers' councils but
criticized measures which weakened central planning.[63] The Yugoslav experience was said to be irrelevant to the USSR on at least two
counts: The USSR was much further along the road to Communism,
and Yugoslavia's economy was so dependent on Western aid that its
economic experience and system were irrelevant to all other socialist
countries. Thus, the Soviets maintained a strategy of claiming a
disinterest in Yugoslav innovations, based on their supposed irrelevance and unsuitability for adoption.

In 1958 Kommunist reacted to the recently announced Draft Program of the Yugoslav Communist Party by rejecting several of its
major tenets: that capitalist states increasingly curb monopoly power;
that it is possible (in the Soviet version) "to arrive at socialism
through a mere increased accumulation of Socialist features"; that
world tensions are caused not by the imperialists alone but by the
existence of two blocs. The Yugoslavs were accused of ignoring the
industrialization experience of the Soviet Union, of ignoring the "world
historic fact" of the division of the world into two antagonistic systems, of talking prematurely of the withering of the state, and of
emphasizing only the aspect of proletarian internationalism which
guaranteed equality of Communist parties and nations, while neglecting
the "necessity for strengthening unity and cooperation of the Socialist
countries." Finally, the Soviets accused the Yugoslavs of "denying
the leading role of the political party of the working class in a socialist state."[64]

Except for occasional sallies at Yugoslav economic failures as
proof that their economic system as a whole, and their lack of collective farms in particular, were failed innovations, the Soviet leaders
focused their criticism on Yugoslav doctrine in general and on Yugoslav positions in international relations, particularly as regards
relations among Communist states. It was not Yugoslav "ideological
deviation in internal policies" but "the interpretation of proletarian
internationalism and the international political orientation of the
Yugoslav state" that caused the Soviet Union to renew the dispute
with Yugoslavia on a large scale in 1958.[65]

Soviet evaluation of Yugoslav systemic innovations, seemingly
never detailed or systematic, fluctuates according to the prevailing
state of Soviet-Yugoslav relations and seems to be a relatively minor
independent influence on those relations. There are two points that
seem to be mentioned no matter what the tone of the overall treatment, namely, the diminution of the role of the party and the

"weakening of the planning element in the economy."[66] In 1967 and 1968, however, some dispassionate descriptions of the 1965 Yugoslav economic reform appeared in Soviet publications, and some articles took a mildly favorable tone.[67] By October 1968 the line seemed to have shifted once more. An article in Kommunist returned to the familiar theme that Yugoslavia's economic difficulties, described in some detail, were due to the "eulogizing of the free market and a disparagement of the planning principle, which is under the socialist state's control." Equal emphasis was placed on "the erosion of the L.C.Y. [League of Communists of Yugoslavia]," with some lesser criticisms of Yugoslavia's attitude toward the 1968 Czechoslovak liberalization.[68]

In sum, the Soviet Union has criticized Yugoslavia mainly for its heterodox position on questions of international relations and the organization of the socialist camp. It has not been particularly hostile—at least explicitly—to some of the innovative institutions of the Yugoslav self-management system. The Soviet Union has been consistently critical of certain doctrinal aspects of Yugoslav Communism, explicitly rejecting such innovations as the withering of the party. It also has been consistently disapproving of the Yugoslav shift to a socialist market economy and of the diminished role of the Communist Party in Yugoslav political life and society. The USSR has expressed its disapproval explicitly and publicly, has not adopted any of the Yugoslav innovations to any significant extent, but has not dealt with the innovations as Stalin would have. That is, instead of trying to undo the innovations by force, or proclaiming that the innovations forced Yugoslavia outside the socialist camp irrevocably, the post-Stalin leadership has allowed itself the option of now embracing, now rejecting Yugoslavia, depending on particular considerations of the moment. Probably calculating that the danger of infection of other socialist countries by Yugoslav ideas and innovations is lessened, owing to declining Yugoslav prestige in East Europe and the availability of the USSR to supply antidotes to such infections, the Soviet leadership does not feel impelled to launch a major onslaught on Yugoslav innovation. By harping on Yugoslav failures it calculates that it can neutralize the attractiveness of Titoist innovation.

Czechoslovakia

If in the Yugoslav case we can postulate that power considerations preceded ideological rationales for sanctions against a nonconforming part of the empire, in the Czechoslovak case we see ideological considerations as primary in motivating the USSR to impose power sanctions on a deviant member of the alliance.

The defining characteristics of the Prague Spring can be outlined as follows:

1. The devolution of the power of the Communist Party, whether intended by the party leadership or not, by permitting new political actors to appear on the scene (Club 231) or allowing old ones to assume new, more vital roles (trade unions, union of writers, youth organizations, Socialist and People's parties).

2. The gradual erosion of party control of the mass media, paralleling the yielding of party monopoly of political activity and organization.

3. Tentative feelers to like-minded deviant associates of the socialist camp (Yugoslavia, Romania) and some overtures to the West, largely in the form of exploration of economic opportunities, particularly with regard to West Germany.

4. Public criticism of the Soviet Union, both in the Stalinist period and as regards contemporary policy. There was much play given in the Czechoslovak media to the trials and purges of the 1950s and to the role of Soviet advisers in the terror period. There was also criticism aired of the position of the USSR regarding international relations among Communist states, and there were frequent criticisms of Czechoslovak—and, by implication or explicitly, Soviet—foreign policies, such as the stance on the Middle East.

5. Some Czechoslovaks made claims that they were developing a model of socialism which could be profitably emulated by other developed countries, socialist and nonsocialist. The official party slogan was that Czechoslovakia was building "socialism with a human face."

6. An extensive economic reform plan, originally articulated and approved under the Novotny regime, was adopted as an integral component of the new program.

7. There was a thorough revision of nationality policy, including federalization of the country, benefiting the Slovaks, with ancillary benefits accruing to other nationalities, particularly Hungarians and Ukrainians in Slovakia.[69]

8. In August 1968 new draft statutes for the Czechoslovak Communist Party were published. While maintaining the principle of "democratic centralism," the statutes contained some significant new provisions: secret ballots for elections to party organs, a time limit for holding offices, a curb on the power of professional party employees, attempts to prevent the accumulation of great power in the hands of any one person, the federalization of the party, allowing differing opinions to be voiced "provided these do not result in activity conflicting with the program and statutes of the party."[70]

Soviet response to these innovative actions and programs escalated from studied indifference, to interested neutrality, to criticism, to condemnation, and, finally, to repression by force. In January and February 1968 the Soviet press paid scant attention to the changes in regime and subsequent developments in Prague, later increasing coverage of Czechoslovakia but emphasizing international affairs and Soviet-Czechoslovak relations rather than internal developments. Soviet criticism began to appear in May and June and escalated subsequently. Individuals, institutions, and officially approved innovations in ideology and political life were attacked. A survey of the major Soviet statements on developments in Czechoslovakia shows that the following themes were consistently emphasized: ideological revisions which downgrade the Leninist component of Marxism-Leninism; "discrediting" and "weakening" the Communist Party and its role in public life (abandonment of the principle of democratic centralism); the seizure of the mass media by "antisocialist and revisionist forces"; opposition to Soviet-Czechoslovak friendship; "statements that all of Czechoslovakia's 'woes' were related to the circumstance that until recently it was guided in its development by what someone called 'the Soviet model of socialism'"; "proposals for replacing principles of planning with unregulated market relations"; and, finally, revisions of Czechoslovak foreign policy in ways that would weaken the alliance of socialist states in Europe.[71]

The Czechoslovak case is a very good illustration of how particular East European political innovations, or, indeed, a political innovation of systemic proportions, become inputs into interest group conflict in the Soviet Union. On one level, Soviet difficulties with liberal intellectuals at home may have sharpened interest in and fear of the prominence of liberal intellectuals as key political actors in Czechoslovakia. The trial of Galanskov, Dobrovolskij, Ginzburg, and Lashkova took place in January 1968. In May Pravda criticized Soviet intellectuals who were not grateful enough to the CPSU and strongly implied that critical intellectuals were not to be legitimated as a political force.

On a more direct level, it has often been remarked that there were important linkages between liberalization in Czechoslovakia, intellectual unrest in the Ukraine, which was concerned not only with general political issues but with Ukrainian national grievances, and the intellectual community of the USSR as a whole.[72] Peter Potichnyj and Grey Hodnett have convincingly demonstrated that there was a difference of opinion in the Ukrainian political leadership wherein Piotr Shelest, first secretary of the Ukrainian party, spoke often and sharply against Ukrainian nationalistic manifestations, emphasized the great dangers raised by events in Czechoslovakia, and stressed

the principle of central planning in economics, while V. V. Shcherbitskii, chairman of the Ukrainian Council of Ministers, seemed to lean
toward experimentation with economic reform, displayed no undue
anxiety over Ukrainian nationalism, and did not press the Czechoslovak
issue.[73]

> As the Czechoslovak crisis unfolded, dogmatic forces in the
> Ukraine found it necessary and/or tactically desirable to
> expose to public view more directly . . . the political mean-
> ings which were at stake in their struggle with the Ukrainian
> dissidents, and to hint that elements within the Party might
> have been finding these meanings congenial to their own
> way of thinking . . . . Political attitudes were probably the
> aspect of Soviet system most significantly affected by the
> situation in Czechoslovakia . . . . The context here was
> the struggle between orthodox and liberal national-communist
> definitions of Ukrainian political realities; a struggle which
> had been going on for some years . . . . The importance of
> the battle of meanings was accentuated by the "ideological"
> character of Soviet politics and political culture, and by
> the assumption that "correct" doctrine has international
> validity. Although members of the liberal Soviet Ukrainian
> intelligentsia were undoubtedly the most avid consumers in
> the Ukraine of cultural and political wares produced in
> Czechoslovakia and Presov [the Ukrainian center in Slo-
> vakia] , it is unclear whether this group drew upon Czecho-
> slovakia for theoretical concepts so much as for factual
> information and moral support. It is also difficult to dis-
> tinguish the Czechoslovak influence from the more inclusive
> influence of liberal Marxist thought in Eastern Europe as a
> whole . . . . Given the "internationalist" (or imperial)
> outlook of Soviet officialdom, it is not difficult to imagine
> that it quickly projected onto the Czechoslovak scene fears
> and resentments which owed their origin to domestic ideo-
> logical struggles in the Ukraine itself.
>   Czechoslovak "inputs," especially those originating
> in Presov, added a valuable component to the already-
> existing non-official communications network in the Ukraine.
> Presov played a substantial role in amplifying the dissemi-
> nation of heterodox interpretations of political reality into
> the network who were not inhibited by ordinary Soviet
> controls.[74]

There was a two-way flow in this linkage, with Soviet Ukrainians
exploiting the "dual" political system by using the media in Presov

to transmit messages which could not be admitted by the Soviet media, "but which nevertheless could not expediently be labelled 'counter-revolutionary' when expressed through officially approved media in a fraternal 'socialist' society."[75] Thus, there was a linkage between Ukrainian interest groups in the USSR and Czechoslovakia, and through these linkage groups some of the outputs of the Czechoslovak innovations were transmitted to the Soviet Union where they became inputs into interest group and factional debates centering around domestic issues. These inputs could be used for contrary purposes. While a Shcherbitskii or a Ukrainian "nationalist" intellectual could choose to emulate or regard with benevolent interest the innovations in Czechoslovak nationality and political policy, a Shelest and other Soviet officials could point to them as object lessons in the dangers of such innovations.[76] Czechoslovak influences had been superimposed upon processes indigenous to the Ukraine, processes visible as early as the first years of the 1960s. For Soviet leaders of "hawkish" inclination, the Czechoslovak "threat" to the Ukraine might well have provided one extremely convenient peg on which to hang their case. It vividly dramatized the danger of developments in Czechoslovakia, and did so with reference to the "Ukrainian question"—a problem about which many members of the Central Committee were more likely to have been anxious than well informed.[77]

The case just discussed sharpens and clarifies some of the contemporary rules of the game of the diffusion of political innovation from an East European state to the Soviet polity, and also illustrates the way in which externally generated political innovations can become inputs into political debate in the Soviet Union.

Hungary

Our third case study is very much in progress—the elaboration and implementation of economic reform and political adjustments in Hungary in the late 1960s. This is a further test of the rules of the game and a great deal of attention has been paid to them by the Hungarian innovators. This case will again illustrate the use of East European innovations in Soviet politics. The Hungarian innovators of the 1960s seem to have profited greatly from two historical lessons—their own searing experience of unsuccessful deviation in 1956, and the more recent, and perhaps equally instructive, fate of the Czecho-slovak innovators.

Some important differences between the ways in which the Czecho-slovak and Hungarian innovations have been formulated ought to be pointed out before presenting a profile of the Hungarian innovations.

While both the Prague Spring and the less dramatic reforms in Hungary were (are) attempts to reestablish the legitimacy of a political regime, and even of a system, which had suffered a severe loss of authority, the Czechoslovaks tried to reintegrate state and society largely on a normative basis, whereas the Hungarians have stressed the use of material incentives for reintegration. The Czechoslovak reformers appealed to the population on the basis of a new political program containing modified values, whereas the Hungarians have deemphasized value and ideological elements in their attempt to offer better material prospects as a way of reconciling the Hungarian population to the system. Since the Czechoslovak reintegration was attempted on a normative basis, it was forced into explicit ideological revisions, evoking a great deal of Soviet concern and anxiety. Furthermore, since the Soviet leadership does not perceive the need for ideological revision of its own system, it was difficult for it to empathize or even sympathize with its counterparts in Prague. The Hungarians, however, by focusing on material incentives and changes in the production and distribution of those incentives, have not been forced to confront ideological issues or articulate them in as direct a way as the Czechoslovaks. Moreover, since the USSR itself has perceived the need to tinker with the economic structure and reward system of its own socialist economy, its leadership can better understand Hungarian motivations and actions.

Second, while the Czechoslovaks were forced by their normative concerns to present their innovations as innovations indeed, the Hungarians are better able to present the changes in their system as mere tinkering with a fundamentally unchanged system, one which basically remains a replication of the Soviet model. The Hungarians see little if any advantage in presenting their innovations as having great systemic implications, and they have tried to avoid discussing their innovations in abstract, ideological terms. This may be one reason why Andras Hegedus, who tried to initiate a discussion on the "alternatives of social development," was criticized and demoted, the proposed discussion never really taking place in the way Hegedus seems to have urged.[78]

A third important difference between the two cases is that the Czechoslovak innovations were evolved in the heat of political battle by a new, unstable political leadership not very well known to the Soviet leadership. The Hungarian innovations were mapped out gradually, in relative calm, by a leadership which was stable, apparently united, and, from a Soviet perspective, reliable and trustworthy. Because of leadership stability, Hungary could go slower, while in Czechoslovakia both the population and rapidly evolving events themselves pressured the leadership for immediate change. In Hungary the existing machinery was able to contain and process the innovative proposals, while in Czechoslovakia the machinery itself was in the process of transformation and was being fought over. Finally, just as the Poles had learned the limits of change from the Hungarian experience of 1956, the Hungarians learned from the Czechoslovak experience in 1968.

Harry Shaffer points to another difference that seems significant. In the 1960s Hungary's economic progress was neither as rapid as that of Bulgaria or Romania, nor as weak as that of Czechoslovakia and Yugoslavia

> where corrective steps became a matter of utmost urgency. Hence, while radical changes in Hungary's economic system were necessary if economic performance was not to deteriorate, the house was not on fire and there was time for thorough preparation for whatever alterations were to be introduced.[79]

Our profile of the Hungarian innovations will be somewhat more detailed than the Czechoslovak one since they are less well known and less dramatic:

1. The Hungarians constantly stress that the leading role of the party is in no way diminished by the economic reforms which went into effect January 1, 1968. One Hungarian spokesman clearly implied that the Hungarians would not fall into the Czechoslovak heresy on the question of the party's role.[80] A Soviet author, writing in the authoritative party journal Kommunist, noted that in the period of economic reform party ideological work was all the more crucial and that the Hungarian party

> appears as the leading and directing force in the political union of Communists and non-Party people . . . . The growth in the leading role of the HSWP [Hungarian Socialist Workers Party] is inseparably linked with the further perfection of the organizational structures of the Party and the development of intra-Party democracy.[81]

"The economic reform embraces our entire society and is of great political significance because the leading force of society—the Party—must manage its determination," said a Hungarian economist writing in a Soviet economics journal.[82] Of course, rhetoric and reality may not coincide, and it remains to be seen whether the Hungarian party, in a low profile position ever since 1956, will maintain or increase its role in the political, social, economic, and cultural spheres.

2. The Hungarian economic reform itself is perhaps the basic element in the more general reform. "While the fundamental features of the Hungarian reform may be similar to those of the reforms already introduced in other Communist countries, the extent to which the reform has been carried is more far-reaching in Hungary than anywhere else in Eastern Europe except Yugoslavia."[83] Without detailing the major features of the reform, we can mention the introduction of a flexible three-category price system, the power given to large enterprises to make their own export contracts with foreign enterprises, the application of reform principles in agriculture as well as industry, and a degree of independence for enterprise directors which "appeared to be greater than elsewhere in the bloc. Finally, the Hungarians were the first to realize that in the changed conditions of the new economic model, the role of the trade unions would have to undergo significant reassessment." One of the essential characteristics of the Hungarian reform is that

> The central [planning] organ is to fix only the long-term
> tasks to be fulfilled, but the details of these tasks will be
> set by the enterprises themselves according to the market
> requirements. It will be the duty of the superior organs to
> harmonize these market requirements and national
> interests.[84]

By and large, the Hungarians seem to have deliberately avoided discussing the economic reform in the wider context of systemic crisis and the need for systemic change. That is, they have avoided the kind of rhetoric that characterized the work of Ota Sik, for example, perhaps simply because the Hungarian reform was not an emergency response to a deeply felt crisis but a measure taken rather deliberately, as something which ought to be done sooner rather than later to avoid the kind of system breakdown confronting the Czechoslovaks. This enabled the Hungarians to present their reform more as a technical adjustment in the system than as a major overhaul and reevaluation of its basic machinery and workings. "Instead of chasing 'hazy pictures' or the model of an 'abstract' democracy which can be realized nowhere, the Hungarian regime seeks solutions corresponding to domestic realities."[85] Jozsef Bognar put it clearly:

> It is not expedient to include in the debate and to expose
> to social confrontation the practical and theoretical multi-
> plying effects of the changes when the reforming movement
> is launched, for in this case the battle-lines become con-
> fused and this, as a rule, encourages the opponents of the

change . . . . It is better to deal with the secondary and accessory consequences when agreement has been reached on basic issues.[86]

3. Part of the economic reform has been an increase in the power of the trade unions. The New Labor Code gives workers the right to share in enterprise profits and makes the unions responsible for the protection of the material interests of the workers by giving them the right to a decisive voice in determining the percentage of profit which is to go into the profit-sharing fund. The unions also share with management the duty of drawing up the annual collective contract which outlines the fundamental duties and rights of all parties in the enterprises. This is based on the recognition that managerial and production personnel may have interests which are not congruent. The most novel labor right included in the New Economic Mechanism is the right to exercise a veto in three kinds of situations: when enterprise actions violate the terms of the collective contracts, when working conditions fall below minimum safety standards, and when the enterprise takes steps which violate "socialist morality." The use of the veto can halt implementation of managerial action until the dispute is settled by a governmental body. In a dispute in the Athenaeum publishing house, the union vetoed a managerial plan to impose overtime work whereby the funds for the overtime would come from the profit-sharing fund. When the dispute was arbitrated, the union won a complete victory.[87]

4. It is important to note that changes in the status of the labor force took place by altering existing institutions, not by creating new ones. For example, the Hungarians might have created workers' councils of some sort to replace or supplement the trade unions, but they refrained from doing so, probably because of their own unhappy experience with such councils in 1956 and because this would unnecessarily dramatize the nature of the changes taking place, perhaps rousing Soviet fears that a Yugoslav model was being experimented with.

5. The Hungarian government has extended the economic reform to the agricultural sector. By 1966 about two-thirds of all collective farms had adopted the system, first introduced on the Nadudvar collective, whereby each family or other field unit is assigned a particular parcel of the land and the collective farmer gets a specific percentage of the total crop produced on that parcel, no matter how high the yield. "This payment is in addition to the income from the work units accomplished [trudoden'] and is paid for in cash."[88] This guarantees the farmer a minimum income no matter the size of the yield and helps improve and stabilize peasant income. "It is perfectly clear that a most important and fundamental tenet of collectivization

has been repudiated, if not entirely abrogated, by Nadudvar: collective membership working collectivized land for the common (collective and state) good."[89] As shall be seen, this innovation became an input into a Soviet debate.

6. Just as in the labor sector familiar institutions have been given new rights and powers, so in the political sphere instead of elaborating new institutions and processes the Hungarians have given parliament new importance, strengthened the National Front, and changed the electoral system. Beginning in 1967, or perhaps a year or two earlier, a new legislative style was inaugurated,

> thanks to which the members of the House no longer simply approved of the bills worked out by the government, but actually "made" the laws themselves by participating in the elaboration of the drafts . . . . The new, correct, and now established practice is to place the drafts of bills prepared by the competent ministers before the pertinent standing committee in order to enable its members to suggest modifications. Subsequently, the ministries draw up the final draft, which comes before the Council of Ministers for approval with a view to the changes recommended by the standing committees. This means that the bill submitted by the Council of Ministers to the Plenum of the House already "incorporates" the views of the deputies sitting in the various standing committees. [Speaker of the House Gyula] Kallai disclosed that the standing committees of Parliament had held 34 meetings and that there were "brisk" debates over the drafts of bills.[90]

In an interview in Izvestiia, Kallai stated that "in spite of the fantasies coming out of some of the capitalist countries, reality confirms that the parliament plays an indispensable role, with great significance in a socialist society in general, and especially in the current stage of development of our country." He pointed out that ministers have been challenged on the floor of Parliament and that

> the work of parliament was noticeably animated, discussions were set off more often, creating a healthy critical spirit. The minister-speakers on this or that question now not only "give a speech" but also lend an ear to the discussions. . . . We are trying to develop the initiative of the deputies . . . to encourage the deputies to join in as initiators of discussions in parliament of important government problems.

Kallai also stressed the importance of the right of interpellation by a deputy.[91]

7. The Hungarian regime has conducted a limited experiment in allowing several candidates to stand for a single office, and it has changed the electoral system so that each district elects a deputy. Kallai claimed that allowing two or more candidates to stand for Parliament resulted in a greater feeling of responsibility toward the constituency on the part of the deputies and a greater familiarity with constituency sentiment.[92] In the April 1971 parliamentary elections, 49 of 352 parliamentary seats were contested, and in local elections over 3,000 of 70,000 offices were contested.[93]

8. The general tenor of the Hungarian reforms is that of reconciliation with an alienated population. Kadar's famous 1961 formulation of "He who is not against us is with us" is a succinct expression of the Hungarian attitude toward the population and the willingness of the regime to resocialize the population gradually, settling for a slow increase in the political consciousness and loyalty of the population. This is accompanied by a "struggle on two fronts," an attempt to walk a middle path between the Scylla of "dogmatism" and the Charybdis of "revisionism." The Hungarians are attempting to avoid the excesses of both the Rakosi regime and the short-lived Nagy period, and to choose a middle way between, say, a Romanian or Bulgarian posture and a Czechoslovak (1968) experiment.

The preference of the Hungarians for concentrating on "small deeds" rather than "senseless dreams," to borrow terms from Russian history, is reflected, for example, in the quiet filling of every one of the many vacancies that have existed in the Catholic church hierarchy for about 18 years.

> This quiet mutual acceptance of an uneasy status quo
> attempted to normalize the internal situation and thus
> placed the entire Mindszenthy case . . . in the perspective
> of a meaningless anachronism. This across-the-board
> agreement between the Catholic clergy and communist
> authorities . . . attests to the internal stability and sur-
> prising consolidation of the Janos Kadar regime.[94]

Another symptom of the regime's posture is the truly astounding fact, especially in the East European context, that "For a decade the regime and the literati have been living together in peace, avoiding any dramatic clashes. This peaceful coexistence was preserved even at the height of the Czechoslovak crisis."[95]

Although Hungarian officials would probably object to the use of these terms, there has been a gradual depoliticization of some areas of Hungarian life, literature being only one instance. A crucial step was the deemphasis on political criteria for managerial personnel in the economy and an increased emphasis on professional criteria. "The campaign against party hacks began early in the 1960's when the Kadar regime started appointing non-Party experts to important administrative posts."[96] Class and other social criteria were dropped in considering applications for admission to institutions of higher education. The very definition of "proletarian" was broadened so that people who were not workers at the bench could enjoy the rights and privileges of the working class. "In other words, the insuperable cleft between a significant portion of worker and intellectual occupations has ceased to exist, and this characteristic feature—one could say qualitative change—of the workers' class is valid many times over with respect to Communist workers."[97] According to the editor of Nepszabadsag, the alliance of the party with non-Communists is a necessary precondition "of successful Communist construction. . . . We regard the further development of socialist democracy to lie in the strengthening of this alliance."[98]

In sum,

We have carried out this social conciliation in accordance with the changes in social and political conditions, neither sooner nor later than the given situation required because both possibilities would have caused damage. And even in recent years we have been involved in constant debate both with those who unreasonably and rashly tried to push us forward and with those who wanted to push us back to a conservative standpoint which abhors democracy.[99]

9. Throughout the period of economic and political changes, the Hungarians have stressed that the alliance with the Soviet Union is not diminished but strengthened, and that Hungary is very much aware of its responsibilities to the socialist community. The prime minister emphasized that in conceiving the NEM the regime was careful to ensure that "international public opinion," and especially the "socialist community," would understand what was being done and, hopefully, would agree with it. "Our place is at the side of the Soviet Union, which is the fundamental force in the socialist concentration, in the struggle against imperialism and in the reshaping of internationalist unity."[100] Soviet commentators, as well as Brezhnev himself, have frequently noted with approval the emphasis that the Hungarians place on their alliance with the USSR:

The Party attaches great importance in its propaganda to the idea of proletarian internationalism and socialist

patriotism, to the further development and consolidation of
the friendship between the Hungarian people and the people
of the Soviet Union and other fraternal countries, to the
strengthening of the unity of socialist cooperation and the
world communist movement. The Party consistently and
decisively denounces chauvinist anti-Soviet "national
communism."[101]

Obviously, invidious comparisons with wayward Czechoslovakia are
implied, especially in the Soviet sources.

At the Tenth Congress of the Hungarian Socialist Workers' Party
in November 1970, Brezhnev praised Kadar as "the true son of the
Hungarian people, an outstanding and respected figure in the international Communist and workers' movement." He went on to praise
the economic reform, the policy of "struggle on two fronts," and, in
much vaguer terms, the political reforms ("expansion of socialist
democracy").[102]

10. Closely connected with the emphasis on ties to the socialist
community, and to the Soviet Union in particular, is the theme of
Western misinterpretation and misuse of the developments in Hungary.
This is in keeping with our rule of not being made to look in the Western media like a deviant from Soviet norms. Imre Pardi wrote that

in the West, beginning with the political aspirations and
calculations of reactionary circles, the reform is depicted
as a sort of liberalization process in social life resulting
in a weakening of socialist social relationships . . . an
estrangement from the Soviet Union and a weakening of
socialist international cooperation. I consider that there
is no need to waste words on the fabrications spread by
Western bourgeois circles.[103]

Izvestiia's correspondent in Budapest wrote an article, significantly
titled "Dynamism Without Sensationalism," in which he pointed to
Western attempts to exploit changes in Hungary for antisocialist and
anti-Soviet purposes. A Hungarian journalist devoted an entire article
in Izvestiia to this subject,[104] and the Izvestiia correspondent wrote
a heavily sarcastic article about a Zurich newspaper's depiction of
Hungary as "disillusioned and insulted."[105] Several articles in this
vein have appeared in the Hungarian press as well.[106]

11. Connected with this effort to play down the liberalizing nature
of Hungarian innovation is the insistence that Hungary is not elaborating a competitive or even distinctive model. Prime Minister Fock
argued that the Hungarians had rejected "provincial" interpretations
of socialism and that NEM is not a Hungarian invention since similar

problems and solutions had been discussed in other socialist countries.[107] Hungarian commentators have repeatedly pointed out that, on the one hand, their experience proves that there is no one single model which all Communist countries must follow, but, on the other hand, Hungarian variations on socialist themes do not constitute a comprehensive and distinct model, and certainly not one which can be presented as an alternative to the mythical Soviet model. Thus, the Hungarians seem to have been very careful to observe our cardinal rule of the game.

HUNGARIAN INNOVATIONS AND
SOVIET DOMESTIC POLITICS

We conclude with an examination of Hungarian innovations as inputs into Soviet domestic issues. First, we must note that the generally favorable treatment the USSR has accorded the Hungarian innovations, particularly the NEM, is due to the nature of the innovations themselves and Hungary's ability to abide by the rules of the game. It is far too simplistic to say, as William Robinson does, that

> the Soviet attitude has tended to confirm that in many cases
> it is really not the nature of the ideological "heresy" which
> arouses the condemnation of the CPSU, but the trustworthi-
> ness of the "heretic" instead. That is to say, the Soviet
> Union has confidence in Kadar's ability to handle reform
> and trusts him to safeguard bloc (i.e., Soviet) interests.
> Dubcek, however, was never held in such "high esteem."

This is only a small part of the explanation, as we have tried to demonstrate.

When we speak of the Soviet reaction to Hungarian innovation, we can pretty much exclude adoption by the Soviet Union of the entire package of Hungarian institutional innovations, simply because both parties agree that some Hungarian experiences are irrelevant to the Soviet Union, especially in view of the greatly different sizes of the two countries.[108] We hypothesize, however, that Soviet political actors who favor further economic reform in the USSR, whether along Hungarian lines or not, have chosen the Hungarian reform as a surrogate for arguments about Soviet reforms and have praised NEM as a way of pointing to the potential advantages of a Soviet NEM. By the same token, Soviet opponents of economic reform raise questions about the NEM as indirect opposition to reforms at home.

Similarly, some Soviet citizens have commented favorably on political changes in Hungary in order to recommend similar changes at home.

It may be assumed that those Soviet correspondents and commentators who are reporting favorably about innovations in the Hungarian system either are themselves enthusiastic about them or are following the wishes of higher-placed people—editors and politicians—who are anxious to show the Hungarian reforms in a favorable light. Correspondent Rodinov went so far as to say that Hungary was "taking the lead, in fraternal union with the USSR" in socialist construction. The same correspondent praised Hungarian reforms in agriculture and pointed to the powers enjoyed by the Hungarian National Council of Cooperatives, and used to protect Hungarian farmers, while no such protective devices exist in the Soviet Union. Since the article appeared at a time when the Soviet authorities were working on a revised charter for Soviet collectives, it may well have been directing attention to Hungarian institutions as a model for emulation.

> The ground rules for a decompression of a centralized agricultural system . . . have been staked out in the Izvestiia account . . . . The zest with which Izvestiia covers the Hungarian experience nourishes the hope that ultimately a similar development of Kolkhoz democracy and market order will be allowed to flower in the Soviet Union.[109]

There seems to have been a clearcut difference of opinion in the Soviet agricultural establishment on the Nadudvar system. The secretary for agriculture of the Soviet party's Central Committee inspected the Nadudvar collective in 1964, the chairman of the collective visited the USSR, and an article on the Nadudvar system (written by a Hungarian) appeared in Kommunist in the same year. "Publication of this article was an important sign of Soviet willingness to discuss, and even reconsider, the uncompromising Soviet system of collectivization; it also indicated approval of Hungarian agricultural policy."[110] The USSR then experimented with the Nadudvar system in a few of its own collectives and in some ways seems to have carried the experiment even further than the Hungarians. While this was going on, the generally conservative agricultural newspaper Sel'skaia zhizn' maintained complete silence on both the Hungarian and the Soviet experiments, apparently a sign of opposition to the innovation. In March 1967 a Pravda editorial came out against changes in central planning and increased incentives in agriculture, but in August 1968 Pravda's correspondent in Hungary published a laudatory article on Nadudvar.[111] All this seems to add up to continued debate within the Soviet agricultural hierarchy on the merits of various systems of agricultural organization and incentives. In this debate the Hungarian innovation at Nadudvar, clearly an innovation with systemic implications, serves both as a model and as a symbol.

Similar Soviet interest group activity can be observed around the Hungarian NEM in general. Aside from the laudatory treatments of the NEM, there have appeared in the Soviet press some carefully worded critical commentaries. Professor Rem Belousov, an official of the Soviet Planning Commission (Gosplan), said in an interview for a Western newspaper, "We are attentively watching how it [Hungarian NEM] turns out. Should it fail, then the Soviet Union can help Hungary. We ourselves, however, must be very careful with such far-reaching experiments."[112] Belousov was expressing mild skepticism about NEM itself, but he was also expressing more clearly his doubts as to its relevance to the Soviet Union. He may have had a valid point when saying that the Soviet Union could bail Hungary out in case of the NEM's failure, but who could bail the USSR out in case its enormous economy suffered reverses as a result of economic reform? Not Hungary, certainly. Therefore, the USSR "must be very careful" with such ventures.

A second Gosplan official told a Western economist that the Hungarian reform is very similar to the Czechoslovak, as indeed it is. "We do not like to criticize our Hungarian comrades, but we think their approach to central planning is totally incorrect; and we should know, because we here in the Soviet Union have had 50 years of experience with central planning."[113] Two things are worth pointing out: A Soviet official claims that by virtue of its historical position the USSR can better evaluate proposed innovations than can its junior partners; Soviet experience with central planning is much greater than that of Hungary and therefore, perhaps, the Soviet experience ought to be emulated. It is very important to note that the two Soviet economists we have cited as somewhat opposed to NEM and its adoption by the USSR are associated with Gosplan, the main agency involved in central planning. Their institution, and their own personal positions, would be diminished in importance and power by the adoption of an NEM-type reform which deemphasizes central planning. These Soviet officials have a personal stake in opposing innovation of the NEM type. A recent report from Moscow also emphasizes that Gosplan has been opposed to the kind of decentralization involved in economic reforms Hungarian style. "At a recent press conference, A. V. Bachurin, the agency's deputy director, said that recent events 'graphically have shown where the illusions spread by some theoreticians can lead' " and he quoted Lenin as supporting central planning, promising that the next Soviet five-year plan will "give priority to tighter planning and more centralization, not less as reformers originally envisaged when Premier Kosygin made the reform public in 1965."[114]

Two other examples of the use of external inputs in internal debate may be cited. One is a statement appearing in Novyi Mir, generally considered to be a medium of expression for Soviet liberals. Reviewing several Soviet publications, V. Savin made so bold as to mention political innovations which he suggested might be tried in the USSR. For example, he quoted Lenin—always a good political tactic—to the effect that opinion groups ought to be allowed to publish petitions and the like in the public press. Considering the nature and source of some recent Soviet petitions, this was a bold proposal indeed. Savin also mentioned that "several scholars . . . have suggested the necessity of increasing the importance of voting in the elections to the Soviets. This suggestion, it seems to us, deserves discussion. For example, in socialist Hungary recently the following electoral system was introduced," and he went on to describe the reforms discussed earlier, adding that "a similar system exists in some other socialist countries."[115] The tactics employed by Savin are instructive: Yugoslavia has developed the electoral system to a much greater extent than Hungary, but Yugoslavia is not as "respectable" in the USSR; Poland also has multicandidate elections, but the Polish regime is certainly no symbol of liberalization nor, on the other hand, has it gotten as good a press recently in the Soviet Union as has Hungary. Finally, Hungarian agitprop methods were favorably commented upon by V. I. Stepakov, then head of the CPSU Central Committee's Agitprop Department, following a tour of Hungary. According to Aryeh Unger, Stepakov was very much involved in a debate as to whether the traditional Soviet agitator was to be replaced by a "politinformator," and he used the purported Hungarian success in agitprop as evidence of the soundness of his own position.[116] Once again, we observe the use of a foreign innovation as a surrogate for Soviet issues and, more than that, as a model explicitly held up for emulation.

INNOVATION AND POLITICAL CHANGE
IN COMMUNIST EAST EUROPE

The history of the diffusion of political innovation from East Europe to the USSR is instructive in pointing out certain aspects of the Soviet-East European relationship and in highlighting some of the goals and priorities of both the Soviet and East European leaderships. The tortuous and uncertain course of innovation diffusion vividly illustrates the changing and highly unstable relationship of the USSR to East Europe in the post-Stalin era. It points to the likelihood that the East European states will continue to be caught in the dilemma of having to innovate in order to strengthen their own internal legitimacy, efficiency, and stability, but at the same time having to satisfy their external audience as well. The partial autonomy gained by the East European states in the last fifteen years has made their political task more difficult, for they are now expected to achieve domestic successes on their own and without the weapons of coercion, while at the same time the ways in which they can move toward such successes are severly circumscribed by the USSR.

Second, attempts at innovation diffusion in an era of polycentrism and relative institutional experimentation dramatize and bring into sharper relief the prevailing institutional and ideological orthodoxies obtaining in the USSR, even though it appears that those orthodoxies are quite often latent, activated only by challenges from within and without. The uncertainties of Soviet orthodoxy and policy are what make the innovative process so risky, and the process itself helps to establish in practice the nature and degree of change in Soviet theory and practice.

Finally, the recent experiences of the East European innovators yield clues as to the short-range possibilities and probabilities of internal change in East Europe as well as in the Soviet-East European relationship. The history of the Czechoslovak and Hungarian innovations and their treatment by the USSR point out the severely constraining boundaries within which change in the socialist systems of Europe is possible.

NOTES

1. Anatole Shub, "Lessons of Czechoslovakia," Foreign Affairs 47, no. 2 (1969): 273.

2. Richard V. Burks, Technological Innovation and Political Change in Communist Eastern Europe, RAND Memorandum RM-6051-PR (Santa Monica, Calif., August 1969), p. 59.

3. Zbigniew K. Brzezinski, "The Organization of the Communist Camp," World Politics 13, no. 2 (1961): 204.

4. Ghita Ionescu, The Break-up of the Soviet Empire in Eastern Europe (London, 1965), pp. 7-8.

5. V. Kotyk, "Some Aspects of the History of Relations Among Socialist Countries," Ceskoslovensky casopis historicky (Czechoslovak historical journal), no. 4, (1967), presented in Radio Free Europe, Czechoslovak Press Survey, no. 1973, p. 14. For an interesting and original treatment of relations among socialist countries in the Stalin era, see V. Kotyk, Svetova socialisticka soustava (The world socialist system) (Prague, 1967), pp. 5-103.

6. Ole Holsti and John D. Sullivan, "National-International Linkages: France and China as Non-Conforming Alliance Members," in James N. Rosenau, ed., Linkage Politics: Essays on the Convergence of National and International Systems (New York, 1969), p. 164.

7. R. V. Burks, "The Communist Policies of Eastern Europe," in Rosenau, ed., Linkage Politics. The classic work on the evolution of Communist East Europe is Zbigniew K. Brzezinski, The Soviet Bloc (Cambridge, Mass., 1961 and 1967).

8. Irving Louis Horowitz, "Consensus, Conflict, and Cooperation: A Socialogical Inventory," Social Forces 41, no. 2 (1962): 187. Jowitt applies Horowitz's distinction in "The Romanian Communist Party and the World Socialist System: A Re-definition of Unity," World Politics 23, no. 1 (1970).

9. For a useful summary of debates on "different roads to socialism," see Paul Kecskemeti, "Diversity and Uniformity in Communist Bloc Politics," World Politics 13, no. 2 (1961).

10. See Fundamentals of Marxism-Leninism (Moscow, 1963), esp. chapter 25; Sh. P. Sanakoev, Mirovaia sistema sotsializma (The world system of socialism) (Moscow, 1968), esp. part two.

11. Nish Jamgotch, Jr., Soviet-East European Dialogue: International Relations of a New Type? (Stanford, Calif., 1968), p. 127.

12. Jan Triska, "The World Communist System," in Jan Triska, ed., Communist Party-States (New York and Indianapolis, 1969), p. 33.

13. Lawrence B. Mohr, "Determinants of Innovation in Organizations," American Political Science Review 62, no. 11 (1969): 112.

14. Karl W. Deutsch, The Nerves of Government (New York, 1966), pp. 207, 221.

15. Ibid, pp. 247-48.

16. Jack L. Walker, "The Diffusion of Innovations Among the American States," American Political Science Review 63, no. 3 (1969): 889.

17. H. G. Barnett, Innovation: The Basis of Cultural Change (New York, 1953), p. 375.

18. Ibid., p. 376.

19. Everett M. Rogers, Diffusion of Innovations (New York, 1962), pp. 124-31. On the importance of compatibility with previous value patterns; see also Deutsch, The Nerves of Government.

20. Rogers, Diffusion of Innovations, p. 148.

21. Walker, "The Diffusion of Innovations," p. 897.

22. Deutsch, The Nerves of Government, p. 147.

23. James Q. Wilson, "Innovation and Organization: Notes Toward a Theory," in James D. Thompson, ed., Approaches to Organizational Design (Pittsburgh, 1966), p. 208.

24. Ibid, p. 210.

25. Rogers, Diffusion of Innovations, p. 99.

26. Karl W. Deutsch, "External Influences on the Internal Behavior of States," in R. Barry Farrell, ed., Approaches to Comparative and International Politics (Evanston, Ill., 1966), p. 11.

27. Ibid., p. 24.

28. Warren G. Bennis, "Theory and Method in Applying Behavioral Science to Planned Organizational Change," in Warren G. Bennis, Kenneth D. Benne, and Robert Chin, eds., The Planning of Change (New York, 1969), p. 77.

29. Ibid.

30. Barnett, Innovation, p. 93.

31. Bennis, "Theory and Method," p. 76.

32. A. L. Kroeber, "Diffusionism," from an article by that title in Edwin R. A. Seligman and Alvin Johnson, eds., The Encyclopedia of Social Sciences, (New York, 1937), vol. 3. Excerpted in Amitai Etzioni and Eve Etzioni, eds., Social Change (New York, 1964), p. 143.

33. Goodwin Watson lists five sources of resistance to change in social systems: (1) conformity to norms or habits; (2) systemic and cultural coherence; (3) vested interests; (4) "the sacrosanct" ("The greatest resistance concerns matters which are connected with what is held to be sacred"); (5) rejection of "outsiders." By defining characteristics we mean something like Watson's "sacrosanct." See Watson, "Resistance to Change," in Bennis, Benne and Chin, The Planning of Change. For another listing of factors inhibiting innovation acceptance, see Ronald G. Havelock, et al., Planning for Innovation through Dissemination and Utilization of Knowledge (Ann Arbor, Mich., 1969), pp. 6.7-6.10.

34. Deutsch, "External Influences," p. 11.

35. Rogers, Diffusion of Innovations, p. 280.

36. Herbert A. Shepard, "Innovation-Resisting and Innovation-Producing Organizations," in Bennis, Benne, and Chin, The Planning of Change, p. 520.

37. Ruth Leeds, "The Absorption of Protest; A Working Paper," in Bennis, Benne, and Chin, The Planning of Change, p. 199.

38. On the notion of transitive and reflexive goals, see Lawrence B. Mohr, The Concept of Organizational Goal, Institute of Public Policy Studies Discussion Paper no. 9, University of Michigan (September 1969).

39. On "Trained Incapacity," see Robert K. Merton, Social Theory and Social Structure (Glencoe, Ill., 1949), pp. 153-56.

40. Leeds, "The Absorption of Protest," pp. 201-02.

41. Ibid., p. 204.

42. Ibid., p. 207.

43. Ibid., p. 208.

44. Rolf P. Lynton, "Linking an Innovative Subsystem into the System," Administrative Science Quarterly 14, no. 3 (1969): 400.

45. Burks, Technological Innovation, p. 33.

46. See Zvi Y. Gitelman, "Power and Authority in Eastern Europe," in Chalmers Johnson, ed., Change in Communist Systems (Stanford, Calif., 1970).

47. Holsti and Sullivan, "National-International Linkages," pp. 164-65.

48. Zbigniew Brzezinski, "Deviation Control: A Study in the Dynamics of Doctrinal Control," American Political Science Review 61, no. 1 (1962): 6.

49. Jamgotch, Jr., Soviet-East European Dialogue, pp. 105, 108.

50. Holsti and Sullivan, "National-International Linkages," p. 166.

51. For use of this tactic in organizations, see Wilson, "Innovation and Organization," pp. 211-13.

52. Horace Kallen, "Innovation," in Seligman and Johnson, The Encyclopedia of Social Sciences, reprinted in Etzioni and Etzioni, eds., Social Change, p. 429.

53. See Milton Rokeach, The Open and Closed Mind (New York, 1960) esp. pp. 55, 268-88. Kenneth Jowitt makes imaginative and productive use of the "open-closed mind" distinction in his Revolutionary Breakthroughs and National Development: The Case of Romania (Berkeley, Calif., 1971).

54. Vernon V. Aspaturian, The Soviet Union in the World Communist System (Stanford, Calif., 1966), p. 84.

55. "The degeneration of steering performance and learning capacity may be the direct consequence of survival and success themselves." Deutsch, Nerves of Government, p. 228.

56. See Zygmunt Bauman's Chapter 3 in this volume.

57. James N. Rosenau, "Toward the Study of National-International Linkages," in Rosenau, ed., Linkage Politics, p. 45.

58. Shepard, "Innovation-Resisting," p. 520.

59. Zbigniew Brzezinski, "Deviation Control," pp. 16-18.

60. See "Letter from the Central Committee of the CPSU to Comrade Tito and other Members of the Central Committee of the Communist Party of Yugoslavia," March 27, 1948, in Royal Institute of International Affairs, The Soviet-Yugoslav Dispute (London and New York, 1948), pp. 15-63.

61. Adam Ulam, Titoism and the Cominform (Cambridge, Mass., 1952), p. 108.

62. Joint Soviet-Yugoslav Declaration, Belgrade, June 2, 1955, in Robert Bass and Elizabeth Narbury, eds., The Soviet-Yugoslav Controversy, 1948-1958 (New York, 1959), p. 57.

63. Pravda, November 23, 1956, quoted in ibid., pp. 78-81.

64. Kommunist, no. 6 (1958): quoted in Bass and Narbury, eds., The Soviet-Yugoslav Controversy, pp. 143-63. See also Khrushchev's speech at the Fifth Congress of the Socialist Unity Party of Germany, in Pravda, July 12, 1958, pp. 2-3.

65. Vaclav Benes, Robert F. Byrnes, and Nicholas Spulber, The Second Soviet-Yugoslav Dispute (Bloomington, Ind., 1959), p. xxx.

66. See Yuri Zhilin and Vadim Zagladin, "Yugoslavia Today," New Times, no. 34 (1963): 6-8, and the continuation of this article in no. 5 (1963): 3-5. See also V. Zagladin, et al., "Yugoslavia Today: Journalists' Notes," World Marxist Review 7, no. 3 (1964).

67. See Natalia Sergeyeva and Irina Trofimova, "Yugoslavia: Economic Reform in Action," New Times no. 49 (1967) and L. Tyagunenko, "Yugoslavia's Economic Reform," New Times no. 17 (1968).

68. Yu Georgiyev, "Yugoslavia: New Variant of Socialism?", Kommunist, no. 15 (1968), translation in Current Digest of the Soviet Press 20, no. 52 (1969): 3.

69. The literature on developments in Czechoslovakia is extensive and probably familiar to most readers. Perhaps the best single English-language source is Robin Alison Remington, Winter in Prague (Cambridge, Mass., 1969). Another useful publication is Studies in Comparative Communism 1, nos. 1-2 (1968). For the most important official documents, see Rok sedesaty osmy (The sixty-eighth year) (Prague, 1969). A good secondary analysis may be found in Philip Windsor and Adam Roberts, Czechoslovakia, 1968 (New York, 1969).

70. Studies in Comparative Communism 1, pp. 294-95.

71. Based on F. Konstantinov, "Marxism-Leninism: A Unitary International Theory," Pravda, June 14, 1968; "The Train Jan Prochazka Missed," Literaturnaia gazeta (Literary newspaper), May 8, 1968; I. Alexandrov, "Attack on the Socialist Foundations of Czechoslovakia," Pravda, July 11, 1968; The "Five-Party Letter" from the Bulgarian, East German, Hungarian, Polish, and Soviet Communist parties to the Czechoslovak party, July 14-15, 1968; "Defense of Socialism as the Highest International Duty," Pravda, August 22, 1968. For very similar statements by East Germans, see On the Situation in the Czechoslovak Socialist Republic, n.d.

72. See, for example, Richard Lowenthal, "The Sparrow in the Cage," Problems of Communism 17, no. 6 (1968): 10; and especially "Pro-Czechoslovakian Mood in the Ukrainian SSR," Radio Free Europe, July 16, 1968.

73. Peter J. Potichnyj and Grey Hodnett, The Ukraine and the Czechoslovak Crisis, Australian National University, Department of Political Science and Research, School of Social Sciences, Occasional Paper no. 6, (1970).

74. Ibid., pp. 102, 115-16, 117.

75. Ibid., p. 75.

76. "While the Soviet leadership stood to lose from the exposure of the Ukrainian intelligentsia, youth, and public at large to greater knowledge of the Czechoslovak reforms, it probably stood to gain from the exposure of many Ukrainian officials to these threatening phenomena. Thus, 'public opinion' losses were to some extent offset by a gain in support for repressive action from within the Soviet political machine." Ibid., p. 120.

77. Ibid., pp. 122-23.

78. See A. Hegedus, "On the Alternatives of Social Development," Kortars (Contemporary), June 1968, presented in Radio Free Europe Hungarian Press Survey, no. 1947 (September 13, 1968).

79. Harry G. Shaffer, "Progress in Hungary," Problems of Communism 19, no. 1 (1970): 49-50.

80. Matyas Toth, "Hungary: Strengthening the Leading Role of the Party," World Marxists Review 12, no. 8 (1969): 24.

81. L. Mosin, "Slavnyi put' bor'by za mir i sotsializm" (The glorious path of the struggle for the world and socialism), Kommunist, no. 17 (1968): 86-87.

82. Imre Pardi, "The Experience of the New System of Managing the National Economy in the Hungarian People's Republic," Ekonomicheskaia gazeta (Economic newspaper), no. 46 (November 1968), translated in William F. Robinson, "Hungary's NEM: A Documentary of Soviet Views and Magyar Hopes," Radio Free Europe, May 30, 1969.

83. Shaffer, "Progress in Hungary," p. 51.

84. Michael Gamarnikow, Economic Reforms in Eastern Europe (Detroit, 1968), pp. 56-57. This book is useful for comparing the Czechoslovak and Hungarian economic reforms, as well as for comparison of East European economic reforms in general.

85. Nepszabadsag (Freedom of the people), September 1, 1968, quoted in "Hungarian Reform After the Invasion," Radio Free Europe, October 14, 1968, p. 24.

86. Jozsef Bognar, "Economic Reform and International Economic Policy," The New Hungarian Quarterly 9, no. 32 (1968): 84.

87. "Party Daily Urges Bolder Use of Veto," Radio Free Europe, June 6, 1969. On the new status of the unions, see Sandor Gaspar, "Increased Role and Tasks of the Trade Unions in Our Country," Radio Free Europe Hungarian Press Survey, no. 1745 (September, 1966); "Characteristic Features of the New Hungarian Labor Code,"

Radio Free Europe, January 15, 1967; "Hungarian Trade Union Activities: Where Politics and Economics Meet," Radio Free Europe, January 31, 1969; and Gamarnikow, Economic Reforms, pp. 147-54.

88. Fred E. Dohrs, "Incentives in Communist Agriculture: The Hungarian Models," Slavic Review 27, no. 1 (1968): 25.

89. Ibid., p. 27.

90. "Socialist Democracy on the Move: Kallai Outlines Parliament's Action Program for 1968," Radio Free Europe, March 8, 1968, p. 2.

91. "Otvetsvennost' pered vremenem" (Responsibility to the times), Izvestiia, July 25, 1968, p. 5. See also Reszso Nyers's call for a further increase in the role of the Parliament in "L'Unita Interviews Reszso Nyers," Radio Free Europe, July 22, 1969.

92. "Otvetsvennost'," p. 5.

93. Clyde Farnsworth, "Hungarians Vote for Parliament," New York Times, April 26, 1971.

94. Andrew Gyorgy, Nationalism in Eastern Europe, Research Analysis Corporation Report, RAC-R-89, January 1970, p. 46.

95. "The Literary Scene in Hungary," Radio Free Europe, June 13, 1969.

96. Gamarnikow, Economic Reforms, p. 120.

97. Imre Vertes, "The Workers' Party, The Workers' Policy," Nepszabadsag, May 1, 1969, quoted in "What is a Proletarian?," Radio Free Europe, June 25, 1969.

98. Janos Gosztonyi, "The Party, Workers' Power, and Socialist Democracy," Pravda, June 1, 1969, quoted in Radio Free Europe, June 25, 1969.

99. L. Rozsa, "The Road of Our Democracy," Nepszabadsag, September 1, 1968, in Radio Free Europe Hungarian Press Survey, no. 1950 (September 18, 1968). Barnabas Racz takes a dim view of Hungarian political change in "Political Changes in Hungary After the Soviet Invasion of Czechoslovakia," Slavic Review 29, no. 4 (1970).

100. Jeno Fock in Magyar Nemzet (The Hungarian nation), September 26, 1968, and Nepszabadsag, September 22, 1968, quoted in "Hungarian Reform After the Invasion," Radio Free Europe, October 14, 1968.

101. Mosin, "Slavnyi," p. 87. See also Pravda, July 4, 1969, and the article by V. Gerasimov in Pravda, July 8, 1969. V. Gutsev and M. Petunin in Mezhdunarodnaia zhizn' (International life), no. 6 (1968), emphasize Hungary's fidelity to the Warsaw Pact and Comecon, as did Brezhnev at the Tenth Party Congress in November 1970.

102. Pravda, November 25, 1970.

103. Pardi in Robinson, "Hungary's NEM," p. 17.

104. Tibor Pethe, "Rovnyi pul's Budapesht" (The even pulse of Budapest), Izvestiia, January 18, 1969.

105. B. Rodionov, "Verdni sochinitelei iz 'Veltvokh' " (Fantasies of the authors of 'Die Weltwoche'), Izvestiia, November 27, 1969.

106. See, for example, J. Horvath in Nepszabadsag, December 7, 1970, in Radio Free Europe Hungarian Press Survey, no. 2109 (January 21, 1971); Z. Lokosz in Magyar hirlap (Hungarian news), December 6, 1960, in Radio Free Europe Hungarian Press Survey, no. 2108 (December 30, 1970).

107. "Hungarian Reform After the Invasion," p. 9. See also the very important editorial, "Where Are We Going?," Nepszabadsag, September 22, 1968, in Radio Free Europe Hungarian Press Survey, no. 1953 (October 9, 1968).

108. "Hungarian and Soviet Reforms Compared: Nyers' Statement," Radio Free Europe, September 16, 1969.

109. "Izvestiia Approves Hungarian Farm Council," Radio Free Europe, March 25, 1968.

110. Dohrs, "Incentives," p. 36.

111. "Pravda Personalizes Nadudvar," Radio Free Europe, August 19, 1968.

112. Handelsblatt, December 2, 1968, quoted in Robinson, "Hungary's NEM," p. 33.

113. Shaffer, "Progress in Hungary," p. 59.

114. Bernard Gwertzman, "Soviet Lag Stirs 'Self-Criticism'," New York Times, March 26, 1970.

115. V. Savin, "Problemy i perspektivy sotsialisticheskoi demokratii" (Problems and perspectives of socialist democracy), Novy Mir (New world), no. 5 (1969): 268.

116. Aryeh L. Unger, "Politinformator or Agitator: A Decision Blocked," Problems of Communism 19, no. 5 (1970): 34.

2

**EAST EUROPEAN INFLUENCES
ON SOVIET ECONOMIC
THOUGHT AND REFORMS**
Leon Smolinski

The interesting question is not that East European economic thought and reforms have influenced the Soviet Union but that this influence has been so limited.

During the 1930s the standard term applied to the early five-year plans was "The Great Experiment." That was, of course, a misnomer. Controlled experiment implies the existence of a control sample. With a sample consisting of one economy, the results of the Soviet experiment could be attributed to factors other than planning: size of market, endowment with resources, historical antecedents, the degree of backwardness at the time the experiment was initiated. Furthermore, the Stalinist model consisted of a number of interrelated policies and institutional solutions and their criss-crossing positive and negative effects were difficult to disentangle. To quote a classical work on problems of experimentation in social sciences:

> In a controlled experiment, the experimenter can manipulate at will, even if only within limits, certain features in a situation (often designated as "variables" or "factors") which are assumed to constitute the relevant conditions for the occurrence of the phenomena under study, so that by repeatedly varying some of them (in the ideal case, by varying just one) but keeping the others constant, the observer can study the effects of such changes upon the phenomenon and discover the constant relations of dependence between the phenomenon and variables.[1]

Let the phenomenon be, in our case, the planners' objective (such as the rate of growth of national income) and the variables be various key ingredients of the Stalinist recipe for achieving that objective.

One sees how inconclusive the prewar Soviet experience was and how qualified would have to be any systemic inferences based upon it.

The situation has changed radically as, in the aftermath of World War II, the size of the sample was increased from one to eight with the emergence of the Soviet bloc in East Europe. Conditions for a grandiose social experiment in socialism were now present to a much greater degree than in the 1920s.

One can visualize at least two alternative scenarios under which the communist governments could take advantage of these conditions. The first possibility was a selective and creative adaptation of the Soviet model of economic planning and development to the differing initial conditions of each country: its level of development already achieved, resource endowment, dependence on foreign trade, and so on. Adaptation would include avoidance of Soviet mistakes, especially those already repudiated in the USSR itself, such as gigantomania. Such a selective adaptation might influence the Soviet economy by making possible, even necessary, a more balanced appraisal of the Soviet model, by isolating its various components and separating necessary features from historic accidents and random factors. It may be added that the relatively ample supply of well-trained, creative economists working on problems of economic planning, especially in such countries as Czechoslovakia and Poland, meant that at least one necessary condition for such a task was met. The possible payoffs from such an approach were obvious. The results of experimentation with different variants of socialist planning and development could be (once again selectively) utilized by the Soviet directors in appraising and streamlining their economic system. As a limiting case, one might even expect variants developed in advanced industrial countries such as Czechoslovakia or East Germany to be in some respects more suitable for the USSR of the 1950s than its own variant created during the early years of industrialization.

The development of multiple variants of socialist planning also could have made that system more acceptable to uncommitted countries reluctant to adopt the monistic Stalinist solution. Under our scenario these countries could choose from a whole spectrum of tested models adjusted to different degrees of economic development. Finally, this solution would have made socialism more palatable to and effective in the East European countries themselves. This polycentric scenario might have resulted in the maximum possible influence of East European economic thought and practice upon the Soviet Union itself and upon the future of the socialist economic system.

Needless to say, this would have hardly endeared the solution in question to the Soviet system's directors. Let us therefore consider an alternative scenario that could provide the USSR with an experimental base without affecting its unique position in the world communist movement. Under that approach, East European economies would introduce the Soviet economic model without essential modifications and adaptations, as they actually did, but then would be able to freely adjust its features in the light of its performance. Under this solution of a rigid implantation and flexible implementation, they could freely develop new incentive systems, planning methods, and other partial reforms if the original Soviet solutions did not lead to optimum results. The Russians would then observe the outcome of such reforms and selectively utilize them in their own planning. The necessary conditions for the success of this approach would then include a free flow of unbiased reports on the performance of the Soviet model in the East European settings, a freedom to act on the basis of such reports by instituting partial reforms, and in general a substantial degree of openmindedness and institutional flexibility on the part of the East European systems' directors, planning officials, and economists. Once again, the availability of economic and managerial talent in various East European economies would facilitate such critical appraisal of and flexible response to symptoms associated with the transplant of the Soviet model into the new economic organisms.

Instead, as is well known, a short-lived interlude of a quasi NEP of the late 1940s (which in turn might be viewed as a modified version of the Soviet system of the 1920s) was followed by a period of rigid, unimaginative imitation of Soviet institutions, strategies, tactics, and even occasionally of random, accidental practices. Oskar Lange relates an extreme example of such imitative development. The Polish garment industry asked the planners to carry out an anthropometric survey of that country's population in order to determine an appropriate frequency distribution of sizes for readymade clothing. Planners rejected that request on the grounds that "we can obtain such data from our comrades in the Soviet garment industry." As a result, for years to come, readymade clothes in Poland provided good fits for Soviet visitors but not for Polish buyers. In a more serious vein, Lange concludes:

> The Stalinist model of industrialization presupposed the large land areas, rich endowment in natural resources and considerable population reserves available in the Soviet Union. It was not suitable for a mechanical transplantation to Poland, a country with completely different economic and geographic conditions . . . . A miniature of Soviet-type industrialization was forced upon [that country].[2]

The reasons for this course of events are complex and a separate essay would have to be written to analyze them. Soviet pressures probably played the decisive role. They were compounded by East

European planners' recognition that borrowing from "the Soviet comrades" was often the safest and quickest way of promoting their personal careers, and in a number of cases by a sincere conviction that
following the established Soviet path was also the safest and quickest
way toward socialism.

For the purposes of this essay, what matters is that severe maladjustments brought about by the slavish imitation of the Soviet model
contributed decisively to the subsequent reaction—to reform movements
in Yugoslavia during the early 1950s, then in Poland and, with more
or less substantial lags, in other countries. Until that reaction set
in, as long as the imitative development pattern continued, the scope
of potential influence on the USSR was rather limited. Potentially,
even with the prevailing rigid implantation and implementation of the
Soviet model, such influence could be exerted by East European economists who, unlike their Soviet colleagues, had kept up with modern
economics and were better equipped to appraise the Stalinist model
critically. In practive, the economists' ability to engage in such criticism was severely limited. Lange subsequently compared their plight,
until 1956, to that of an astronomer whose telescope had been taken
away. Deprived of statistical information and of freedom to publish,
they were increasingly reduced to silence or (like Lange himself) to
writing laudatory commentaries upon Josef Stalin's "Economic Problems of Socialism." The contemporary Polish saying that "our only
economist was Stalin and he was not an economist" was descriptive
of the situation in other bloc countries as well. Their virtual inability
to influence the Soviet Untion under these conditions also was related
to the intellectual climate there. Not unlike post-Ricardian economists
a hundred years earlier, the Soviet system's directors seemed to
believe that the Marxist theory of political economy had achieved a
fairly final form and that their economic institutions were a satisfactory embodiment of that theoretical system. Their East European
counterparts could then only congratulate themselves at having available Soviet solutions from which to copy.

It is true that even at the height of Stalinism the copies in question
were less than perfect and that the East European economies continued
to preserve some of their peculiarities. For example, forcible collectivization was proceeding at a slower pace than it had in the Soviet
Union and individual peasant farms still survived. But Soviet observers
found little reason to study such vestigial remnants of the past, let
alone imitate them and dismissed them as temporary, tactical concessions that would soon find their way to the garbage heap of history.
As early as 1950 authoritative Soviet expert N. D. Kazantsev, anticipated that throughout East Europe

at a certain stage of the fight against the kulaks, an all-out
collectivization will be achieved and it will become feasible
to liquidate the kulaks as a class . . . . Their confiscated
land will be given in perpetual use to the kolkhozy and all
land in the country will be declared state property . . . .
All land will be nationalized in people's democracies, as
dictated by the interests of the state.[3]

The view that people's democracies were destined to pass through
all the stages of Russia's road to Stalinism, albeit with occasional
differences in tempo, prevailed in other areas of economic policy as
well. It might have delighted Karl Marx ("An undeveloped country
sees in a developed one a mirror-image of its own future"[4]) and,
possibly, Walt Rostow. But the East Europeans themselves were less
and less pleased with it.

POTENTIAL CHANNELS OF EAST EUROPEAN
INFLUENCE ON SOVIET PLANNING

The imitative economic development that set in with varying lags
in East European countries resulted in periods of theoretical innovation, economic experimentation, and institutional change.

Now that autonomous change was rapidly taking place in economic
theory and practice, it appeared plausible to expect that Soviet theorists and practitioners would closely follow these developments and
occasionally be influenced by them. This expectation was made even
more plausible by the fact that in the Soviet Union itself a thaw succeeded the intellectual and institutional stagnation of late Stalinism.
The peak of economic debate and experimentation in Poland, for
example, coincided with the partial break-up of the rigid Stalinist mold
in the Soviet economy, the Sovnarkhozy reform, the sale of Machine-
Tractor Stations (MTS), the shift to cost reduction as the main managerial success indicator, the revival of mathematical economics after
a quarter-century of dogmatic slumber, and many other symptoms
of openmindedness and willingness to question traditional assumptions
and solutions.

Thus, it appeared reasonable to expect that in their search for
new solutions the Soviet system's directors and economists might
be influenced by the experimentation going on in Eastern Europe
during the late 1950s, especially in Poland (the most "autonomous"
experimenter in those years), but also to a smaller extent in Czechoslovakia, Hungary, and East Germany. As time went on and, toward
the end of the 1950s, Soviet influence was firmly reestablished in once

heretical Poland and Hungary, one also could expect (in line with our earlier discussion) that the USSR might in some cases use these countries as laboratories for induced experimentation (such as large-scale application of mathematical models and computerization of economic planning) before trying such methods in the Soviet Union itself. Poland, with its highly creative group of mathematical economists and cyberneticists, and with its headstart in developing input-output tables and computers, appeared a likely candidate for such a role. Such experiments, such a concerted intrabloc division of labor, could then be an important way for East Europe to influence the Soviet economy. Expectations along these lines were held by some Western economists at the time.

We will be concerned with the extent to which these expectations were met. Before discussing this matter, let us pause briefly to consider some possible channels through which East European influences could operate. In 1956 Soviet and Polish economists voiced a complaint about the paucity of their contacts: "there are few personal contacts as regards research activities and there is hardly ever an opportunity to participate in scholarly discussions."[5] There is no reason to believe that the situation in other countries differed greatly. Thereafter somewhat closer contacts were established. Visits of Soviet economists to East Europe became more frequent, in part so they could participate in such international conferences as the first international conference on the application of input-output methods in economic planning, organized in Warsaw in 1959, or the December 1958 conference in Prague dealing with the improvement of planning methods in countries of the Soviet bloc. East European economists visited the Soviet Union on similar occasions or to give lectures. Some of their works were published in Soviet translations, especially books dealing with mathematical economics. In addition, Polish publishers made an interesting attempt to bring out Russian translations of Polish monographs or collections of theoretical articles for which Soviet publishers, apparently, had not shown enough interest.[6] At least one of these collections, containing the first Russian translation of Kalecki's celebrated growth model, appears to have aroused considerable interest on the part of some Soviet theorists.[7]

One also finds occasional references to original, untranslated sources (mainly Polish and Czechoslovak) in Soviet economic literature. These deal almost exclusively with specialized monographs and articles in various branches of mathematical economics and economic cybernetics and their applications in planning. Soviet users of such sources show critical acumen and discernment, their citations usually referring to original contributions (for example, Henryk Greniewski's pioneering research on economic cybernetics) rather than to popularizations or compilations. We may finally mention straws in the wind, such as evidence that Polish economic journals have a number of noninstitutional subscribers in the Soviet Union.[8] This indicates enough interest on the part of their Soviet readers to undertake the effort of reading specialized texts in Polish, a language sufficiently different from Russian to require some study. Of course mere interest does not imply influence, but a potential vehicle for carrying such influence is there.

An increasingly important channel through which East European economists convey novel theoretical concepts or reform proposals to their Soviet colleagues is, apparently, the various commissions of Comecon.[9] It is an open question how receptive Soviet representatives are to such ventures since they reportedly tend to be recruited from among practitioners (the closest analogy to whom might be found among the graduates of American colleges of business administration) who find the less pragmatic and more theoretically minded arguments of their East European colleagues somewhat baffling. And yet, in the long run such official contacts among government officials may be at least as conducive to the spread of new ideas as the more publicized meetings among professors of economics.

One should perhaps mention the somewhat amorphous, diffuse, and difficult to define influence that people's democracies may exercise upon visiting Soviet citizens. From informal conversations one gathers that they tend to be impressed with the better quality and greater variety of consumer goods, the availability of fashionable clothing in privately owned stores, and similar amenities. The difference between, say, Warsaw and Moscow reportedly was more striking in these respects during the late 1950s, when the Poles were engaged in some limited reforms of their planning and incentive system while the Russians had done far less in that direction. This point was made repeatedly in Polish and Hungarian literature describing that period. One readily concedes that Soviet visitors may have been impressed and may have voted with their rubles, by stocking up on East European consumer goods, but it is highly unlikely that they made the connection between these phenomena and, say, differences in national planning systems, or that their propensity to reform their system was in any way affected.

These, then, are some of the potential channels through which East European influences could enter the Soviet economy. To what extent have they done so?

EVIDENCE OF INFLUENCE:
AGRICULTURAL AND INDUSTRIAL MANAGEMENT

Let us begin with the most important long-term departures from the Soviet model: the prevalence of individual peasant farming in Poland and Yugoslavia, and the Yugoslav system of industrial management through workers' councils. Neither has had any appreciable influence upon Soviet economic theory or practice, but one is hard put to find any evidence of a serious interest in these path-breaking innovations, or any analytical studies by Soviet economists of, say, comparative performance of private and collective farming, of the operation of workers' councils, of their theoretical significance and practical implications.

In a fairly representative statement, the well-known Soviet economist Gatovskii criticizes the Polish economists' view that socialism can be built in the nonagricultural sector alone while individual peasant farming survives indefinitely in agriculture. Instead, Gatovskii states that a gradual conversion of private into socialist farming is inevitable.[10] A similar attitude is taken with respect to Yugoslav agriculture, even during the periods when the Soviet leadership was assiduously wooing Tito: "For the time being, small-scale peasant farming represents the prevailing form of land tenure in Yugoslavia. . . . The Yugoslav government pursues the policy of expanding and strengthening the socialist sector both in the city and in the village, of assuring the victory of socialism."[11] This is hardly consistent with the view that the Soviets are ready to concede the possibility of diverse forms of socialism. Private ownership of farms in Yugoslavia is angrily denounced during periods of strained relations; at other times it is ignored or dismissed as a temporary vestige of the past that has no permanent doctrinal or practical importance. A similar attitude prevails with respect to peasant farming in Poland; Soviet commentators usually stress any developments that could be interpreted as strengthening the position of the surviving collective farms.

Thus, the agricultural revolution in Yugoslavia and Poland has received scant attention from Soviet analysts. However, one institutional innovation associated with the disbanding of collective farms in Poland in the fall of 1956 may have conceivably influenced subsequent Soviet policies: the decision to greatly reduce the role of Polish machine tractor stations. Most of the machinery was then transferred to the remaining collective farms and even to the so-called "agricultural circles"–genuine, voluntary agricultural cooperatives then being created. The only function left with the MTS was to perform repairs. In February 1957 Pravda attacked these reforms as violating the principles of socialism. But a year later the Russians in turn disbanded their machine tractor stations[12]; as pointed out by a French economist who studied that decision in depth, the Soviet decree coincided in its essential features with the Polish solution. While noting these similarities, one cannot prove conclusively that the latter influenced the former, especially since it was clearly not in Khrushchev's interest to explicitly acknowledge any such influence. The Polish innovation was part of a broader reform allowing the peasants to leave collective farms when they desired. Had Khrushchev mentioned Poland in the context of his MTS decision (which was being criticized anyway on doctrinal grounds by Suslov), this might have aroused dangerous associations of ideas.

Khrushchev was less cautious when speaking of the other major departure from the Soviet model, the Yugoslav workers' councils, on the occasion of his visit to Yugoslavia in August 1963. He started by criticizing Soviet industrial management: "Our industrial establishments have become so huge that a plant director could become a dictator, were it not for the existence of a sensitive public opinion." He then spoke favorably of Yugoslav workers' councils and continued: "the situation in the Soviet Union has become ripe for democratization of industrial management. As it is, we have too much bureaucracy." Khrushchev also announced that a special delegation would be sent to Yugoslavia to study the workers' councils and to prepare proposals for the Soviet government.[13] Characteristically enough, the Soviet prime minister's statements, although widely publicized in the Yugoslav and Western press, were never published in the Soviet Union itself. Workers' councils may have influenced, for a while, the mercurial Khrushchev, but censorship prevented the Soviet public from knowing his views.

This curious incident seems to indicate that the Soviet establishment (to use a much abused term) was reluctant to recognize even the remote possibility that it might learn something from the Yugoslav experience with such fundamental innovations as the workers' councils.

EVIDENCE OF INFLUENCE: MATHEMATICAL ECONOMICS

The same impression is reinforced as we pass to our next case study: East European influences on the development of Soviet mathematical economics and its applications in planning.

In this area, the advent of the computer age and econometric models found the Soviet Union woefully unprepared. After a brilliant start during the 1920s when such outstanding pioneers as E. Slutzky,

A. Kenius, N. Kondratief, and G. Feldman were among the world's leading mathematical economists and econometricians, work came to an abrupt halt during the first five-year plan. The "mathematical deviation in planning" was condemned on Stalin's personal order, and mathematical formulas disappeared for a quarter-century from Soviet economic literature and curriculums.[14] The long fight for the rebirth of Soviet mathematical economics began about 1957 under the leadership of V. Nemchinov and L. Kantorovich. Their well-entrenched conservative opponents attacked the bourgeois character of various branches of that science, its incompatibility with Marxist economic theory, and its sterility and uselessness in a centrally planned economy. One might assume that in their search for allies and precedents, and for the technical know-how, the Nemchinovites would be eager to take advantage of the considerable experience accumulated in this field by Yugoslav economists.

The first textbook on mathematical economics in East Europe, by Aloizij Vadnal, appeared in Yugoslavia as early as 1951, followed in 1955 by The Mathematical Introduction to Econometrics.[15] In 1956 the same author, in an excellent paper at the European Congress of Econometricians at Aix-en-Provence, dealt explicitly with the methodological problem that was to occupy Soviet contestants for years to come: the applicability of advanced mathematical methods in socialist economic planning. He reached the conclusion that there are no methodological objections or insurmountable practical difficulties to such applications and that, the more highly developed a socialist economy becomes, the more it can benefit from them.[16] At about the same time, Albin Orthaber explored in a long article the practical problems of applying input-output methods in economic planning, availability of statistical data for that purpose, and so on.[17] Finally, at the econometric conference that convened in Belgrade on November 5, 1957, a general agreement was reached that mathematical economics and econometrics are fully compatible with Marxist theory and it was decided to apply them widely in Yugoslav economic research and planning, proceeding from the theoretical foundations of Marxist economics. Work already was in progress on such practical problems as an adaptation of Dutch and Indian planning models to the needs of Yugoslav planning, antedating by a number of years Soviet explorations of that kind.[18]

To return now to our point of departure, it comes as an anticlimax to note that, to my knowledge, all this work, all pioneering attempts to cope with problems that were to occupy Soviet economists for years, passed virtually unnoticed by either the Nemchinovites or their opponents. Was this because, in spite of official protestations, the Yugoslavs were not considered bonafide Marxists and their economy not a planned one? Hardly. Such an attitude might explain the

Nemchinovites' silence, but not that of their opponents. Or was it
because none of the participants in the great Soviet econometric debate
bothered to read Yugoslav economic literature and none of the afore-
mentioned books, articles, and reports appeared in languages other
then Serbo-Croatian? Whatever the reason, in spite of several impressive firsts scored by the Yugoslavs in this important area, one detects
no influence upon the Soviet Union.

At the same time the Russians felt no compunction about acknowledging assistance in this area from economists from other East
European countries such as Poland and Hungary. In particular, the
fact that mathematical methods had already found acceptance in those
economies obviated the need for importing them directly from the
capitalist West and thus deprived the Soviet antimathematicians of
one of their favorite arguments. For example, one finds that the first
textbook on linear programming (using the more easily computable
Danzig method rather than Kantorovich's multipliers) published in
the Soviet Union and used in training economists was translated from
the Hungarian.[19]

As early as 1957 Polish economists argued, at a Moscow conference, for the use of mathematical growth models and input-output
methods; the first international conference on the use of such methods
in economic planning met in Warsaw in 1959.[20] In a number of
instances, such countries as East Germany continue to lead the USSR
in the development of actual applications of input-output tables in
economic planning.[21] Exchanges of experience in these areas have
played an important part in introducing mathematical methods into
Soviet planning. In a more general way, such exchanges have been
promoted by coordination of economic plans in Comecon countries,
resulting in joint recommendations aimed at improvements in planning
methods.[22]

A special mention must be made of the role played by the distinguished Polish economist Oskar Lange. A founder of modern mathematical economics, he also was a highly placed Communist politician,
the vice president of Poland's State Council, and a widely influential
and original Marxist thinker. From the viewpoint of the Nemchinovites,
one might almost say that if such a person had not existed, he would
have had to be invented. His prestige has helped make mathematical
economics respectable in the Soviet Union and neo-Marxist economics
respectable in the West. He also entered the Soviet debate directly
by trying to reconcile input-output methodology with Marx's growth
model in an article that was soon translated into Russian.[23]

While East European influence in this strategic area was very
real, one should not exaggerate its significance as a causative factor
behind the mathematical revolution in Soviet economics. Both the
Nemchinovites and their opponents were occasionally turning to East

European experience to find support for their opinions, rather than to search for inspiration and factual evidence. Even in the case of Oskar Lange, who undoubtedly enjoys the strongest influence of all the East Europeans, one cannot resist the impression that the Russians were sometimes more interested in using his prestigious name than in ascertaining and learning from what he actually said. A Russian translation of his Introduction to Econometrics did not appear until 1964, six years after the original edition and long after translations of several texts by bourgeois economists. Amusingly enough, its anti-Nemchinovite editor carefully removed all complimentary mentions by Lange of such authors as Nemchinov and Kantorovich.[24]

EVIDENCE OF INFLUENCE:
ECONOMIC POLICY AND REFORM

In any event, East European influences on Soviet economic theory have been strongest in the area of methodology just discussed. They were far less pronounced in the working out of more substantive problems, such as growth models, or theory of optimal decision making, with the possible exception of borderline problems pertaining to information theory, cybernetics, and general systems analysis, where Polish, Hungarian, and Czechoslovak influences appear at times.

To come now to the field of economic policy and reform, we shall limit ourselves to three case studies: Liberman-type reforms of success indicators and incentive funds, mergers, and the introduction of interest charges.

Most reforms of enterprise incentive funds proposed by Liberman had been experimented with in selected groups of enterprises, or even introduced in industry as a whole, in various East European countries during the late 1950s. (for example, it was decided at the Communist Party Central Committee meeting in Czechoslovakia, on February 25, 1958, to adopt the principle of long-term material incentives in industrial enterprises. Enterprise incentive bonus was set as a function of the total amount of profits earned; the formula was adopted for five years in advance, just as Liberman proposed. The general principle was adopted that "the share of total profits earmarked for bonus payments should be as stable as possible so as not to impair the effectiveness of the incentive systems."[25] This measure was adopted before Liberman's proposals became widely known in the USSR (that is, four years before his Pravda article) but after the original statement of his views on this matter (in Kommunist in 1956).

A more clearcut case of East European reforms preceding the publication of a corresponding proposal by Liberman occurred in Poland. New Polish rules determining the principles of formation of a bonus fund, introduced in selected enterprises in 1958 and extended by 1960 to most branches of industry, provided that payments into the bonus fund were to be related to the improvement in the rate of profitability; more important, the official decree included a table showing the relationship between the two magnitudes. The relationship in question is determined according to a sliding scale that was introduced into Liberman's proposals only in August 1962, or more than two and a half years later.[26] The Polish priority in this case appears fairly conclusive. But does the priority in publication unequivocally imply a Polish influence on Liberman? It might, but we cannot exclude the possibility that Polish reformers had knowledge of Liberman's sliding table approach prior to its publication.[27]

Let us now consider just a few features of the Kosygin reforms of 1965 which had been tried out in Eastern Europe in earlier years. The proposal that enterprises have control over their depreciation allowances was made in Poland as early as May 1957, and the legislation introducing an enterprise development fund to be used for financing decentralized investment was passed in October 1958. The term "direct links" among enterprises is used to describe East German legislation passed on February 11, 1958.[28]

One could readily multiply such cases where an economic reform was first adopted in an East European country years before being introduced in the Soviet Union. In the cases mentioned above it is also known that the reforms were mentioned in Soviet periodicals. However, these are at best necessary but not sufficient conditions for establishing without doubt that the Soviet reforms were influenced by the East European ones that preceded them. One hardly ever finds any specific acknowledgment to this effect in the Soviet economic literature. Even more significant is the fact that until the late 1960s one usually found only casual cataloguing of East European reforms and experiments, without analysis of the actual experience. What is more, such analysis was rarely available even in the economic literature of the East European countries. For example, numerous experiments were carried out in Poland from 1955 on using various principles of formation of the enterprise wage fund and various methods of wage payments to individuals. But as late as 1962 no analysis of these experiments was available, nor were the results made available to economists.[29] No wonder that after initial enthusiasm there was growing exasperation with the endless economic experiments among Polish economists. When in 1965 a hesitant but more comprehensive reform was finally proclaimed, one of them stated characteristically: "At last things have begun to move. We have finally broken

out of the vicious circle of experiments, more experiments, and
nothing but experiments."[30]

One wonders how influential East European experiments in the
USSR could be under these circumstances. As for the actual reforms,
the Russians' ability to benefit from them may have been impaired
by the well-known characteristic of Soviet-type economies: Once a
reform gets introduced, it often becomes part of the official party
line and, as such, is not subject to critical appraisal in economic
literature. There were exceptions to this rule, such as the periods
of relatively free discussion in Poland in late 1950s and in Czechoslovakia in 1967-68, but those also were the periods during which
the countries in question were being looked at with the greatest suspicion by the Soviet system's directors and, consequently, when their
potential influence upon Soviet developments was at its low ebb.

The history of introduction of interest charges in cost accounting
and pricing in socialist enterprises of the Soviet bloc provides another
interesting illustration of the rather typical sequence of events. As in
the case of mathematical economics, the practice in question is con-
troversial and, ever since its abandonment by the Soviet Union under
the first five-year plan, is alleged to violate Marx's labor theory of
value. Again, as in the case of mathematical economics, the Yugoslavs
were the first to break the taboo by making interest charges part of
enterprises' costs of production in 1957. As a rule, interest charges
are set at the level of 3.5 percent of the value of capital assets, except
at some less profitable branches, which are charged 1.7 percent.
Once again, the Poles launched a lively theoretical discussion beginning with Kenryk Fiszel's proposal in May 1956 and culminating in
the recommendation to introduce interest charges on fixed capital
assets, issued by the Council of Economic Advisors in the Spring of
1957.[31] But then, nothing happened. Both the Yugoslav breakthrough
and the Polish economists' recommendation were, for all practical
purposes, ignored for a number of years. Then on January 1, 1964,
Hungary introduced interest charges on fixed capital (at the level of
five percent in manufacturing and one percent in extractive industries).
Poland followed suit in June 1965, the Soviet Union in September 1965,
and then, once the innovation had been made respectable by the Soviet
acceptance, other countries of East Europe rapidly introduced it.
There was, however, no uniformity in this area and each country
appears to have followed its own preferences as regards the level
and the methods of calculation of interest charges. Thus in Poland
and Czechoslovakia interest charges are computed on the replacement
value of capital assets, while Bulgarians, East Germans, and Hungarians use the original value. The rate of interest used varies from
three percent in Bulgaria to five percent in Poland and Hungary and

six percent in East Germany and Czechoslovakia and is thus, roughly, inversely correlated with the respective countries' level of economic development, a rather unexpected finding.[32]

In summary, we find that neither the Yugoslav decision in 1957 to introduce interest charges into cost accounting, nor the imaginative Polish theoretical discussion of the problems involved at that time had any influence upon Soviet developments. The Hungarian experience, since January 1, 1964, was mentioned in Soviet publications and may possibly have been taken into account in the Soviet decision taken in September 1965. However, the extent of such influence (if any) cannot be ascertained. Finally, the Soviet acceptance of that innovation seems to have convinced the more conservative people's democracies that it was ideologically respectable, but there was no attempt on their part to faithfully imitate the solution adopted in the USSR. One sees evidence of "follow the leader" attitudes, but not of the "ape the leader" policy of the Stalinist years.

Our last case study deals with what has been the most significant organizational innovation in Soviet industry during the last decade on the level of an enterprise[33]: the development of sovetskie firmy by the merger of several establishments producing homogenous or related products. East European (notably Polish and Czechoslovak) influences did affect the early formative stage of development of these units and also can be expected to be taken into account in future Soviet policies.

What is the economic rationale of these mergers? Under the traditional policies of output maximization and seller's market in Soviet-type economies, the tendency toward interplant specialization by process and/or product is often offset by the reluctance of each producer to become dependent on outside sources of supply. In shoe manufacturing, for example, each factory tends to produce a wide variety of products and to engage in all stages of production. This raises the cost of production since each process is performed on a relatively small scale.

The first Soviet firm, Progress, was created in Lviv in October 1961 by merging one large modern shoe factory with four small high-cost producers, located in the Lviv sovnarkhoz. Some stages of production for all five producers were now concentrated in the big "leading enterprise," others delegated to the smaller plants. Each participant became specialized in a narrow range of products. Additional savings were achieved by drastically reducing the managerial staff of the smaller plants while the staff of the "leading enterprise" came to perform managerial functions both for itself and for the firm as a whole. Under another variant of this setup, participant factories other than the leading enterprise lose their identity altogether and become, for all practical purposes, mere branches.

Finally, there is an altogether different type of firm, where the participating enterprises are of a more equal size and on an equal footing. None of them "leads"; each retains its management, balance sheets, and bank accounts, and savings achieved are almost exclusively due to economies of specialization.

It is interesting to note that the emergence of firms, which after the modest beginning in the Lviv sovnarkhoz gradually spread throughout the Soviet economy, seems to represent one of the few known cases of a significant institutional reform coming into being as the result of local initiative, taken by officials and economists of the Lviv sovnarkhoz. It was not until 1963 that the central government recommended widespread experimentation along these lines.

There is strong evidence that the creators of the first Soviet firms were inspired by the so-called VHJ (vyrobna hospodarka jednotka) introduced in Czechoslovakia early in 1959, and possibly by similar Polish institutions created in November 1960 after the Czechoslovak prototype.[34] One finds in early Soviet firms institutional solutions adopted in Czechoslovakia, especially in the so-called VHJ Type II firms, which also were organized around a leading enterprise (vedouci podnik) and had a similar division of rights and responsibilities among participating enterprises. The economic justification offered for the creation of Soviet firms also parallels Czechoslovak and Polish discussions. The first experiments with Polish firms took place in the leather and shoe industries, just as was later the case in the Lviv sovnarkhoz.[35] The resemblances are too close to be coincidence. The geographical location of the first Soviet firms also supports the hypothesis of their East European origin. In particular, the local press offers evidence of economic and cultural contacts between Western Ukraine and Poland.

At present, a major difference between a typical Soviet and East European firm is that the former embraces a few or at best a few dozen enterprises, usually located in the same geographic area, while the latter is an industrywide cartel-like association of all enterprises producing a given group of products. There is a growing interest among Soviet economists in the latter solution, and this is one of the few cases where Soviet analysts anticipate that the future development of Soviet industrial organization is likely to follow the path already taken by advanced East European economies.[36] They admit accordingly that the Russians may learn useful lessons from solutions already adopted in these countries. "In particular such problems merit our attention as the [decision-making] rights of a production association, principles according to which its bonus funds are formed, its optimal size, rules of apportioning enterprises among associations, etc."[37] The author adds that lessons should be learned not only from

East European achievements but also from their mistakes since, unless forestalled, "these defects can crop up in our country as well."[38]

This insight is increasingly shared by other Soviet analysts of the East European scene, not only as regards the future of Soviet firms but also in various other areas of economic reforms. The future East European influence may therefore increasingly be felt in a negative way: by making Soviet planners aware of pitfalls ahead, by preventing the occurrence of undesirable phenomena. If a future trend may be plotted on the basis of what are, so far, just a few isolated statements by Soviet specialists on East Europe, that area may yet belatedly assume the role of an economic laboratory, as discussed at the outset of this essay. Should this be the case, East European influences on Soviet decision making will become even more difficult to detect. It is hard enough to associate them with any concrete step that Soviet reformers have taken. It will be even harder to give East Europeans due credit for mistakes that the Russians will have avoided, for steps they will not have taken.

SOVIET RESISTANCE TO EAST EUROPEAN MODELS

Will such negative feedback from East European reforms be limited to the relatively minor, technical details of implementation and design such as we have discussed? Hardly. The aftermath of the Czechoslovak events of 1968 makes it abundantly clear that too radical attempts at reform in an East European economy may arouse so much hostility in the Soviet system's directors as to slow down the pace of Soviet reforms or even alter their direction. The Czechoslovak experience may have been a historical accident rather than a historical necessity of economic decentralization.[39] The political implications of the Czech experiment (rather than any specific characteristics of the economic reforms) appear, nevertheless, to have put new weapons into the hands of Soviet conservatives. And Soviet proponents of reform were put once more on the defensive and, instead of attacking the evils of overcentralization, they spend more and more time trying to prove the harmlessness of decentralization.

In using the Czechoslovak experience on the domestic front, Soviet conservatives appear to follow some such strategy. The ultimate goal of Czech reformers, they claim, was market socialism, which Soviet commentators identify with full autonomy of enterprises, hence with a complete decentralization. But this would amount to a restoration of capitalism. Hence any step in that direction, any degree of decentralization greater than the one traditionally accepted in

Soviet-type economies, represents a major threat to socialism and a
violation of Marxism-Leninism. To convey the flavor of this reasoning,
a few quotations from articles on Czechoslovak reforms may be useful: "Even the most insignificant reduction in the role of central
government's planning is fraught with the most serious consequences
for the economy."[40] Czech economists favoring market socialism
"in reality attempted to turn the country upon the road to capitalism"
and wanted to justify "their vicious concept of abandoning central
planning and replacing it with market mechanism which would regulate
macroeconomic proportions and provide the criteria for economic
decision-making."[41] Czechoslovak reformers wanted to give full autonomy to enterprises. But this amounts to repudiation of state ownership of industry. Also, "full autonomy of enterprises and all its
implications enter into conflict with the basic principles of Marxist-
Leninist economic theory."[42]

The common denominator of such comments is that the Czechoslovak reformers' ultimate objectives are made to appear more radical
than they ever actually were. This enables the commentators to repudiate various steps actually taken by the reformers as allegedly
leading inevitably toward such objectionable ends. In turn, by establishing such associations of ideas, it becomes easier to attack such
steps when they are proposed or actually taken in the Soviet Union.
Soviet reform proposals then come under criticism because they
resemble Czechoslovak practices.[43] The antireformist reaction in
the Soviet Union was encouraged and actually was preceded by Polish
antiliberal spokesmen such as an obscure professor, Wieslaw Iskra.
As early as April 1968 he attacked some of the most creative and progressive Polish economists (including W. Brus, S. Kurowski, J.
Drewnowski) whose "strategic purpose is to distort Marxist political
economy, to orientate it westward, to turn its interests away . . .
from the goals and tasks of the Party."[44] In November 1968 Gomulka
himself joined in condemning "economists who attempt to replace
central planning with a free interplay of market mechanisms" and
pronounced what might be looked upon as the common slogan of conservatives in all Soviet-type economies: "We want to strengthen the
role of central planning."[45] It is a saddening indication of how far
Poland has traveled from the "Spring in October" of 1956. But the
extent of Gomulka's influence on the Soviet Union was probably no
greater in his last years, when he promoted the cause of counter-
reformation, than it had been in 1956 when he headed the Soviet bloc's
most progressive government.

CONCLUSIONS

In general, in this writer's opinion, the influence of East European economic theory and reforms on Soviet counterparts remains rather limited. The Czechoslovak debacle is no exception. Soviet hostility appears to have been aroused not so much by the Czech economic revolution as by a fear of a political counterrevolution. Political developments in Czechoslovakia have influenced those in the USSR by strengthening the hand of Soviet conservatives. This in turn may lead eventually to a certain recentralization of Soviet economic decision making, or prevent decentralization that might otherwise have taken place. But, whether positive or negative, the influence of Czech economic developments as such remains limited, even though the domestic economic reformers' position may be weakened by conservatives associating them with the discredited Czechoslovak reforms. Such practices would merely serve as additional rationalizations of domestic policies (such as future recentralization, if it should occur) decided upon on other grounds.

This does not preclude the possibility that in the future East European experience may exert a more significant influence upon some of the Soviet partial reforms, upon concrete institutional solutions and modes of implementation. There are some signs that point in that direction.

One is the emergence of a growing body of economists specializing in East European affairs and also well acquainted with the technical problems of Soviet economic reforms. In this connection, the character of monographs and articles dealing with East European economies has been changing. They have become less descriptive and more analytical, and they often freely concede that in some cases East European countries may have developed more advanced, more perfect solutions to problems of incentives, wage formation, industrial organization, and such than has the USSR. Their work is accordingly centered around analysis of East European practices that may point the way for Soviet reformers, on the solution of these limited, concrete problems. All this a far cry from the belief that what happens in an East European country might induce the Russians to adopt "socialism with a human face" or "socialism without the kolkhozy," or some other such systemic breakthrough. Instead, the possibilities of evolutionary influences rather than of a revolutionary breakthrough appear to be the order of the day for such young economists as B. Rakitskii.[46]

In a recent issue of Voprosy ekonomiki, Rakitskii provides an interesting survey of areas of economic reform in which some East European countries are ahead of the Soviet Union and have lessons to

offer. By implication, this survey also suggests some directions that
Soviet reform is expected to take in the future.

One, already mentioned, is the formation of industrywide associations of enterprises producing a certain group of commodities. This
has been accomplished throughout East Europe and is only beginning
in the Soviet Uniton. Rakitskii finds evidence of monopolistic abuses
that would represent an even greater threat to efficiency in the USSR
where, due to the geographical extension of the country and large
distances separating member enterprises, the administrative problems
of managing a giant cartel would be compounded. It may therefore be
more desirable to depart from the East European solution and set up
several associations instead of one in any given industry. Rakitskii
then criticizes the Soviet economists who apparently believe that the
Russians have more to learn from the organizational experience of
large American corporations than from other Soviet-type economies.
One wonders whether they share Galbraith's belief that the logic of
the new industrial state is stronger than ideological or systemic
differences among countries.

Rakitskii then points to another area where East European countries have succeeded in solving a problem awaiting solution in the
USSR: the abandonment of ceilings upon enterprise wage funds. In
this area, however, he believes their experience to be useless for
Soviet planners, since they have to cope with a much larger volume
and variety of output of consumer goods which have to be adjusted to
any such solution if inflationary pressures are to be avoided. Thus
the differences in the size of the economies may preclude the larger
one from adopting the solution successfully tried out in the smaller.

According to Rakitskii, the main lesson to be drawn by the Russians from planning reforms in East Europe is the new interpretation
given to the concept of stability of plans. It amounts to a stability of
broad, general objectives of the system's directors and the mainte -
nance of stable rules of the game, coupled with flexibility of specific
targets. The author anticipates a similar development in Soviet
planning.

Soviet planners also may learn from East European experience
in decentralization of pricing decisions: "The experience of [East]
European socialist countries indicates that . . . we suffer considerable
losses due to excessive rigidity of our prices."[47] It suggests that
prices should be fixed in terms of floors and ceilings, thus allowing
more flexible, decentralized responses to changing business conditions.
The author emphasizes that the transplantation of East European
experience in this field might facilitate the anticipated partial transition from central allocation of supplies to wholesale trade.

Finally, Rakitskii approves of the recognition in recent years
throughout East Europe of the role of stochastic factors and of the

need for the creation of strategic reserves at various levels of decision making. He views it as a necessary condition for combining
planning at the center with an autonomy of execution at the periphery,
"with a full utilization of socialist market mechanisms."[48]

The distinction between "socialist market mechanisms" and
"market socialism" may appear subtle, but it is apparently very real
to Soviet economists appraising recent developments in East European
economies.

In the future, if the past experience provides any reliable guide,
we may expect the extent of East European influences on Soviet economic thought and policies to vary as the function of Soviet domestic
developments rather than the other way around. These influences may
be expected to strengthen liberalizing developments (if any), but not
to give rise to them in any important area of Soviet economics.

NOTES

1. E. Nagel, The Structure of Science (New York, 1961), p. 451.

2. O. Lange, an interview with Trybuna ludu (The people's tribune), December 5, 1956, in O socjalizmie i gospodarce socjalistycznej
(On socialism and socialist economy) (Warsaw, 1966), pp. 257-58.

3. N. D. Kazantsev, in Izvestiia Akademii Nauk SSSR, otdelenie
ekonomii i prava (transactions of the Acacemy of Sciences of the USSR,
division of economics and law), no. 4 (1950): 256-58.

4. A view rather different from the laissez-faire ideas held by
his contemporaries theorizing on comparative advantage.

5. O. Lange, speech of June 7, 1956, Pisma ekonomiczne i spo-
leczne 1930-1960 (Writings on economics and social science 1930-60)
(Warsaw, 1963), p. 396.

6. For example, Ocherki po teorii sotsialisticheskogo vosproiz-
vodstva i tsen: izbrannye sochineniia polskikh ekonomistov (Essays
in the theory of socialist reporduction and prices: selected works by
Polish economists) (Warsaw, 1964). This is an interesting collection
of contributions to macro- and microeconomic theory.

7. Judging by a long review of the above volume in Ekonomika i
matematicheskie metody (Economics and mathematical methods), no. 5
(1966): 787-92.

8. Information obtained from Polish economists.

9. Information collected from Czechoslovak economists.

10. A. Gatovskii, Voprosy ekonomiki (Problems of economics)
(Moscow), no. 12 (1957): 21-22.

11. K. Danilov, Voprosy ekonomiki, no. 2 (1956): 8.

12. Pravda, February 4, 1957, and January 25, 1958, as reported by H. Wronski in Kultura (Culture) (Paris), no. 4 (1965): 149.

13. Khrushchev's speech in Rakovia, Yugoslavia, as reported in The Guardian, August 22, 1963, and in New York Times, same date.

14. See my "Planning Without Theory," Survey (London, 1967), pp. 120-21.

15. A. Vadnal, Matematicni uvod v ekonometrijo (Mathematical introduction to econometrics) (Ljubljana, 1955).

16. Reported in Statisticka revija (Statistical review) (Belgrade), no. 4 (1956): 323-25.

17. A. Orthaber, "Pitanje primena sistema tebela 'Ulaza-Izlaza' kod nas" (Questions on our application of 'Import-Export' tables), Ekonomist (Belgrade) no. 2 (1956): 121-221.

18. Ekonomist, nos. 1-2 (1957): 129-31.

19. B. Kreko, Lektsii po lineinomu programmirovaniu (perevod s vengerskogo), Sibirskoe otdelenie Akademii Nauk SSSR (Lectures on linear programming, translation from Hungarian, Siberian division of the Academy of Sciences of the USSR) (Moscow-Novosibirsk, 1958).

20. B. P. Miroschnichenko, ed., Planirovanie v evropeiskikh stranakh sotsializma (Economic planning in European socialist countries) (Moscow, 1962), p. 29; Voprosy ekonomiki (Problems of economics) (Moscow, 1957), pp. 90 ff.

21. On East German experience see V. Petrova, Planovoe khoziaistvo (The planned economy) (Moscow), no. 5 (1968): 73-79.

22. Miroshnichenko, Planirovanie, p. 37.

23. In V. S. Nemchinov, ed., Primenemie matematiki v ekonomicheskikh issledovaniakh (Applications of mathematics in economics research) (Moscow, 1959), pp. 214-50. Originally published in Sankhyaa, an Indian journal, in February 1957.

24. Ekonomika i matematicheskie metody, no. 1 (1965): 157.

25. M. Rositskii, Voprosy ekonomiki, no. 8 (1958): 55ff.

26. The Polish table is reproduced in a decree of the Polish Council of Ministers of January 25, 1960, discussed in M. Misiak, ed., Bodzce ekonomiczne w przedsiebiorstwie przemyslowym (Economic incentives in an industrial enterprise) (Warsaw, 1963), pp. 50, 64; and in B. Glinski, Teorie i praktyka zarzadzania przedsiebiorstwami przemyslowymi (The theory and practice of management of industrial enterprises) (Warsaw, 1963), p. 224. Liberman's proposal of a similar table was published in Voprosy ekonomiki, no. 8 (1962) and in Pravda, September 9, 1962.

27. A well-informed Polish economist spoke in 1958 of the great interest Liberman's early (1955-56) publications had aroused among Polish economists (private conversation).

28. Zycie gospodarcze (Economic life) (Warsaw), no. 22 (1957); Central Planning in Poland (New Haven, 1962), p. 302; K. Mikulskii,

Voprosy ekonomiki, no. 7 (1958): 147. The latter source translates the German terms as "priamye sviazi mezhdu predpriatiami," thus anticipating the common use of this term at present to describe Soviet reforms in that area.

29. Misiak, Bodzce.

30. A. Paszynski, Polityka (Politics) (Warsaw,), no. 21 (1965).

31. H. Fiszel, in Nowe Drogi (New paths) (Warsaw), no. 5 (1956): 45-46; Zycie gospodarcze, no. 22 (1957).

32. Exceptions are allowed for, as well as differentiation of the interest charges by sector. For example, in Bulgaria construction enterprises pay 2 percent and small-scale industry 1 percent; extractive industries pay lower rates ranging from zero to 2 percent in Czechoslovakia, 1 percent in Hungary, etc.

33. As distinct from organizational innovations above the enterprise level, of which Khrushchev introduced a great many at various times.

34. Glinski, Teorie, p. 162.

35. Decree of Council of Ministers, November 17, 1960, Monitor Polski (Polish legal courier) (Warsaw), no. 94 (1960).

36. B. Rakitskii, Voprosy ekonomiki, no. 3 (1969): 138.

37. D. Butakov, Voprosy ekonomiki, no. 8 (1968): 76.

38. Ibid., p. 76.

39. Although Wlodzimierz Brus, a Polish economist, saw the connection between the two as early as 1956; see Trybuna ludu, June 10, 1956.

40. R. Evstigneev and V. Kaiia, Voprosy ekonomiki, no. 10 (1968): 105.

41. D. Allakhverdian, Voporsy ekonomiki, no. 9 (1969): 113.

42. Ibid.; Evstigneev and Kaiia, op cit., p. 106.

43. Cf. New York Times, March 26, 1970.

44. Trybuna ludu, April 22, 1968.

45. Pravda, November 12, 1968.

46. B. Rakitskii, Voprosy ekonomiki, no. 3 (1969): 137-40.

47. Ibid., p. 139.

48. Ibid., p. 140.

3

**EAST EUROPEAN AND
SOVIET SOCIAL SCIENCE:
A CASE STUDY IN
STIMULUS DIFFUSION**
Zygmunt Bauman

This essay examines a form of stimulus diffusion that occurs in situations where the cultural pattern as such encounters no resistance to its spread but there are impediments to the transmission of its content. Thus, to use an example cited originally by Alfred Louis Kroeber, there is no historical evidence of an actual link between Buddhist monasticism and the Christian monasteries of the Middle East and Europe. Nevertheless there is a striking similarity in the general formal patterns and ideological frameworks of the two. The case is illuminating because the wandering of ideas and stimuli, contrary to the displacement of relatively bulky material objects, leaves behind slight traces, if any:

> After all, the fundamental idea of the institution is a simple one, and it need not have impressed more than one or two individuals of unusual intensity of conviction and persuasiveness, for them to apply it in the setting of an entirely different religion, and, when the "time became ripe," for the institution to take root and flourish.[1]

The methodological consequences of the peculiar elusiveness of the actual diffusion process are far-reaching and rather discouraging. In each case of an intuitively convincing analogy between cultural patterns in neighboring or even distant cultural systems, we are entitled to suspect an underlying process of stimulus diffusion but we will rarely be able to prove or disprove our conjecture. Moreover, not even in the absence of verified historical evidence of the genuine transfer of cultural information can we be finally convinced that the case for stimulus diffusion is irrevocably lost. Thus, the whole problem becomes metaphysical gibberish for the scientific purist, but no less real and significant for anybody interested in the actual development of sociocultural systems.

Nevertheless, the methodology designated by the stimulus diffusion theory seems to provide the most promising approach for the type of studies described in this volume. Gordon Childe in 1952 warned over-enthusiastic believers in the power of diffusion that "diffusion is not an automatic process. . . . one society can borrow an idea . . . only when it fits into the general pattern of the society's culture—in other words, when the society has evolved to a stage which allows of the acceptance of the idea."[2] Actual diffusion is always an intricate inter-action between "giving" and "accepting" cultures, in the course of which both partners significantly evolve and the object of cultural transmission changes fundamentally.

The stimulus diffusion concept, by focusing attention on the internal changes of the diffused items, asks the right kind of scientific questions. The migration of ideas rooted in the sociocultural systems of East Europe, rapidly carried over from the out-group into the in-group of the Soviet Union and thus becoming in one shot more eligible for institutional imitation, is indeed a typical case of stimulus diffusion. Nothing was just taken over by Soviets; nothing could be just taken over. Acceptance is possible only on the condition of adaptation, and adaptation means transformation. The required adaptation may on some occasions leave to the initial pattern the role of a first push only.

Transformation is a global process, but it can be split analytically into two dimensions. First, there are changes in the internal structure of the diffused item; on opposite sides of the watershed identical terms sometimes connote sociocultural phenomena of highly divergent composition and with substantially different hierarchical ordering of parts. Second, the diffused item as a rule acquires a new function in the new sociocultural setting. This functional dimension of transfor-mation in the process of diffusion is, from the point of view of systematic analysis, the crucial one, shedding light on the meaning of the process as a whole as well as its driving forces.

It goes without saying that, in spite of its leading role in molding and countenancing the new status of the adopted item, the receiving system seldom if at all avoids far-reaching alterations in its own structure. The sociocultural system is not a cluster of unconnected units; every new addition affects the status of most of the older units as well as the total web of their relationships. This process provides a third dimension to our analysis.

Therefore, I have distinguished three analytical aspects of the problem that I feel could and should be treated separately:

1. Comparison between composition and structuring principles of the diffused item in the mother system and in the fabric of the adopting system; in other words, what was lost and what was gained on the way from the first system to the second.

2. Comparison between the function performed by the diffused item in the framework of the mother system and in the fabric of the adopting system.

3. Comparison between the relevant parameters of the adopting system before and after the adoption; in other words, how and to what degree the sociocultural identity of the adopting system was influenced by the adoption.

The penetration of East European social science into the Soviet system will be scrutinized in terms of these three aspects. Before considering that issue, however, it is advisable to get a relatively clear picture of the two interacting systems before the adoption. It also will be necessary to examine briefly why, among all other proposals on the world social science market, the Eastern European proposals, although relatively humble in absolute terms, represented a peculiarly attractive object for adoption to the Soviets.

THE SCENE OF ENCOUNTER

The East European countries destined to serve as a source of inspiration for emerging Soviet social science were politically included in the in-group of Soviet Russia immediately after World War II. However, the actual encounter in the sociocultural meaning of the word did not start until the late 1950s and gained impetus only in the 1960s. The reason for delay was relatively simple. Although the acknowledgment of plurality and diversity of forms compatible with the officially approved label of socialism had been made under the Stalin regime, Stalin was sufficiently conscious of the possible consequences of this concession to take all desirable precautions against a genuine cultural exchange. The principle of unidirectional communication (westward) was ruthlessly enforced, and a cultural ban was placed on the idiosyncrasies of the new members of the socialist family. To the closed system of the Stalin state, every inflow of information offering alternative solutions was dangerous. To Stalin, firmly entrenched and unchallenged at home, the new dominions meant additional fields of expansion and convenient extension of Soviet rule. After Stalin's death the East European countries became significant factors in the internal Soviet balance of power. It was only natural that Stalin's would-be successors would consider it a minor and relatively cheap concession to the people's democracies to lift the ban on their cultural peculiarities. It is difficult to ascertain whether at any single point of post-Stalin history this fateful change was consciously contemplated or openly debated. It was rather a by-product of the contingencies of the war of succession: it was practically inconceivable to claim that, say, Polish or Czech support should be taken seriously while simultaneously labeling Polish-ness or Czech-ness the heritage of an inferior and valueless social order. One way or another, the ban was lifted and the chain reaction Stalin had so shrewdly prevented was set off.

When the curtain was lifted, it uncovered a picture totally different from everything known to the contemporary generation of Soviet social scientists. This did not apply in equal measure to all people's democracies, however. The relatively weak and meager tradition of native or imported sociology in Bulgaria, Hungary, and Romania was effectively extirpated during the Stalinist rule and left no visible traces in intellectual and cultural life there. The perseverence of the Stalinist order in Czechoslovakia kept the relatively rich tradition of Czech social science dormant and inactive for the time being. In Poland, however, the Stalinist regime was broken early enough to secure the practical continuity of intellectual development, and Polish social scientists stood alone as independent partners with something of value to offer. (When Czech sociologists began to gather their strength in the mid-1960s they had to wisk away the dust that for a whole generation had covered the memory of Thomas Masaryk's sociology of praxis; the critical realism of Arnost Blaha, J. L. Fischer, and Emanual Chalupny; the sociography of Anton Stefanek; or the structuralism of Jan Mukarovsky.)

Polish sociologists owed this exception status to the unbroken line of scientific tradition. Administrative measures to eliminate the non-Marxists from university instruction and the publishing market were initiated only in 1950; the government never went so far as to exterminate them. The period of reconstruction began as early as 1954, when the highly revered professors of the period, who constituted the living link between old Polish tradition and the modern period of sociological expansion, were returned to their chairs. Against the background of approximately 70 years of sociological study, this recess looked and proved to be imperceptible. Besides, even by itself it was not a wasted time; expansion of Marxism, even (for the time being) in its degraded and distorted form in the final account enriched rather than impoverished the Polish sociological scene. For the role played by the Polish social sciences in their encounter with Soviet would-be sociologists several years later, this absorption of Marxism accomplished during the fateful period of 1950-54 was by all means a necessary condition of successful diffusion.

The scarce resources of an underdeveloped and stagnant country prevented the development of mass sociological research and the expansion of academic sociology in prewar Poland. In spite of the unfavorable conditions, however, the extension of the social sciences in Poland at this time was far better than average. Set on the cross-roads of West and East, Polish intellectual life fed on mental currents, fashions, and fads coming from both sides and processed them in a most original way. A constant intellectual anxiety, supported by inevitable social criticism and deep interest in the world scientific development, magnified by the incessant search for solutions to grave domestic problems—these factors and others contributed to the exceptional sophistication and originality of Polish sociological thought. Not many countries in the prewar world could rightly claim three fully developed and original schools.

The first school was connected with Ludwik Krzywicki, the head of the Institute of Social Economy, an independent center of socioeconomic study. Krzywicki foreshadowed in word and deed the close alliance between the Marxist analytical approach and the survey and field research methods developing at the time. An ardent supporter of the not yet fully accepted idea that any sound generalization should be based on carefully checked empirical data, Krzywicki made enormous efforts to mobilize the institute's resources to collect facts and record the parameters of Polish society. He and his institute left an invaluable collection of studies on Polish society between the wars. The peculiarity of Krzywicki's method lay in using both sociological and economic analytical frameworks. What proved the most important factor from the perspective of our theme, however, was an attribute common to Krzywicki and the founders of the other two schools: the peculiar intertwining of scientific interests with sociopolitical reformatory commitment, known to the West from the experience of the muckrakers Charles Booth and Seebohm Rowntree.

Elaborating on Max Weber's casual assessment of sociology as "the power of the powerless," Krzywicki and his disciples challenged the sacred beliefs of a tradition-ridden, economically stagnant, and politically paralyzed society and chose for scientific scrutiny the least flattering and most debunking aspects of the semidictatorial misrule. It was a fighting, militant, indomitable, and disobedient sociology. Krzywicki himself defined the tasks of his institute as "sweeping away the sources of poverty and injustice from the Polish soil." Among the numerous collaborators and disciples of Krzywicki who grew up in the intransigent atmosphere of the institute were Oscar Lange, Julian Hochfeld, Edward Strzelecki, Andrzej Grodek, and several others who entered the Polish postwar scientific scene as the active bearers of the tradition that intellectual defiance was the mission of sociology.

The second school was concentrated around Warsaw University and the remarkable personality of Stefan Czarnowski. The most important characteristic of this highly original thinker was the belief that both the social strucure and a culturological approach are indispensable to fruitful and sound sociological thinking. Czarnowski's own studies included penetrating analyses of the most neuralgic points of the Polish class structure together with outstanding research in cultural anthropology and the theory of cultural change. The scientific contributions of his disciples were characterized by continuous efforts to bring together the achievements of sociology, anthropology, and social psychology, and by an extreme sensitivity to the historical dimension of social facts.

But we also find the same deep sense of sociopolitical involvement we noticed in the case of Krzywicki's institute. Czarnowski and his disciples focused their scientific analysis on the central issues of the politically unhappy Polish society; they investigated multiplying signs of fascist tendencies and forcibly opened the eyes of dormant public opinion to the deepest sources of social oppression and harassment. Only the highest scientific standards can serve public purposes but only this service makes them worth the scientists' toil. Loyalty to this principle was introduced into postwar Polish social science by Czarnowski's disciples and heirs: Stanislaw Ossowski and Nina Assorodobraj-Kula.

The third school is best known in the United States because its founder, Florian Znaniecki, spent most of his creative life there. His analytical or humanistic school, with an affinity to the Chicago interactionists, focused its attention on discovering the latent structure of values that shape behavior. The representatives of the school expounded and inspired studies of memoirs of the kind of people who usually do not express their views in print. It was felt that this unique material could enable social scientists to look into "the other image" of social reality; that is, into an unknown mental world that in itself amounts to an alternative social reality. The methodological preoccupations and slightly more one-sided "academic" rationale did not transform this branch of Polish prewar sociology into a disengaged and uncommitted scholarly affair. The very choice of the milieus the school used as a source of memoir writers—the unemployed, young peasants, migrants in search of their daily bread—reflected its understanding of the social role of sociologists. The Znaniecki school, at least as far as its Polish offshoots are concerned, was by no means an exception from the general rule. In its professional ideology it sided with supporters of the idea that social scientists serve social progress by their independent position and unlimited right to criticize.

   Thus social science entered postwar Polish history determined
to continue, to the best of the nation's interests, its role as a spokesman
for the oppressed and neglected. No authority has succeeded in taming
this obstinate and unyielding will. The Polish intellectuals, who enthu-
siastically accepted the promise of the postwar regime to uproot
social injustice, hoped that the new government would endorse their
right to independent criticism as an indispensable means of correcting
unavoidable errors in social policy. The intellectuals themselves
stated quite clearly what their active participation in the nation's
history should mean. An unbroken line connected the call of the writer
Tadeusz Borowski ("let us look after our [Polish] democracy") with
the blunt dilemma of the philosopher Leszek Kolakowski: "If the
socialist system needs us at all, it needs us in the capacity of critics;
there is no profit for socialism in the yes-man docility of the intellectuals." Delusive perhaps, but expectations enhanced and reinforced
the inherited propensities of the postwar social scientists. At first,
at least, they saw the practical embodiment and implementation of
their dreams in the audacious blueprints of the new regime; but from
the very beginning they considered themselves equal partners of the
regime, limited by nothing but objective truth and scientific conscience.
   This particular aspect of the social scientists' attitude obviously
was the immediate cause for the attempt to eliminate them from the
universities in the dismal first half of the 1950s. Punishments and
persecutions were most severe and unconditional in the case of sociologists (such as Professor Ossowski) who refused, as a matter of
principle, to accept command, rather than mutual agreement, as the
basis of their participation in work.
   Social commitment, which by this time had already become an
integral feature of Polish social science, was reinforced both by the
gloomy experience of the short but violent Stalinist period and by the
circumstances of the dramatic comeback of the ousted sociologists.
The first factor added unexpected weight to the premonitions of
Borowski or Jan Strzelecki; nobody could now deny the dangers
involved when intellectuals submit to political power. It was now
clear that it was impossible to comply with the mounting demands of
an unchecked totalitarian power and simultaneously to retain the
intellectual's traditional role. The consciousness of the inherent
conflict between the role of an obedient party member and the role
of a social scientist became more poignant as it was corroborated
by practical experience. Another factor, however, proved decisive
for the shaping of Polish social sciences from 1954 on.
   The social scientists' comeback occurred during a dramatic
national awakening. Countless social conflicts and class grievances,
formerly suppressed, were about to explode at the first sign of any
weakening of power. The intellectuals promptly assumed the leading

role in the impending upheavals. They constituted the only stratum capable of articulating grievances and the only group used to expressing its rationale in the generalized terms of scientific concepts and moral values; these terms were sufficiently broad to include almost every private complaint. Moreover, at this troubled period of Polish history it was enough to be against, and to be sufficiently loud, to secure an enthusiastic (although unfortunately short-lived) applause that only too easily could be taken for a sign of well-founded political support. Many a leader of the 1956 national revolt was misled and jumped to premature conclusions concerning the ephemeral union of class interests in general and the political maturity of workers in particular. But this subject belongs to another story; what is important for us in the present context is that the intellectuals themselves, and a prevailing majority of the politically involved element, sincerely believed that intellectuals were destined to play a leading role in the forthcoming process of national reconstruction, and that it was their duty to offer an alternative political formula and to supervise its implementation.

The force of historical circumstances imposed duties on the Polish social scientists that were far beyond their real capacities. Emerging from the dark years relatively unblemished and untarnished, they seemed to offer a genuine alternative to the discredited politicians of what was rapidly becoming the "ancien regime." The first university lectures of the expelled professors turned into a minor national festivity in the presence of hundreds of auditors totally uninterested in scholarship, dozens of newspapermen, and the incessant crackle of flashes. Since the sociologists had been taken for political oracles, every single word they casually dropped aroused enormous popular interest. The very word sociology, formerly banned, became a symbol of national renewal and aroused an excitement compatible only with the intensity of popular cravings for change. The nation, too long fed by a stale concoction of wishful thinking and bombastic revelations of eternal truths, was hungry for the rye bread of brute facts. Newspapers kept their front columns open for everything labeled sociological report; there was no better merchandise than statistical tables. The depth of the truths revealed by sociologists was of no importance; one could hardly expect substantial discoveries in such a short time. The public wanted and paid for the symbols of political intransigence. The revival of Polish sociology was defined not so much by its scientific achievements as by the political attitudes it connoted in its "virtual identity."

It took many years of corruption and intimidation to subdue and disarm an institution born of the national wrath. At the time of its encounter with its Soviet neighbor, Polish sociology was far from being tamed. When Polish sociology was discovered by the Russian would-be sociologists, it played—whether successfully or not—the role of a spokesman for national grievances and an instrument for correcting the rulers' mistakes.

The Soviet partner had entirely different background, interests, and expectations. There was no tradition of intransigence in Russian prerevolutionary sociology, particularly in its official, university branch. It was looked upon by the political movements of the time as an abstract academic discipline, if not a particularly insidious version of the ruling ideology. The Communist Party, at a very early stage of its history (in the course of Plekhanov and Lenin's intellectual showdown with the populists), distinguished between historical materialism as the revolutionary social theory of the militant proletariat, and sociology as the bourgeois "pseudo-science" designed for the sole purpose of leading astray the incipient gravediggers of class rule. Lenin's disdain for "bourgeois objectivity" left little room for conjectures as to the probable fate of this social science in the event of the party's victory. Perhaps this was an additional factor for the subsequent academic seclusion of official, and incidentally not very developed, Soviet sociology, which had as its task the confirmation of the opinions of former professional revolutionaries.

The prerevolutionary record of reciprocal miscomprehension and animosity determined the uneasy relations between Russian sociologists and the now victorious Bolsheviks during the short period of truce immediately after the revolution. There is no evidence that the old establishment sociologists were inclined to resist actively the advent of the new regime. One can even surmise that, used to their respectable and shaded university life, they would try to the best of their ability to comply with the demands of the new rulers—if the rulers were ready to leave them in peace. The uneasy armistice was brutally broken by the fateful paper in which Lenin condemned Pitirim Sorokin for publishing a research report on the dynamics of divorces that gave unfavorable testimony to the new regime. It is difficult to overestimate the grave consequences of the paper. For many years it formulated the terms on which the new system was prepared to accept or tolerate the social scientists. The steadfast principle of the priority of immediate propaganda purposes over all possible scientific aims was promulgated. Not even an auxiliary technical role was conceded to social research. Sociology as an institution ruled by its own standards and norms was thus doomed to extinction. The few prerevolutionary sociologists of any scientific standing drew the necessary conclusions and left the country.

One can employ many different points of view in explaining the consistent resentment by the new revolutionary powers of sociology as a descriptive science of society; indeed, many explanations—the most obvious and "convincing" (owing to the primitiveness of their motivational premises)—already had been given. However, one rather subtle epistemological reason seems, so far, to have been overlooked. Sociology as a descriptive science of the autonomous social reality was born from the experience of the failure of French revolutionary leaders to impose their intellectually conceived normative order on the obstinate and indomitable social structure. The need for and legitimacy of sociology in the above sense could be recognized only if the myth of the normative, legislative origin of social reality had been disposed of—which had indeed happened in the aftermath of the French Revolution. The October Revolution of 1917 granted the old myth a new lease on life; it was hoped that power concentrated in the hands of a proletarian state would transform the kingdom of necessity into the kingdom of freedom; thus the discussion of normative principles rather than the tracing of objective trends was the new systemic prerequisite. The sudden interest in sociological research, dating in the Soviet Union from the 1960s, testifies to the gradual crumbling and disintegration of the myth, parallel to the process that took place in another part of the world a century and a half ago.

The 1920s brought some efforts to initiate sociological studies that were politically without reproach and had mainly practical or abstractly theoretical purposes. These efforts were undertaken by the new, highly educated, and brilliant generation of Marxist scientists—before part of it was exterminated and the rest called to order by Stalin. A. I. Todorovsky investigated social change in the village of Vesegon district under the impact of the revolution; V. S. Nemchinov initiated field research in village communes; S. G. Strumlin applied survey methods to investigate correlation between cultural advancement and time budgets; S. G. Vasilevsky and A. V. Tchaianov elaborated original methods of social research. These and other representatives of the Sturm und Drang generation still cherished the vain hope of a successful union between the experimenting government and the people in order to make the experiments successful. The false hopes were duly dispersed before they could crystallize into an original model of applied social sciences adjusted to the conditions of a socialist society.

There is no need to recall what happened in the dismal 1930s. The idea of professional social science as an independent source of valuable knowledge completely disappeared. The spirit of the epoch was lucidly expressed by a typical leader of the ideological front, M. D. Mitin: "The further advancement of Marxist-Leninist theory . . . is associated with the name of Comrade Stalin. In all of Stalin's practical achievements, and in all his writings, the totality of the experience of the struggle of the world proletariat, the whole rich stock of Marxist-Leninist theory was accumulated." The terror of

the late 1930s finally brought what was left of Soviet social science to
a complete standstill. The period of nonexistence was long enough to
cut off every thread of tradition. There was no living link to connect
the frail pre-Stalinist sprouts of sociological interests with the Soviet
sociology of today, which is of a technological, managerial nature.

The politics of suppressing any independent scientific social
research was continued during the 1940s and well into the 1950s. Any
empirical research undertaken by social scientists on their own was
said to be inspired by a bourgeois "idealistic philosophy," the nature
of which was defined by A. A. Zhdanov in his speech on G. Aleksandrov's History of Philosophy: "The experience of our victory over
fascism taught us to what a dead end idealistic philosophy had led
whole nations. Now it has presented itself in a new repulsively filthy
garment, which reflects the very depth of the limbo into which the
decaying bourgeoisie has sunk. Pimps and criminal delinquents in
philosophy—really, here you have the peak of corruption and foulness."[3]

These words were spoken in 1947, when in other countries of the
socialist camp, and above all in Poland, the social sciences still
flourished. Zhdanov was apparently conscious of the potential dangers
in encouraging a two-way flow of communication between these countries and the in-group. His speech contains precise instructions on
this matter: "From the embers of war the states of the New Democracy
and the liberating movements of colonial nations emerged . . . . Who
else, if not we, the country of victorious socialism and its philosophers—
should assist our foreign friends and brothers in throwing the light
of scientific socialist consciousness upon their struggle for the new
society? Nobody but we can and should enlighten them and supply them
the spiritual armament of Marxism."[4] Thus the unidirectional relationship was firmly established: the Soviet philosophers in the role
of givers, not takers. The Soviet philosophers warned their "foreign
friends and brothers" but assured them that everything they said was
of value on the sole basis of the socialist character of the country
from which it came.

Perhaps Eugene Kamenka is right when he calls the increase in
scholastic treatises following Zhdanov's speech a kind of miniature
"Carolingian renaissance;" but it was not until Stalin's death that the
first signs of a qualitative shift became visible.[5] Much has been
written about the complex changes in Soviet society that brought about
a partly voluntary, partly enforced shift in traditional attitudes and
evaluations. Not one of these changes can be neglected if the sources
of the new Soviet sociology are to be properly understood, yet there is
no place here for an exhaustive analysis of the problem.

However, some factors seem particularly important in the awakened interest in the social sciences in the non-Soviet meaning of the

word. As students of current Soviet history have not paid these factors
the attention they deserve, it seems worthwhile to mention them here.

The first was, of course, a freshly awakened curiosity in deep-
rooted, heretofore overlooked social institutions whose amazing vita-
lity and immunity to prescriptions from above was discovered the
moment the smokescreen of official ideology was dispersed. Traditional supports of cognitive self-assurance were irretrievably shattered
by the downfall of Stalin's monopoly of knowledge. The slogan "back
to facts" was the natural replacement, above all in the eyes of young
reformers who sought prestigious support for their unorthodox ideas.

The second is the far-reaching effect of the end (although never
complete) of the "besieged fortress" complex and thus of the prolonged
period of the Soviet Union's self-enforced isolation. It does not matter
whether Nikita Khrushchev thought about the repercussions of the chain
reaction he would set in motion when he initiated his extensive travels
abroad. Whether or not deliberate, the new style of political life and
the new formula of a Soviet presence in the world brought the Soviet
"fighters of the ideological front" into direct contact with their
Western counterparts. The very fact that certain professions were
defined as relevant was a fateful deviation from the sacred principle
that an unbridged gap existed between Soviet historical materialism
and everything being done, regardless of label, in non-Soviet societies.
The historical materialists were now forced to fight their ideological
battles on sociological territory. Moreover, since any definition of a
relevant partner is by the same token a self-definition, the Soviet
philosophers somehow had to handle the previously avoided and awk-
ward question of the relation and division of competence between
historical materialism and sociology.

Had it been merely a question of cultural contact, the Soviet philosophers would have been sufficiently immune to undesirable influences
to emerge intact and untarnished. Due to their status at home, however, the Soviet participants considered this harmless exchange of
views for mutual benefit as a fateful battle, to be decided as battles
are in most cases: by dividing the partners into victors and vanquished.
Perhaps this helps to explain the notorious discrepancy between the
scarcity of informal Soviet scientific contacts and the otherwise understandable attention paid in the Soviet Union to international congresses
of formal organizations. In no other country in the world are the
"proceedings" of the International Sociological Association (ISA)
congresses treated so seriously and cited so frequently. The Soviet
philosophers went abroad to win—unfortunately only to discover that
there is no victory without rules and that they must start by learning
the rules.

Another important factor was related to new developments in the field of social mobility and the circulation of elites. One foremost institutional pattern of the Soviet system from its very beginning was its swift and smooth absorption of the coming generations. This was achieved by securing the prompt inclusion of the most capable, potentially elitist youths into the established web of power and influence. The main institution serving this process was, traditionally, the continuous (and for one generation, wholesale) purge. The purge as an institution simultaneously served two important system-maintaining functions: It prevented the crystallization of inimical or even independent elites; and, by building active and militant loyalty into the very process of individual promotion, it secured an early and steadfast self-identification with the established system. For reasons already extensively described by many writers, the Soviet system since the 1950s has abandoned the institution of mass purge. Nonetheless, the effective absorption of the potentially elitist youth segment has remained an important prerequisite of the system, which tries-so far successfully-to weave social change into the preservation of establishment. With purge as the means of change and the element of flexibility, the ideological formula represented stability of the system and sanctity of its basic institutions. One social process underlying the post-Stalinist transformations was the establishment's active effort to turn itself, the "privileged class," into a "class of privileged"—that is, to put a steady foundation beneath the present positions of privileged individuals. Some price had to be paid; the institution of purge was the first and most obvious victim, but the second (and perhaps unexpected) victim was the traditional sacredness of the "one and only" ideological formula. The focus of the system's stability and preservation shifted from the plane of principles to the plane of groups-in the sense of unified aggregates of people.

When a young and unemployed actor comes to a stage where all parts are already distributed, he has only two options: either to prove that he is able to perform one of the part currently on stage better than an older actor or to postulate an enlarging of the present script to make room for some new actors without impinging on the rights of the veterans. When purge was abandoned, the first option was reduced to proportions incommensurate with the giant task of elevating a significant part of every new generation; the second was the only option left. Instead of the coupling of extreme flexibility of role distribution with extreme stability of institutional and ideological patterns, which occurred under Stalin, the model implemented since the 1950s combines the relative stability of role ascription with an ideological structure flexible to the point of almost secularizing every institutional pattern except the stability of personal status.

Were Stalin's model still in force, the young ambitious scientists of the late 1950s could have imitated Mitin or Yudin's pattern of the early 1930s and tried to compete with the elders of the profession within the framework of the established definition of their professional role. As this was no longer the case, they looked eagerly for uninhabited territories. Khrushchev's idea of romantic adventure on the virgin lands of Kazakhstan—a means of unloading the dangerous demographic bomb in the European urban centers—provided a pattern and symbol for the new style of mobility problem solving. Sociology was indeed a convenient fallow waiting for young and ambitious tillers. The one thing that had to be done to make the desert inhabitable was to mold a new ideological formula rationalizing its eventual usefulness for the system.

It is exactly at this point that the role of the people's democracies comes into the picture. We have mentioned that the war of succession after Stalin's death elevated the people's democracies to the role of nominally equal members of the socialist family of states, that is, units with something significant to say and with weight and prestige attached to their statements. In order to preserve the supreme ideological definition of the Soviet system, the basically socialist character of these units had to be acknowledged. Furthermore, the assumption could no longer be made that the institutional solutions of the people's democracies, if different from the Soviet Union's, were necessarily inferior and expressed a relatively backward stage of sociopolitical development. That is why it would have been much more difficult for young Russians to inhabit the sociological desert if sociology had been only an American or French affair. The fact that Polish socialism already accommodated something called sociology and had not been rendered infamous made the venture incomparably easier. The function played by Polish sociology in its respective system and/or the originality of its ideas and approaches were irrelevant. The only thing that really counted was that sociology had already been made legitimate in a socialist state and therefore could be imitated. The Soviet enthusiasts of the new scientific profession were perfectly conscious of both the capacities and limitations of the Polish colleagues. For the kind of discipline they wanted to build they could find—and indeed have found—much more reliable teachers elsewhere. Still, the Polish example was priceless as a source of and rationale for stimulus diffusion.

These are some of the factors that determined the encounter of Soviet and Polish sociologies that finally took place in the late 1950s and early 1060s. Each partner brought his own intellectual tradition, molded by the previous history of the discipline in his own country and by the present institutional prerequisites of the respective sociopolitical systems. The dissimilarity of traditions did not rule out

TABLE 3.1

The Intellectual Premises of Social Science According
to Polish and Russian/Soviet Tradition

The Polish Tradition	The Russian/Soviet Tradition
1. Science and ideology belong to two different theaters. Ideology is not an independent source of knowledge. Science can contribute to ideology but cannot serve it. It is better, although not always possible, for science to abstain from any kind of ideological inspiration.	1. Science and ideology are two closely connected and complementary aspects of human knowledge. Ideology is superior to science and provides both rationale and goals for scientific activity. Science is right only when in accord with ideological premises.
2. The freedom of scientific endeavors is limited solely by the requirements of truth. Only if pursuing the truth can science be of any value to society.	2. The freedom of scientific endeavors is limited by the interests of the society. Not every truth is socially useful; science is right only when useful for society.
3. Scientists submit what they do to professionally specified criteria only. Other criteria are irrelevant in the framework of science.	3. There are no specific criteria of science different from criteria applied widely in the rest of society. Men of practice can use their criteria to evaluate scientific statements.
4. The pursuit of science is the task and domain of professional scientists only. The domain is exterior to the field of immediate social practice.	4. Social science develops by joint or parallel efforts of professionals and social activists. Not only are both contributions of equal value but opinions of spokesmen for practical experience are superior as representing the final test of truth.
5. The function of social scientists is to supervise the rulers.	5. The function of social scientists is to help the rulers.

Source: Compiled by the author.

diffusion but made the substantial transfiguration of the diffused object the condition sine qua non of the diffusion itself. That is why, to complete the description of the scene of encounter, it is necessary to sum up these scattered remarks on the peculiarities of the two traditions to which the partners had to conform. They can be summed up conveniently in five points (see Table 3.1).

DIFFUSION THROUGH DIVERGENCE

The late 1950s and early 1960s saw a great deal of activity along the Polish-Soviet sociological front. The editors of the monthly Problems of Peace and Socialism summoned a small conference to Prague with the obvious intention of bringing together the top representatives of Polish sociology and several young pioneers of a "sociological movement" in the USSR who have come to occupy the central positions in institutionalized Soviet sociology today. At that time they apparently expected to avail themselves of the prestige already enjoyed by the established Polish sociology and intended to use this as a significant asset in the struggle to legalize their new and suspicious trade. At that very time all positions of importance and influence in the realm of social science in the Soviet Union were held by old and ignorant men who saw the struggle against modern sociology as the last battle for their own survival. They would never have voluntarily accepted any kind of sociology different from the vague and shallow interpretive ideology they had been producing. Therefore, to get access to the sector of the social system reserved for the social sciences, the young people had to make it clear from the very beginning that what was at stake was an entirely new formula, totally unconnected with what was traditionally meant by social science. By proclaiming that their trade belonged to a separate realm, the young men could and would be able to avoid having antiquated fossils as either allies or enemies in their struggle.

Shortly afterward a group of leading Polish sociologists arrived in Moscow to deliver a series of lectures on Polish field research. The meeting was crowded; the sour faces of the old contrasted with the sincere enthusiasm of the young. The Polish contributions were rather modest, too mundane to explain the ardent zeal of the younger members of the audience; what was important was the fact that "socialist friends" (and not capitalist scarecrows brought in to be "mercilessly criticized") were publicly proclaiming the good news of field research being carried on in a socialist country.

I have continuously stressed the seemingly tactical aspect of Soviet interest in Polish sociologists. From this the conclusion should

not be drawn that the ideas and findings of Polish sociology had no
influence on the profile of the nascent Soviet social science. Although
Polish sociology was much less appropriate to the uses the Soviet
pioneers intended for their trade than, say, the Lundberg-Mayo-
Lazarsfeld branch of American sociology, it offered some tangible
assets. It is true that the young Soviet sociologists tried hard to avoid
any hint that their discipline was somehow connected with anything
that could be judged and evaluated as Marxist or non-Marxist (the
very terms would arouse the antiquated academic stooges, used to
treating everything taxed as Marxist as their exclusive domain and
everything labeled non-Marxist as something to be exterminated).
Nevertheless, they simply could not ignore the tacit conventions of
the system in which they acted. Never having been forced to consider
the problem as a clique politics issue, Polish sociologists had no
reservations about accepting the Marxist contribution to modern
sociology and themselves made significant contributions to the promotion of a modernized and empiricized version of Marxist sociology
and to the enrichment of modern sociological thought with the valuable
elements of Marxist tradition. Thus Polish sociology offered the Soviet
pioneers a number of original solutions relevant to their own problems;
many of them, besides, frankly believed that the sociology they were
about to launch should be Marxist and thus different from the bourgeois.

Second, by the early 1960s the Polish sociologists had already
accumulated quite a number of research projects, questionnaires,
scales, and tests adjusted to the specific issues and conceptual system of a socialist society. These readymade instruments could not
have been derived directly from, say, the American experience, even
if it had been (and it was not) advisable to draw openly from the American experience at this precarious stage, when the very existence of
Soviet sociology was still at stake.

For these two reasons, at the initial phase of their activity the
Soviet sociologists borrowed heavily from the writings and unpublished
research documents of their Polish colleagues. One cannot estimate
the real scale of this borrowing from the usual indicators—mention
of names, acknowledgments, notes, and references; higher political
considerations excluded a public acknowledgment of debt. For a
number of reasons—fluctuations in the political climate, the unpredictable whims of foreign (and by now independent and prestigious)
rulers, the USSR's status as a great power, and/or the complete
absence of legal regulations for cultural exchange—the Soviet academic institution preferred to circulate the translated works of
Polish sociologists in mimeographed form and through official
channels rather than make them available to the general public. The
ups and downs of political hopes and fears caused the authors to write

and rewrite the indexes of cited names several times in the course of preparing a single book for print. There were sociologists who, to play it safe, did not mention the names of Polish colleagues whose research they copied without the slightest modification. To insiders, however, the reality was clear enough and the crucial role of Polish sociology as not only a protective cover but also a rich source of inspiration and a catalyst was not contested.

This incubatory period was rather brief, however; after it had consolidated, Soviet sociology quickly found other patrons and partners. Several years later one representative personality of Societ sociology, N. Osipova, in an article written for the Polish quarterly Studia Socjo-logiczne (1967) stressed the differences between Soviet and Polish sociologists. In a somewhat euphemistic way these differences were ascribed to "1. differences in the level of development of the social relations which provide the subject for sociological analysis; 2. differences of the sociological traditions to which sociologists refer; 3. also, perhaps, from the divergent understanding of the function of sociological research and sociology itself as a scientific discipline."[6]

Her formulations rightly express the real reasons for the inevitable break—but perhaps reversing the genuine hierarchy of factors. The student of psychologically oriented sociology will find the second factor most important; a political scientist probably will opt for the third. Both will agree that the first formula is best explained as a projection of the other two.

Indeed, the choice of a specific understanding of the function of sociology was the crucial political decision made by the young Soviet team and this choice determined its view on the other aspects of the issue. A small and ambitious group of sociologists emerged, especially in centers far from Moscow politics. Today this group has assumed the positions of importance in the new sociological establishment and is about to shape the profile of official Soviet sociology for years to come. This group attached paramount importance to focusing the public image of its discipline around an issue with which it could deal well.

In 1956 in The Functions of Social Conflict, Lewis A. Coser described the situation in American sociology as follows:

The majority of sociologists who dominate contemporary sociology, far from seeing themselves as reformers and addressing themselves to an audience of reformers, either have oriented themselves toward purely academic and professional audiences, or have attempted to find a hearing among decision-makers in public or private bureaucracies. They center attention predominantly upon problems of adjustment rather than upon conflicts; upon social static

rather than upon dynamics. Of key problematic importance
to them has been the maintenance of existing structures and
the ways and means of insuring their smooth functioning.
They have focused upon maladjustments and tensions which
interfere with consensus. Where the older generation discussed the need for structural change, the new generation
deals with adjustment of individuals to given structures.
In the dominant trend of contemporary American sociology,
the psychological subsumes the structural and hence individual malfunctioning subsumes social conflict.[7]

Coser chose Elton Mayo and his human relations group as the
typical example of described trends:

All of Mayo's research was carried out with the permission
and collaboration of management. It was conducted to help
management solve its problems. To Mayo, management
embodied the central purposes of society . . . . We do not
assert that these men simply took over the views of the
decision-makers under whose auspices they pursued their
studies; but we hope to have shown that they accepted the
decision-makers' choice of problems and that they shared
their perspectives regarding conflict phenomena.[8]

This lengthy citation spares us the necessity of contructing our
own description of the trends dominant in the new Soviet sociology.
The similarity is indeed striking, and it is not our task to decide
whether it speaks in favor of adherents of the convergence theory or
simply results from coincidence. Thus, Osipova sees the tasks of
Soviet sociologists in the field of labor and industry as follows:

The new system of management opens an opportunity to
achieve cohesiveness of the interests of economic authorities,
of industrial administration and working crews. The economic and organizational conditions for harmonious cooperation of the staff are achievable only if the influence of not
only economic, but also political, psycho-social and moral
factors is taken into account . . . . The management of the
working personnel demands to take into account and to
exploit such factors as psychological aspects of the working
process, the degree of democratism in the relationships
between managers and workers, the rewards and punishments system, the mobility of an individual inside the
industrial community, the system of group values and norms,
etc. The use of psychological and moral factors to achieve

the harmonious cooperation of the working crews secures
not only economic, but also social profits.[9]

The main preoccupation of the author is not, as we have seen, far
removed from that of, say, F. J. Roethlisberger: "How can a comfortable working equilibrium be maintained between the various social
groups in an industrial enterprise such that no one group in the organization will separate itself out in opposition to the remainder?"[10]
Harmony and equilibrium, elimination of conflicts ("troubles" or
"disorganizations" in the managers' language), the smooth implementation of managerial decisions—all these provide the focus and
organizing concepts of the new Soviet sociology in the same measure
as they organized the dominant and most vigorous trends of American
sociology, at least until quite recently.

This trend stems directly from the inherent logic of the Soviet
sociopolitical system at its present stage of development. If a group
of young, ambitious, and reform-minded men had wanted to break
through the ossified cliques to positions of power and influence in
Stalin's time, the sociologists undoubtedly would have accused the old
cliques of ideological deviations and tried to impress the rulers with
their willingness to promote the traditional ideological formulas even
more eagerly and loyally than their predecessors. At present the
old-fashioned mechanism of mobility has been replaced; individual
positions are much more secure than they were before and it requires
too much effort to remove a clique from its cosy position. The new
ideological formula of utility is much more effective and not necessarily contradictory to the one previously accepted; it even is advisable
not to underscore the contradiction but to try to make the new formula
look complementary to the old one as much as possible, if only to keep
the established groups neutral. Besides, every group aspiring to participate in power has to meet some indispensable requirements, for
example, by showing that its offers will enhance the present strength
and stability of the existing system and open new ways to promote the
old aims.

The most difficult predicament of all men of power is to get people to conform to some general rules of behavior that are necessary
to bring about a planned and desirable cumulative result. This is the
problem of effective influence, and it can be achieved by attacking the
social action structure from either the first or the second of its two
poles: by manipulating the cognitive-cathetic map of the actor or by
conveniently rearranging the situational array of pressures and attrac-
tions. The generation of Mitin, Yudin, Konstantinov, Fedoseev,
Kammari, Gleserman, Yovchuk, and others has drawn its rationale
from the first task. The right ideological prescription effectively
indoctrinated by a concentrated propaganda effort was considered

the most efficient way to secure the concerted action of the ruled and
to implement the goals set forth by the rulers. Until the 1950s the
second task was practically untouched or was reduced to a crude and
untested system of economic stimuli (revoking belatedly the homo
oeconomicus shibboleth of Adam Smith).

This task was chosen by the new Soviet sociologist to justify his
bid for a separate room in the castle of social influence. The bid has
proved successful, as it has kept well in line with the general formula
of efficiency rationality developed by post-Stalinist rulers. The new
sociologists' offer responded to the call for a rule of experts, for an
increase of professional skills, for "scientifying" the art of management. As a matter of fact the new sociologists' claim hit the bullseye
and placed them, at least potentially, into the very center of the nascent
regime of specialists and highly skilled managers. In a system that
puts more trust in the convincing eloquence of hard reality and the
human search for profit than the mobilizing capacities of tedious
spiritual appeals, the new sociologists felt much more at home than
the old Stalinist stooges. They were an indispensable part of the new
system; they did not invent their role but rather deciphered the new
demands rightly even before the new rulers were able to articulate
them.

That is how and why the paths of Polish and Soviet sociologists
parted, and the gap between them widened with time. The function
chosen or accepted for a scientific discipline determines the structure
of scientific interests, choice of problems, and ways of expressing
results. It has taken many years for Polish authorities to make any
progress in calling the Polish sociologists to order, and their purpose
is still far from achieved. Soviet sociology since its birth has played
the benevolent role of a trustworthy aid to the established authority.
This does not necessarily mean that it cannot on some future occasion,
by the sheer logic of sociopolitical history, be thrown into an entirely
different sociopolitical niche, as is currently happening in the United
States. In a system lacking alternative channels for articulation of
social conflicts and diverging interests, the explosive capacities of
relatively autonomous centers of social thought are multiplied. Some
symptoms of this potential role of sociological research were already
visible in the "wild-cat" sociological initiatives "far away from
Moscow," which the new sociological establishment did its best to
curb. Until recently, however, the dominant function of Soviet sociology seemed to be so different from the principles guiding the growth
of its Polish counterpart that diffusion of stimulus presupposed basic
transformations in the structure of its material correlate.

THE PROFILE OF THE NEW SOVIET SOCIOLOGY

In one of the best empirical studies published so far in the USSR, Man and His Work (1967), the two brilliant Leningrad sociologists, A. G. Zdravomyslov and V. A. Yadov, classified the social tasks of the new Soviet sociology. They distinguish three broad spheres of sociological activity:

1. Analysis of worldwide processes related to the struggle between the two contradictory socioeconomic systems, capitalist and socialist. At this level Soviet sociology should perform "theoretical and ideological functions, which in the framework of Marxism are identical."
2. Study of the internal problems of the socialist society. Sociologists are to supply the necessary information on the genuine state of the society and also perform a "critical" function (the definition given by the authors is illuminating indeed): "in this case sociology is an instrument of estimating the possible ways of solving social problems and contradictions."
3. Investigation of separate subsystems of Soviet society; here "the sociological analysis is submitted to the tasks of the scientific regulation and management of the social processes."[11]

The formulations cited above are typical of the rationale that young sociologists have chosen to justify the utility of their work and try to live up to in their everyday practice. All functions (if we do not attach too much importance to the lip service paid to tradition in the first point) are formulated in an unemotional and ideology-free managerial language; as far as their content is concerned, they give an account of the type of problems that usually face and worry managers. The struggle between the new sociology and the bullheads of historical materialism is a corollary of the broader struggle between managerial and ideological tendencies that has been going on for years inside the Soviet political system. The tortuous fate of the new sociology since its first appearance on the Soviet scene reflects more or less exactly the fortunes of the struggle between the diehards of ideological purity and the ascending generation of pragmatic managers. There were mutual accusations of disloyalty, wrapped in the clumsy phraseology of ideological metaphysics; more and less successful attempts to accommodate new trends in the old framework or to bribe and tame their standard bearers; offers of truce and uneasy compromises broken with the next shift in the floating equilibrium of power. One thing, however, remained constant: The new sociology tied its own fate unilaterally to the lot of the managerial wing. It spoke its language and offered services that made sense only in the framework of managerial rule.

For this purpose the young sociologists were well prepared by their own educational background and the achievements of Soviet science in general. There is no need to stress the well-known achievements of Soviet mathematics and the unprecedented bloom of the formalist school. These two rich and ready-to-use sources of inspiration ensured a privileged start to everybody who wished to lift social study to the level of an exact science in the modern meaning of the term, and to express problems and results in a language understandable and familiar to people who grew up under modern technology. If we add to this Veblen's famous theorem on the privilege of the latecomers, we will have the two conditions that secured the rapid elevation of the new Soviet sociology to the highest level of modernity defined as degree of mathematical sophisitication. Polish sociology, much more traditional in its research techniques, was left behind almost immediately. But the vanguards of Soviet sociology also outrun the highest standards of American sociology, first of all in the theory and application of mathematical models to the study of social problems. The Novosibirsk scientists, who set the standards of methodological sophistication for the rest of the Soviet applied sociological research, came from mathematics rather than from what previously assumed the role of "the science of society." The opinion that a substantial mathematical background is much more important than intensive study in social theory is frequently heard in the leading circles of the new Soviet sociology.

As a result, the ability of the Soviet managerial system to absorb the type of information that the sociologists are already prepared to serve turned out to be the main bottleneck in the further advancement of the new science. Parallel developments inside the party and governmental executive institutions have not gone as far. On the one hand, this is a problem of the managerial personnel, who in many cases are unprepared to formulate their questions in a relatively elaborate form and to make the expected use of the answers they get. Attempts at eliminating this shortcoming are being made through special courses in empirical sociology in the numerous party schools; the art of ordering sociological studies and handling their results has been accepted as a basic skill for future high-level party or government officials. The new sociologists have served as the chief pressure group promoting this fateful innovation. Still, the other side of the problem is much more significant and not as easy to dispose of. The lack of relevant knowledge is not the only or even the main obstacle to accommodating the managerially oriented sociology into the sociopolitical system. Even if they did possess the necessary skills, the managers could hardly make any reasonable use of the data supplied by sociologists if the system in which they function was not adjusted to the continuous input and processing of information. The Soviet system is not now constructed in this way; thus, pushing through even the most advanced and vital ideas requires the removal of too many obstacles to become a routine part of systemic functioning. As the chief architect of the Soviet bureaucracy, Stalin did his best to bring it as close as possible to Weber's ideal type of "black box," cut off from any input but the will of the top. As a result, this bureaucracy was hopelessly unadjusted to the independent search for reliable information and almost completely lacking in the "exploration instinct," which can secure the effective assimilation of the environment and a prompt accommodation of its internal structure. The consciousness that there is something to be gained by ascertaining facts cannot by itself bring practical results if is not backed up by real flexibility and the "informative openness" of the system itself. With this prerequisite, we see the foundations of the Soviet sociologists' role as a pressure group in the service of a specific progressive systemic reform.

The reform sought openly or tacitly by the sociological pressure group amounts to decentralizing the decision-making procedure. Sovietologists frequently confuse two sociological phenomena, decentralization and democratization, or insist there is between them at most a quantitative and not a qualitative difference. It is therefore necessary to clarify the character of the decentralization that makes it possible for Soviet sociology to survive in its present shape and also transforms this sociolgy into a force for reform.

The model of decentralization at stake would inevitably consist of the transfer by the state of its monopolistic control over the means of production to the managers, who would assume the role of private collective owners of the means of production. The second but no less important aspect of this model is the retention of the state's monopolistic political power. The managerial class, while freed from control from above, will nonetheless need to depend on and therefore wholeheartedly support the police powers of the state in order to overcome dissent due to the inequality of distribution and lack of access to control over the production process.

The model of democratization does not necessarily postulate the separation of economic and political powers, and in this sense it is not simply an extension of the second model. Rather, it is an alternative way out of the vicious circle of the model actually in existence. Preserving (as has been the case in the Yugoslav theoretical model) the basic unity and indivisibility of popular sovereignty, it puts both the political and economic aspects of power under the direct control and management of representative democratic organs. The freedom of the underprivileged to organize themselves, according to Raymond Aron's famous definition of democracy, is the most prominent feature of this system, making it qualitatively different from the decentralization model.

The management changes the Soviet sociologists propose and promote belong to the decentralization model. They wish and demand
that relevant sociological research be included in the decision-making
process on every level of the party and government hierarchy. In
practical terms, this means opening each layer of previously closed
systems to independent sources of reliable information; in other words,
to accept a new situation in which the lower levels of the centralized
hierarchy use relatively independent criteria for their decisions,
rather than relying on those derived from above. The consequences,
both accepted and unpredicted, can be far-reaching indeed. At the
present time several high-level republican and district (Belorussian,
Kazakhstan, Uzbekistan, Georgian, Estonian, Sverdlovsk, Voronezh)
party committees have been employing teams of sociologists to investigate specific problems of management and, as far as one can judge,
are making an honest effort to use the results to justify their decisions.
There is a well-pronounced trend toward institutionalization of the new
situation, in which different organs will enjoy their own "sources of
truth" to broaden their own field of maneuver in bargaining with the
higher levels of the hierarchy. Thus, the new sociology can serve to
strengthen the decentralizing tendencies in the Soviet system and make
it more accessible to the inflow of information, including feedback.

It remains to be seen whether these changes, if successfully accomplished will lead to a gradual weakening of the monolithic system and
to qualitative transformation or, on the contrary, to an accommodation
of conflicts and thus to increased flexibility and adaptability in the
present system. Both outcomes are equally plausible; the result will
depend in the last instance on the adaptability of social forces and
their political expression. However, one can hardly point to any
evidence that Soviet sociology in its present form has contributed to
the processes of liberalization or democratization, which were due to
different historical circumstances and cultural traditions—and also so
typical of Polish sociology until relatively recent times. The optimistic opinions sometimes voiced on this matter find their sole justification in the misleading although understandable professional belief that
liberalism and democracy spring from the very essence of the social
sciences. If anyone still cherishes this illusion, the experience of
Soviet sociology, which is not so different from the experience of so
many other countries, the United States included, should indeed convince him of the opposite. From the point of view of its sociopolitical
function, Soviet sociology today is not very different from the kind of
sociology dominant in other highly industrialized countries. If there
is a difference, it may be reduced to the fact that in the USSR only the
dominant type of sociology exists; therefore its managerial function
is even more apparent than elsewhere.

NOTES

1. A. L. Kroeber, The Nature of Culture (Chicago, 1952), p. 352.
2. V. Gordon Childe, Social Evolution (London, 1952), p. 172.
3. A. A. Zhdanov, quoted in G. Aleksandrov, Historia zachodnio-europejskiej filozofii (The history of Western European philosophy) (Warsaw, 1951), p. 34 (this is the Polish translation of Aleksandrov's Istoriia zapadno-evropeiskoi filosofii).
4. Ibid., p. 35.
5. Eugene Kamenka, "Soviet Philosophy 1917-1967," in Social Thought in the Soviet Union, ed. Alex Simirenko (Chicago, 1969).
6. N. Osipova, "Badania socjologiczne w Zeiarzku Radzieckim" (Sociological research in the Soviet Union), Studia Socjologicze (Sociological studies), no. 3, 1967.
7. Lewis A. Coser, The Functions of Social Conflict (London, 1956), p. 20.
8. Ibid., p. 24.
9. Osipova, "Badania socjologiczne."
10. F. J. Roethlisberger, Management and Morale (Cambridge, 1946), p. 112.
11. A. G. Zdravomyslov and V. A. Yadov, Chelovek i ego rabota (Man and his work) (Moscow, 1967), pp. 6-7.

4

**CZECHOSLOVAK AND
POLISH INFLUENCES
ON SOVIET LITERATURE**
Deming Brown

Among the numerous features that indicate the quality of a nation's literary life, the most relevant for the present study would seem to be the civic role of literature (the degree of involvement and influence of writers in public affairs); the thematic concerns of literature (its topical trends, moods, and special interests); esthetic trends (the development of styles and genres); and ideological trends.

Poland and Czechoslovakia have been chosen as representative of East Europe for two reasons. First, the literatures of these two countries recieved more attention in the Soviet Union than those of any other countries in the area. Second, both countries have displayed a strongly Western cultural orientation. This second reason is, I believe, crucial. Poland and Czechoslovakia, have stood as potential cultural bridges between Russia and the West, and the partial revival of Soviet literature since the death of Stalin has been largely although not exclusively the result of increased receptivity to Western influence.

Until 1954 the preponderance of influence in the Soviet Union and East Europe flowed from east to west. The Soviet Union's contribution to Poland and Czechoslovakia was in techniques of party controls over literature—through censorship, writers' unions, editorial and academic bureaucracies, and a variety of administrative and police measures, including the blacklisting and incarceration of writers. In the realm of ideology and esthetics, the Soviet contribution to these two countries was the theory and practice of socialist realism. Although socialist realism was by no means inimical to all writers in these countries, and in fact found many practitioners, its currents ran counter to those that were to prove most attractive in the late 1950s and the 1960s when a modicum of literary freedom returned to both countries.

LITERARY DEVELOPMENT SINCE STALIN'S DEATH

Since the death of Stalin, and particularly since the Twentieth
Congress of the CPSU, the literatures of the Soviet Union, Poland,
and Czechoslovakia have all benefited from increased freedom. All
three countries have experienced a minor literary renaissance at one
time or another during the past twenty years. However, the pace,
quality, and duration of the revival varied. And although the initial
impetus came from the death of Stalin, very shortly thereafter both
the political and the cultural peculiarities of the three countries
shaped literary life in different ways. For this reason, it is appropriate to briefly review the general literary development of each of
these countries over the past two decades.

Soviet Union

Soviet Russian literature entered this period under a special
handicap. Whereas Polish and Czechoslovak literature had suffered
relatively short periods of Communist supervision and control (from
1945 and 1948, respectively), Soviet literature had existed under these
conditions for nearly four decades. Since about 1930, moreover, Soviet
literature had been effectively cut off not only from the West but also
from much of its own rich heritage of the first three decades of the
twentieth century. One of the major accomplishments of the past
twenty years has been the partial restoration of that heritage. Many
writers who were suppressed during the Stalin period were rehabili-
tated and their works reprinted (if only selectively). Their members
included not only those, such as Isaac Babel and Mikhail Bulgakov,
who died under Stalin's rule but also those, such as Anna Akhmatova
and Boris Pasternak, who survived Stalin and, after long periods of
enforced silence, were once again allowed to publish at least some of
their current writings. Such rehabilitations were very often incomplete
and tentative; one must not claim too much for them. Nevertheless,
the fact that these writers, and some of their works, did emerge to
the surface of literary life was an indication of positive change in the
atmosphere.

Similarly, the quality of Soviet literary criticism and scholarship
improved markedly. Although the journals and publishing houses continued to issue vast quantities of narrow and monotonous nonliterary
(essentially political and ideological) commentary of literature, there
was increasing attention by many critics to esthetic, spiritual, and

philosophical aspects. Here again, Soviet literary life began to approach
that of the 1920s, when, together with Marxist criticism of various
shades, esthetic criticism and scholarship flourished for a time.

Soviet Russian poetry during this period began to experience a
revival that, if allowed to continue, could well have become a major
one. Recapturing the techniques, and to a great extent the spirit, of the
symbolist, futurist, and acmeist poets of 1900-25, a new generation
of Soviet poets tried quite self-consciously and insistently to restore
the heritage of the Silver Age. A similar effort took place in Soviet
prose. Repudiating the ponderous, vacuous novel that served to document party theses in Stalinist times, prose writers turned to the
shorter forms of the novella and short story. Somewhat in the manner
of Chekhov, they attempted to cultivate a literature that asks trenchant
questions, avoids prescribed and easy answers, and invites the reader
to form his own—quite possibly unorthodox—conclusions. In both prose
and poetry, there was a significant increase of allegory, of writing
between the lines, and of the Aesopian language in which Russian
literature has traditionally couched subversive ideas and social protest. Not only in this covert manner but also quite openly, Soviet
writers increased the satirical content of literature; the herd of
sacred cows in the Soviet Union became somewhat smaller.

These developments widened the range of topics in Soviet literature and enhanced the variety of treatment. Writing became more
personal and individualized. There was more latitude for the lyric
element in literature; it became possible, for example, to write intimately and idiosyncratically about love and death—although the limits
of erotic intensity and pessimism remained stricter than in the West.
Moral exploration increased: Questions of individual ethical choice,
ends and means, and the conscience—which in the Stalin era were
either unmentionable or governed by collectivist formulas—could now
be examined in some depth. More candor was permitted in portraying
the seamy side of Soviet life—rural backwardness and deprivation,
bureaucratic abuses and corruption, social frustration and inequality.
The publication of occasional outbursts of sharp social criticism was
allowed: Solzhenitsyn's "For the Good of the Cause," Evtushenko's
"Winter Station," Dudintsev's Not by Bread Alone, Yashin's "Vologda
Wedding." Although such works do not question the fundamentals of
the Soviet system, they occasionally penetrate fairly close to its core.

All these developments, and many others as well, were to a certain degree merely byproducts of a trend of de-Stalinization that was
initially inspired by the central authorities and limited in its objectives.
But the trend was erratic and poorly controlled, and the literary
results were surely different from what the central authorities had
desired and anticipated. Much of the literature of the past twenty years
has been retrospective. To correct the Stalinist record, for example,

some writers not only re-told the story of World War II and collectivization in the 1930s but also reexamined aspects of the revolution itself. There was even a brief airing of the most important open secret of all: the concentration camps. The resulting revelations about the past were far from complete and often distorted. (One thinks, for example, of the enormous gaps in Ilya Ehrenburg's memoirs.) What is important, however, is that in the process of resurrecting at least some of the buried facts of Soviet history and embedding them in works of art, writers often added a significant moral dimension. The reexamination of civic themes, halting and tentative though it was, was accompanied by some rather bold and disturbing speculation on the quality and purpose of life.

A measure of the limitations of these developments is the fact that the most profound and eloquent speculations of this sort—Pasternak's Doctor Zhivago, Solzhenitsyn's Cancer Ward, The First Circle, and The Gulag Archipelago, and the writings of Andrei Sinyavsky—have not been published in the Soviet Union. It also is true that the philosophical range of Soviet writing was still severely restricted. Although it is no longer necessary for writers and critics to pay lip service to socialist realism at every turn, and although some do write as if socialist realism did not exist, it is still the only officially accepted literary theory, and it still cannot be attacked openly. A special set of inhibitions, resulting from this phenomenon, seems to confine the Soviet literary imagination to a relatively narrow sphere. The number of permissible themes has increased, but the number of philosophical implications to be drawn from these themes has not grown correspondingly. The shibboleth of decadence remains powerful.

Soviet Russian literature also is confined in another way: The Russians continue to write mainly about themselves. Despite the somewhat wider knowledge of the world that has been available to them in recent years, they seem to lack the confidence, or the daring, to undertake literary excursions to other times and places. There are exceptions: Russian science fiction is flourishing; some writers who go abroad come back with travel essays; the poets sometimes evoke foreign experiences; and historical novels (but with Russian settings) are common. By and large, Soviet writers confine themselves to familiar home ground.

Poland

The period of Stalinist control over Polish literature (1945-55) was shorter and less devastating than in the Soviet Union. (The doctrine of socialist realism was not imposed by party decree until 1949.) Ruthless discipline did succeed in producing a gray literature of socialist realism, in corrupting many authors and driving others into exile, and in silencing many of Poland's finest talents. (The distinguished novelist Maria Dabrowska, for example, wrote "for the drawer" during this period and translated Pepys' Diary.) But these pressures did not entirely prevent the emergence of an authentic, individualized, national literary expression. The stark, brutal concentration camp stories of Tadeusz Borowski, for example, devoid of the slightest tinge of faith and uplift, reached depths of despair that would not have been tolerated in a Soviet writer. And Adolf Rudnicki's documentation of the tragedy of Polish Jews during the Nazi occupation is largely incompatible with the formulas and cliches of socialist realism. Although the voice of Polish literature was muffled and distorted, its latent energies remained powerful as the Stalinist decade came to a close.

The thaw in Poland became evident in 1955, with the publication of Adam Wazyk's fiery political and social protest, "Poem for Adults," and in 1956 with the reappearance of Maria Dabrowska, with her collection of stories The Morning Star, and the angry short stories of Marek Hlasko. There were eloquent condemnations of the Stalinist past, including works by reformed socialist realists such as Tadeusz Konwicki and Kazimierz Brandys. The new treatment of the past involved not only a revised view of Poland's recent political history, a more critical depiction of present social conditions, and a more profound probing into problems of individual conduct and responsibility, but also a reexamination of Polish life during World War II and the German occupation.

The period of sharpest and most direct political and social protest terminated in 1959, when Polish writers began concentrating on more purely esthetic interests. As early as 1956 they had begun quietly asserting the right to cultivate their own gardens, and the authorities had acquiesced by leaving literature free to move in the direction of political aloofness and neutrality. By 1959, in contrast to the Russians, who by and large continued writing on social themes that had a direct and immediate national relevance, the Poles had turned to more general philosophical themes and to more purely literary experimentation. Although partly at the expense of immediate social commitment, Polish literature in the 1960s achieved impressive variety, depth, and sophistication. Its treatment of psychological, moral, and philosophical problems and its speculations on the tragic nature of history (often in the form of parables) moved it prominently into the mainstream of modern Western literature.

The intellectual sophistication and freedom from isolation of Polish literature was manifested in many ways. Jerzy Andrzejewski's novel The Inquisitors–a study of ends and means and questions of individual moral choice, with prominent political implications–has the Spanish Inquisition for its setting. His The Gates of Paradise is about the Children's Crusade. He Cometh Leaping Upon the Mountain, a novel said to be based in part on the character of Pablo Picasso, is set in contemporary France. The reputation of one author of the postwar generation, Jacek Bochenski, was made with a novel about Julius Caesar, and his most recent novel, Tabu, tells three parallel stories of frustrated love: The first concerns a nun in seventeenth-century Spain, the second a woman refugee from France in the 1930s, and the third a woman of the present day who is undergoing psychoanalysis. Two of the most widely read Polish works of recent years–Tadeusz Breza's The Bronze Gate and The Office–are about the contemporary Vatican. It should be noted, however, that the Poles have developed a sophisticated technique of writing between the lines of a historical novel or novel with a non-Polish setting. Although their interests were truly cosmopolitan, they were dealing to a great extent, if indirectly, with the problems of their own country. (This is an aspect of the strong Polish tendency to write in metaphors and allegory in dealing with delicate themes, a practice that goes back to the partitions.)

Polish writing reasserted its ties with the West not only by showing a sympathetic interest in European settings, institutions, and questions but also by adopting a largely Western manner. Tadeusz Konwicki in A Dream Book for Our Time portrays the nightmarish confusion, torment, and moral devastation of his nation in World War II with a combination of novelistic techniques that is thoroughly avant garde. In Polish fiction the antihero (a photographic negative of the traditional Soviet positive hero) became a common figure. Polish poets are as exploratory as the prose writers, perhaps more so. The linguistic experiments of Miron Bialoszewski, his interest in the grotesque and in ambiguous, "meaningless" sounds; the deliberately coarse and "ugly" verse of Stanislaw Grochowiak; the deeply intellectual, sophisticated, and classically compact verse of Zbigniew Herbert; and the ironic, pessimistic, calculatedly crude "antipoetry" of Tadeusz Rozewicz–all are clearly on the frontier of modern literature. Both Rozewicz and Slawomir Mrozek have made major contributions to the theater of the absurd. It should be emphasized, however, that avant-gardism was a major trend in Polish literature before World War II,

exemplified by Gombrowicz and Witacky. The developments represented by these writers were not as dramatic a departure from tradition as similar developments in Soviet literature would have been.

Czechoslovakia

The revival of literary life in Czechoslovakia came about much
more slowly than in either Poland or the Soviet Union. Except for a
brief period of thaw in 1956 and 1957, Czechoslovak literature until
1962 was nearly as stagnant as it had been before the death of Stalin.
In 1956, however, a magazine for young writers, Kveten, was founded,
and this journal became a training ground for a group of talented
poets, critics, and prose writers who were to come to the fore in the
1960s. The first advances were made in poetry, which moved away
from the theme of building socialism and became meditative, satirical,
and even erotic. Czechoslovak prose began to liberate itself politically
from the old patterns by cultivating anti-Stalinist themes (as in Ladislav Bublik's The Spine and Ladislav Mnacko's Delayed Reports), and
by discarding the standard construction novel and the large epic of
socialist development. More important, such prose writers as Josef
Skvorecky moved entirely outside the framework of socialist realism
by producing novels and stories concerned with the human condition,
independent of immediate political and social contexts.

Writing continued about the years of German occupation, the war,
and the resistance. However, such writers as Ladislav Fuks, Arnost
Lustig, and Bohumil Hrabal played down the heroic features of these
events and concentrated on their psychological and moral effects, on
the little man who was their victim, and on the muddled, confused,
often unheroic behavior of individuals caught up in the whirlpools of
history. A drama of political allegory and thinly veiled protest developed, as in the plays of Ivan Klima, together with the satirical drama
of the absurd, splendidly exemplified by Vaclav Havel.

The theme of alienation developed; writers began exploring the
problems of frustrated youth and the psychology of loneliness. The
stories of Hrabal featured the grotesque, at times approaching sur-
realism. In their unconventional form, the subjective, antirealistic
stories and novels of Vera Linhartova approached the French "nouveau
roman." Like Poland, Czechoslovakia developed a school of modern
philosophical poetry, in which the leading figure was the scientist
Miroslav Holub. And, as in Poland, all these developments represented not a sudden turning to or slavish imitation of the West but a
resumption of natural contact with cultural forces that had been

indigenous before World War II, a resumption that the era of Stalinism had postponed.

THE CIVIC ROLE OF THE WRITER

The foregoing sketch of developments in these three national literatures suggests something about the role of writers in public affairs. A somewhat closer look is required, however, because there is not necessarily a high correlation between the literary practices of writers and their political opinions, or indeed between the strength of their political opinions and their political effectiveness. Since the purpose of this essay is to speculate on the influence, if any, of Poland and Czechoslovakia on the Soviet Union, let us look at this facet of literary life.

The civic role of Polish writers has been conditioned by two circumstances not present in either the Soviet Union or Czechoslovakia. The first is the existence of a strong Catholic church, with its constant reminder of ideological and spiritual alternatives to the new official beliefs. The second is that during the greater part of this 20-year period Polish writers enjoyed fairly extensive and direct acquaintance with the West. They traveled in Europe and America, maintained contact with critical and disaffected Polish emigres, and had relatively free access to foreign books, periodicals, and newspapers. After 1956 the works of some contemporary emigre writers were permitted publication in Poland. The influential emigre journal Kultura, published in France, circulated widely in Poland from 1956 to 1966. As a result, Polish writers were able to maintain a dialogue not only with the West but also with other Poles throughout the world, and thereby to reinforce their sense of national identity under the political shadow of the Soviet Union.

The extreme unrest of the Polish writing community burst to the surface in 1955, with the publication of Adam Wazyk's "Poem for Adults." In that year also, the journal Po Prostu was founded, to become a rallying point for rebellious young writers. In close connection with a network of youth discussion groups, the so-called "intelligentsia clubs," this periodical was extremely active in preparing the way for the Polish October. By this time, most of Poland's influential writers—including Communists—were thoroughly estranged from the Communist leadership, so that the literary revolt was led by a combination of disillusioned young Communist intellectuals and older repentant Stalinists. In view of the fact that the Polish October was a national uprising involving many sectors of the population, one cannot conclude that the writers were the decisive political factor, but they were powerful spokesmen of popular discontent and aspirations.

From 1956 to 1959 the Gomulka reforms encouraged a spirit of protest, and Polish writers, many of them ex-Stalinists or passive collaborators with Stalinism, engaged in social criticism with a will. (There were limits, of course; for example, the government closed down Po Prostu in autumn of 1957.) After 1959, as the Gomulka regime became less tolerant of criticism, there was a conscious withdrawal from politics, particularly on the part of younger writers. Turning away from political themes, Polish writers began cultivating their literary art. However, they did remain engaged to some extent. In March 1964, some 34 of Poland's most prominent intellectuals (including the writers Dabrowska, Andrzejewski, Jastrun, Rudnicki, Dygat, Kott, Wazyk, and Slonimski) sent a letter to Premier Cyrankiewicz protesting censorship and other cultural policies. (This was followed by reprisals, including a stop on publication of the works of several of the signatories. The episode caused such an international furor that the authorities organized a counterprotest against the alleged exploitation of the scandal by Radio Free Europe. Among those who refused to sign the protest were 57 Communist writers.)

The expulsion of Professor Leszek Kolakowski from the party in December 1966 brought about an open letter, again protesting against current cultural policies, signed by 22 prominent members of the Warsaw branch of the Writers' Union. Many of these, in consequence, either resigned or were expelled from the party. The situation of dissenting writers became more and more difficult in 1967, and extremely so in 1968 and 1969. When in January 1968 Mickiewicz's patriotic play "Dziady" was banned from the stage of the National Theater because of the "anti-Soviet reactions of the audience," 231 writers and intellectuals petitioned for an extraordinary session of the Warsaw branch of the Writers' Union and, on February 29, passed, over vigorous party opposition, a resolution requesting reinstatement of the production and reforms in the system of censorship. This was followed in March by numerous student demonstrations protesting the closing of the play and censorship in general, and expressing enthusiastic support of the reforms currently taking place in Czechoslovakia. Shortly thereafter the poet Antoni Slonimski was singled out in the press as a prime instigator of the demonstrations, and there followed a series of reprisals against leading writers, who were either expelled from the party or dismissed from their posts. (The play has since been restored to the Polish stage and has enjoyed great success in the 1970s. Likewise, Slonimski has reappeared in print since the coming to power of Edward Gierek.)

When the Soviets invaded invaded Czechoslovakia in August, Slavomir Mrozek, visiting Rome, sent a telegram to the BBC declaring his solidarity with the Czechs and Slovaks. Jerzy Andrzejewski addressed an open letter to Eduard Goldstucker, president of the Czechoslovak Writers' Union, protesting the invasion. But these were the last gasps of liberal expression. In the fierce wave of reaction that swept Poland in the succeeding two years, liberal writers were completely submerged.

In Czechoslovakia the liberalization of literary life came about much more slowly than in either Poland or the Soviet Union. A mild thaw began in the summer of 1955, and in a debate at the Second Czechoslovak Writers' Congress in April 1956 there were demands for the abolition of censorship, the release of writers from prison, and liberation from the shackles of socialist realism. The writers did win a few concessions: Some Stalinist bureaucrats were removed from leading positions in the Writers' Union, censorship became less oppressive, and certain banned authors began to reappear in print. The relief was shortlived, however, and by 1958 the literary bureaucrats had returned to power, enforcing neo-Stalinist policies. Thus, liberally inclined writers were forced to remain silent at a time when their counterparts in the Soviet Union and Poland were being somewhat more outspoken. To a great extent this situation was attributable to the extreme rigidity of the Czechoslovak party leadership, but it was aggravated by the traditional Czech preference for avoiding a struggle against vastly superior forces.

The movement toward genuine liberalization became more evident in 1962 and 1963. Open discontent was evident at a conference of the Slovak Writers' Union in April 1963 and at the Third Czechoslovak Writers' Congress in May there were appeals for an end to stagnation and corruption. Toward the end of 1963 Kulturni zivot, the official organ of the Slovak Writers' Union, published a series of revisionist articles that led in the spring of 1964 to a series of confrontations with the orthodox party press, and with Novotny himself, all of which proved inconclusive. With the political press still tightly controlled, the literary journals gradually became a locus of debate and accumulated great liberal prestige.

Meanwhile, the liberals' influence grew within the Writers' Union itself. In 1966 the union was able to send a delegation to Moscow protesting the sentences meted out to Daniel and Sinyavasky. The trend that had been building since 1962 became decisive in 1967, when at the Fourth Writers' Congress there were strong and open protests against regulation of the arts, and censorship in particular. (A dramatic moment at the congress was the public reading, by Pavel Kohout, of the petition that Alexander Solzhenitsyn had tried unsuccessfully to put before the Congress of Soviet Writers.) There were demonstrations against a whole array of abuses of state power and against the denial of constitutional freedoms. The writers boldly complained of the divergence between the ideals of socialism and its practice in Czechoslovakia, frankly proclaimed their aspiration to rejoin the Western European cultural community (by this time, they had already accomplished much along these lines), and demanded recognition of their right to creative freedom in the form of official public safeguards. From this moment forward, Czechoslovak writers played a leading role in the events that culminated in the overthrow of the Novotny regime.

The political influence of the Czechoslovak writers in 1967-68 was greater than that of any writing community in a Communist country since Hungary in 1956. Like the Hungarians, they achieved this influence by articulating popular discontent. To some extent, the writers generated their political power by themselves, by establishing strong positions within the party and winning the party's support for their cause. When the Novotny regime tried to crush liberal influence by closing down offending magazines and newspapers and juggling editorial staffs, the liberals successfully boycotted them. But the most effective boycotts were conducted by the public itself—the readers. The verdict of history may be that Czechoslovak writers did not so much change the political climate as take advantage of it.

In the Soviet Union since Stalin there have been three main periods in which writers have pressed for and, within severe limits, won freedom to express unorthodox ideas and attitudes, to make original moral evaluations, and to engage in candid criticism of the contemporary scene. All three periods, however, brought about a reaction in which the authorities took fright at what they had allowed to happen and undertook to punish and silence the offending writers and to chastise the offending editors. The first period was 1953-54, when such works as the critic Pomerantsev's essay "On Sincerity in Literature" and the first part of Ilya Ehrenburg's novel The Thaw appeared. A second more extensive liberalization took place in 1956 and 1957, when numerous poems, plays, and prose works were published denouncing Stalinism and its vestiges, pleading for more humanity in both Soviet life and art, and arguing that the legitimate function of literature is to analyze and criticize, not merely to illustrate official policies. Probably the most outspoken work published in this period was Vladimir Dudintsev's Not By Bread Alone. The highlight of the third period, 1962-63, was Alexander Solzhenitsyn's One Day in the Life of Ivan Denisovich. Since the fall of Khrushchev in 1964 there has ensued an unsteady but general erosion of literary freedom.

The last 20 years of Soviet literary life, however, have left a legacy that can be destroyed only by thoroughgoing reaction on a massive scale. The Stalinist form of terrorism no longer predominates:

The incarceration of writers, editors, critics, and academic persons
has ceased to be common. Writers have been permitted to tell more
of the truth about life—both within the Soviet Union and beyond its
borders—than in previous decades. Also, they are somewhat less
isolated culturally than they were 20 years ago. More translations
of foreign literature—and notably that of Western origin—are available.
(A notable breakthrough in this respect is the recent translation of
William Faulkner's The Sound and the Fury.) Writers are freer to
travel abroad than formerly, although permission to do so is granted
as a reward for good behavior and correspondingly revoked as a
punishment for political ideological transgressions. Finally, the
pretense of monolithic unity in the literary community has disappeared.
If only by default, the authorities have seemingly legitimized the existence of loosely defined, fluctuating, but nevertheless distinctly recog-
nizable liberal and conservative camps in Soviet literature. The
resulting clash of ideas and prejudices, although of necessity carried
on at a fairly low level because of the extreme obtuseness of the conservatives, has been a source of some stimulation and ferment.

Nevertheless, Soviet literary life is governed by circumstances
that have been essentially the same for decades. Censorship remains
complete and all-pervasive, and writers must either consciously or
unconsciously tailor their works to fit its demands. There are also
elaborate party and administrative controls over writers, and the use
of police power against recalcitrants has recently been on the increase.
The newest administrative device has been forced emigration from the
Soviet Union—the creation in the professional (and even the private)
lives of such writers as Solzhenitsyn, Nekrasov, Sinyansky, Galich,
Korzhaven, and Maksimov of conditions so intolerable that they must
choose exile. And the same moral conditions prevail, only slightly
modified by the absence of naked terror: Writers must still suppress
the truth, resort to the subterfuge of writing between the lines, and
avoid a vast array of intellectual positions, moods, and literary techniques that are characteristic of writing outside the Soviet Union. The
positive achievements of the past 20 years were largely attributable
to the opportunism of Khrushchev, who used the liberal writing community for his own political ends, and to the vacillation or inattention
of his successors, uncertain of their strength and preoccupied with
noncultural matters.

The activity of the liberal writing community has been manifest
in the editorial policies of certain periodicials, sporadic ferment
within the Union of Soviet Writers, and public or semipublic protests
against official policies governing literature and against the persecution of writers. One hesitates, however, to call the liberal writing
community a political faction, much less an organized political force.

At certain times, and on certain issues, there have been impressive
displays of solidarity among liberals. But their ranks appear to be
loose and easily fragmented; it seems impossible for them, as a group,
to withstand the kind of pressures that the central authorities are
capable of applying in moments of crisis.

In the field of publications—notably, for a time, the journals Novyi
Mir and Junost' and the newspaper Literaturnaia gazeta—the liberals
exerted influence through membership on editorial boards. They were
clearly effective in promoting works, authors, and points of view congenial to their cause. The editorial boards of periodicals, however,
are a precarious political base, since the party, through the Writers'
Union, can and did shuffle these boards at will. The modest and fleeting
successes that the liberals enjoyed in periodical publication came about
through a combination of their own ingenuity and the temporary suffer-
ance of the authorities, and not through a consolidation of real political
power.

The successes attained by the liberals in the Writers' Union itself
likewise proved ephemeral. Their greatest triumph—the use of a secret
ballot in April 1962 to capture control of the Moscow section of the
union—was summarily terminated a year later when Khrushchev
ordered structural changes in the union, eliminating their power. Like
every other Soviet institution, the Writers' Union is ultimately a creation of the party and correspondingly vulnerable to manipulation, and
when the liberals became a sufficiently serious embarrassment to
Khrushchev, he clipped their wings. It is important, however, that in
1962 and 1963 their writings were sufficiently prominent to alarm the
party leadership. Together with artists, composers, and other representatives of the intelligentsia, they were repeatedly convened by
Khrushchev and his cultural lieutenants to be alternately harangued
and cajoled in an effort to keep them in line.

Although they had little power within the Writers' Union, the
liberals did seem to exert some influence through sheer recalcitrance.
In 1966, for example, a number of them refused to lend their names
to the campaign of vilification organized by the union and directed
against Andrei Sinyavsky and Uli Daniel, thus rendering the campaign
somewhat less effective. A number of prominent liberals quietly boycotted the Fourth Congress of Soviet Writers in 1967; when Solzhenitsyn,
in an eloquent letter of protest, petitioned that same congress to debate
the issue of censorship, he received wide although unsuccessful liberal
support. Although heel-dragging, refusal to be mobilized for every
official purpose, and occasional support of outspoken rebels does not
seem to have had much practical effect on the workings of the Writers'
Union, it surely helped to dramatize the liberal cause.

Much of the activity of the liberal writing community, we must
assume, took place in private or in sessions of editorial boards and

organizations of the Writers' Union and party of which there is no
public record. The most insistent public expression of liberal opinion
was in the form of letters of protest and petitions directed to officials
and agencies of the Soviet government, and in a mass of documents
that circulated through Samizdat. This kind of activity seems to have
increased markedly in the past ten years. Its first dramatic manifes-
tation was in 1966 in response to the trial of Sinyavsky and Daniel,
during which hundreds of writers and other intellectuals went on record
opposing the treatment of the two as a violation of socialist legality.
Subsequent and similar manifestations took place in connection with
the trial of Ginzburg, Galanskov, Dobrovolskij, and Lashkova in 1968.
Signed protests of this sort, it should be noted, were directed not only
to government officials and the press of the Soviet Union but also to
the foreign press, foreign Communist organizations, and to agencies
of the United Nations. The liberals were appealing not only to the
Soviet government and public but also to world public opinion.

This kind of activity may, ironically, be more evident to observers
in the West than to the general Soviet population. The Soviet press
almost never prints these protests, and mentions them only sparsely
and indirectly. Samizdat is certainly widespread and appears to be
increasing, but it is impossible to determine the extent of its reader-
ship or its popular effectiveness. Reprisals directed against some
protesting liberal writers would indicate that the authorities consider
them a threat. On the other hand, liberal protest does not seem to
have slowed the trend of repression. One can only conclude, I think,
that the liberal writing community is not a locus of political power;
rather, it is a disorganized but important political irritant.

This is in direct contrast to the situation in Czechoslovakia in
1967-68. For one thing, the protests of Soviet liberals have seldom
found their way into print and have therefore not achieved the fully
public quality of those in Czechoslovakia. By maintaining firm control
over all publication, the authorities have restricted liberal protest to
personal contact, the circulation of letters and petitions, and Samizdat.
Also, Czech and Slovak liberal writers in 1967-68 benefited from the
fact that the Communist Party itself was in rapid transition and, in
those politically unstable conditions, found an opportunity to serve
as spokesmen and catalysts of change. Working within the party and
the Writers' Union, they managed to gain control of literary journals
and newspapers and to transform them into political organs of crucial
importance. On the other hand, the Soviet authorities, by manipulating
the editorial boards of periodicals, have been careful to prevent such
a thing from happening.

The Soviet authorities have been alert to break up any concentra-
tions of liberal influence that threaten to become decisive. This fact
is of course a reflection of the political forces at the top of the Soviet

government. But the Soviet Writers' Union itself also has a longer
history of discipline and a longer tradition of monolithic rigidity than
those of Poland or Czechoslovakia. With a more powerful bureaucracy,
less real democracy, and less room for open debate and discussion,
it provides less opportunity for liberal opposition. For example, no
Soviet writers' congress has approached the level of intense and open
political debate that was attained at the 1967 congress in Czechoslovakia.
And as far as I know, the Soviet Writers' Union has never risked the
public embarrassment of permitting its conservative element to be
outvoted on an issue of national importance, as did the Poles over the
Dziady affair in 1968.

Has the role of Polish and Czechoslovak writers in public affairs
influenced the role of their Soviet counterparts? For writers of conservative or reactionary inclination, I think we can conclude that there
has been no influence; the ideas and practices of Soviet reactionaries
seem to be homegrown. They have no need for ideological models or
instruction in the techniques of defending their vested interests and
fixed positions. On the other hand, Soviet liberals have clearly admired
the periodic developments toward freedom in Poland and Czechoslovakia,
aware that any permanent achievements in Eastern Europe might
enhance their own liberties. There is little evidence, however, that
Soviet liberal writers have done more than enjoy a vicarious gratifi-
cation over the political victories of their neighbors to the west.
Although they may wish to emulate the Czechs and Poles, they behave
as if their experience has told them that it is simply impossible for
them to do so.

The October events in Poland of 1956, for example, raised the
morale of the Soviet intelligentsia; it was reported that Polish newspapers and journals were eagerly bought up, and that many Russians
learned Polish to get access to freer ideas. It need not be emphasized,
however, that this is political activity of the mildest sort. Similarly,
Soviet writers observed the Czech Spring of 1968 with great interest,
enthusiasm, and hope, but their public behavior was not significantly
influenced by those events. In August 1968 there was widespread
disapproval of the invasion of Czechoslovakia. Public acts of protest,
however, were pathetically rare and ineffectual. Nevertheless, a major
reason behind the decision to invade Czechoslovakia was the fear that
the infection of Czechoslovak democratic and libertarian aspirations
would spread to the Soviet intelligentsia. The quiet and resigned
reaction of Soviet writers to the invasion and termination of Czechoslovak freedom, however, would indicate that their potential for decisive political activity was still quite modest.

Soviet writers have visited Poland and Czechoslovakia from time
to time and must have established personal friendships with writers
there. Such contacts might well be extremely influential, but

unfortunately I have very little information about their extent or depth. On a more formal basis, literary contacts have been under the sponsorship of the Soviet Academy of Sciences (through its subsidiary, the Gorky Institute of World Literature), the Union of Soviet Writers, and their Czechoslovak and Polish counterparts. This activity seems to have taken the form, chiefly, of meetings between delegations of literary officials, scholars, critics, and editors, to discuss problems of Marxist criticism, mutual scholarly and translation projects, and the general improvement of contacts between writers' organizations. Often these meetings were bilateral: Between 1960 and 1965, for example, there were three of them between Czechoslovak and Soviet delegations. (The same approach was taken from time to time with Poland, East Germany, Bulgaria, Hungary, and Yugoslavia.) There also were multilateral meetings, such as one is Moscow in 1965 between the leading officials of writers' unions of the "socialist countries."

The Soviet reports for such meetings have a heavily bureaucratic flavor. For one thing, the Soviet side is almost invariably represented by officials and orthodox spokesmen such as Aleksei Surkov and Ivan Anisimov. One suspects that the purpose of such meetings was more to supervise literary contacts than to promote them, and that their main motivation, at least on the Soviet side, was to ensure the ideological correctness of the relationship between the Soviet, Czechoslovak, and Polish literary communities. It is even possible that the main purpose of these meetings was to counteract any pernicious liberal influences that might have come from East Europe to the Soviet Union through less formal contacts.

SOVIET TRANSLATIONS OF POLISH
AND CZECHOSLOVAK LITERATURE

An important indication of possible literary influence is the translation of Polish and Czechoslovak literature into the languages of the USSR.[1] It should be noted, first of all, that the number of translations into the minority languages of the Soviet Union roughly equals the number of translations into Russian. (Translations from Polish are, in descending order of frequency, in Russian, Ukrainian, Lithuanian, Latvian, and Estonian. For translations from Czech and Slovak, the order is Russian, Estonian, Ukrainian, Lithuanian, and Latvian.[2]) This fact is of special interest, for the pattern of publication in minority languages, and notably those of the Baltic republics, differs somewhat from that in Russian. A case in point is the Polish novelist Jerzy Andrzejewski, who appears to have been published in book form four times in Estonian, once in Latvian, once in Lithuanian, and only once in Russian. His novel Ashes and Diamonds first appeared in Lithuanian and Estonian in 1957 (there have been three Estonian editions), and came out in Russian only in 1965. (The novel also was published in Ukrainian in 1968.) One can only speculate on the reasons for the long delay before its appearance in Russian. The novel does give a sympathetic treatment of Poles, who, at the end of World War II, found themselves to have been in the wrong camp of the resistance movement. It is quite possible that the Soviet authorities could tolerate the publication of this politically dubious novel in small minority languages more easily than in Russian.

In selecting works for translation, Soviet publishers seem to have been concerned at least as much with political significance and journalistic interest as with literary merit. The only virtue of many of the Czechoslovakian and Polish authors published would seem to be the political orthodoxy of their writings and, quite possibly, their standing and influence in the party circles of their respective countries. Even among genuinely talented writers, perference seems, not surprisingly, to have been given to those who enjoyed reputations, more or less, as socialist realists—such as Wanda Wasilevska (who wrote in Polish but as a Soviet author), Jaroslaw Iwaszkiewicz and Leon Kruczkowski, and the Czechoslovaks Marie Majerova, Ladislav Mnacko, and Jan Drda.

But many writers also have been published whose sole claim to attention is their talent. Among these were several Polish authors of the 1930s, 1940s, and 1950s who had not been published in the Soviet Union before 1956, and in this sense Soviet readers were provided with a long-delayed acquaintance with modern Polish literature. There also was a modest publication of such first-rate contemporary prose writers as Maria Dabrowska, Tadeusz Konwicki, Adolf Rudnicki, and Tadeusz Breza, and of the poets Wladyslaw Broniewski, Konstanty Galczynski, Tadeusz Holuj, Mieczyslaw Jastrun, and Tadeusz Rozewicz. It is probable that many of these writers were a genuine revelation for Svoiet readers. Breza's accounts of the Vatican, for example, may have provided them with their first relatively objective report of that institution. And the most widely published Polish writer of all in the Soviet Union—Stanislaw Lem, the author of what is ostensibly science fiction—must have startled and delighted Soviet readers with his extremely trenchant social and political allegory.

But a number of Polish writers of great literary merit appear to have been granted merely a token publication or none at all. Such are the poet Miron Bialoszewski and the prose writers Jacek Bochenski, Stanislaw Stanuch, and the late Marek Hlasko. Tadeusz Borowski has been translated only into Lithuanian, Leopoly Tyrmand only into Ukrainian. The most interesting case is that of Slawomir Mrozek, whose volume of stories The Elephant was published in Estonian in

1964, and whose play <u>Tango</u> was published in Estonian in 1967. With the exception of one brief story from <u>The Elephant</u> (this story's political implications happened to be congenial) in <u>Inostrannaia literatura</u>, Mrozek apparently has not been published in Russian.

The number of contemporary Czech and Slovak writers published in the Soviet Union is considerably smaller than the number of Poles. To some extent this is justified by the fact that over the past 20 years Czechoslovak literature has not been as varied and interesting as Polish literature. Nevertheless, the same general pattern of translations obtains as with the Poles. In addition to Majerova, Mnacko, and Drda, the most extensively published contemporary prose writers were Ludvik Askenazy, Jan Otcenasek, and Vladimir Minac. There was modest publication—two or three editions each—of the playwright Pavel Kohout, of the prose writers Ladislav Bublik, Ivan Klima, and Ivan Kriz, and of the poets Jiri Fried and Jiri Taufer. (The last named, who is more politician than poet, obviously was translated for official reasons.)

The omissions are even more striking among Czech and Slovak writers than among the Poles. Prominent prose writers not published in the Soviet Union are Bohumil Hrabal, Vera Linhartova, Josef Skvorecky, and Ludvik Vaculik. The leading poet Miroslav Holub has not been translated, nor has Vaclav Havel, Czechoslovakia's most prominent dramatist of the absurd. Arnost Lustig and Milan Kundera have appeared only in Estonian, Vratislav Blazek only in Latvian, and Jan Prochazka only in Ukrainian.[3]

It seems clear that Soviet writers (as well as readers and critics) who depend on translations for their contact with Polish and Czechoslovak literature—and most of them do—can only have a knowledge that is far from thorough. The Soviet authorities have been selective politically, ideologically, and esthetically. There is adequate exposure to the socialist realism of the Soviet Union's western neighbors, but a relatively slight exposure to trends that deviate from it. This is significantly less true, however, of the Baltic and western regions than of the rest of the USSR. Everything else being equal, Estonian or Ukrainian writers, for example, would seem much more likely to have been influenced by Polish, Czech, or Slovak literary tendencies than would their Russian colleagues.

COMPARATIVE APPROACHES TO LITERARY THEMES

World War II

It is instructive to compare the treatment of certain common topics by the writers of these three countries over the past twenty years. The most prominent of these is World War II. Because Poland and Czechoslovakia were occupied countries during most of the war, their writers have naturally emphasized the resistance, the concentration and death camps, and life under the occupation. Soviet writers, on the other hand, have tended to concentrate on the war's purely military aspects. In general, there also has been a contrasting psychology in the three literatures. Soviet writing has been predominanly heroic and patriotic, featuring the bravery, self-sacrifice, and determination of the Soviet peoples in defense of their fatherland. Although it has not slighted the horrors of war, it has stressed the positive human aspects of a defensive war with a clear national purpose. By contrast, the war literature of Czechoslovakia and Poland (particularly the latter) has primarily a brooding and tragic quality, emphasizing the political confusions and tensions of the resistance, the terrible suffering of the Jews, and the physical and moral devastation that the war and occupation left in their wake.

Before 1956 the function of Soviet war literature, in the main, was to demonstrate the role of the Communist Party leadership and ideology in bringing about the victory over Hitler's armies, to show the indispensability of Stalin's guidance, and to prove that the heroic exploits that won the war could only have been accomplished by the especially endowed Soviet Man. After 1956 writers were permitted to describe the war with somewhat greater candor. The political coloration changed, to show how Stalin's military unpreparedness had permitted the initial rapid German advances deep into Russia, and to suggest that his callousness and blundering had caused needless sacrifices of human life and resources. However, writers have tended to shy away from politico-military interpretations of the war, tied as they are to the unsteady and sometimes reversible process of de-Stalinization.

Soviet writers also have used the conflict as a device for evaluating the more recent past and, by implication, the present. Yuri Bondarev's novel Silence and Vladimir Tendrjakov's Rendezvous with Nefertiti, for example, embrace both the war and the period up to the death of Stalin. Both novels draw a contrast between frontline morality—where individual honesty, loyalty, and cooperation among

comrades are indispensable, and where the single purpose of destroy-
ing the enemy brings about a pragmatic knowledge of right and wrong—
and the complex and corrupt peacetime scene, where falsity and moral
compromise are prominent features of life. Polish and Czechoslovak
writers, on the other hand, do not present such a morally simple and
clearcut picture of the war itself, and seem disinclined to emphasize
this aspect of the differences between wartime and peacetime.

The Poles always have appeared to be freer than Soviet writers
to linger on the macabre aspects of wartime, its demoralizing effects
and its psychic scars. (Borowski's starkly horrible deathcamp stories
and Rudnicki's chronicle of the separate tragedy of the Jews probably
could not have been published by a Soviet author, least of all in Stalin's
time.) Moods of pessimism, disorientation, and despair are much more
prominent in Polish than in Soviet war writing. Even Soviet poetry
about the war, which reaches greater depths of gloom than Soviet prose,
is not as desolate as its Polish counterpart.

The best Czechoslovak writing about the wartime scene had tended
to be antiheroic. Such writers as Hrabal, Fuks, Lustig, and Skvorecky
have used the war and occupation as background for psychological and
moral investigation and tend to be concerned with the problems and
conduct of the victims of Nazi oppression rather than of those who
fought actively against it. A mildly antiheroic strain of a different
nature is discernible in Soviet war writing of the 1960s—the poetry
of Bulat Okudzhava and his story "Good Luck, Schoolboy," which
have strongly pacifistic implications, and Solzhenitsyn's "An Incident
at Krechetovka Station," which emphasizes the ambiguity of moral
decisions in wartime. This trend, however, was so severely criticized
that it now seems to have ended.

It seems paradoxical that the literature of a battered but victorious nation has been less free to explore the war candidly, in all its
ramifications, than the literatures of the two countries it helped to
liberate. It is true that as occupied nations their suffering was of a
different character and, in the case of Poland, may well have been
deeper, both physically and morally. The fact remains that Polish
and, to a lesser extent, Czechoslovak literature have explored numerous dimensions of World War II that Soviet literature has left virtually untouched.

Generational Conflict

Another theme common to the literatures of all three countries
is the conflict of generations. It appeared first and with the greatest
force in Poland in the angry, pessimistic writings of Hlasko. The

writings of this young generation of Poles were in a spirit of deep
disappointment and bitter hostility toward their elders, whom they
portrayed as morally callous, cynical, and spineless. In Czechoslovakia the theme of "fathers and sons" was expressed first by such
young lyric poets as Sotola, Kundera, and Florian, who wrote of the
search for moral ideals to replace those of a discredited and defeated
older generation and insisted on the need to defend the inner world of
feelings against the pressures of conformity. Prose works featured
the confused searchings of young people trying to find a place in a
society but mistrustful of a world of heartless careerism and smug
vulgarity. Such works, usually narrated in the first person, tended to
be laconic and highly colloquial, reflecting the revulsion of the young
against the hollow and corrupt phraseology of a generation that ceased
to be able to think as individuals. In both countries, however, young
writers went beyond the stage of polemics against the society of their
fathers to argue against the very necessity that literature have a social
orientation. Young writers and critics alike demanded an "authentic"
literature—one that involved the pure self-expression of the author,
in contrast to the "engaged" writing of the previous generation, which
usually was subordinated to the extraliterary aims, which conceived
of man as a purely socially conditioned being, and which tended to
ignore existential problems.

Young writers were not the only ones who dealt with the conflict
between generations. The theme was used by more mature writers
as well, but usually as a device for examining the bad conscience of a
nation, of those who had compromised under totalitarian pressures,
by contrasting their spiritual fatigue and blunted moral sense with the
idealism and uncorrupted mentality of their children. This theme was
particularly prominent in Soviet literature, which dealt with the same
issues: the guilt, passivity, and defeatism of the Stalin generation, and
the impatience and moral searching of young people who cannot accept
the solutions and prescriptions of their fathers. In the Soviet Union,
however, it was distinctly the younger writers who made the most of
this theme. Many of the most prominent writers who are now in their
thirties and forties—Evtushenko, Aksenov, Gladilin, Voinovich, Bitov—
established their reputations largely by writing of fathers and sons.
Although the theme was timely and of great social and ideological
importance in the Soviet Union, these writers also derived significant
esthetic value from it. Some of the most interesting writing, as such,
in the past 20 years has been based on the psychology of the younger
generation and its fresh use of the vernacular. In this respect, it is
worthy of note that the writers of all three nations owe a debt to the
American J. D. Salinger.

There are, however, two major differences between Czechoslovak and Polish writing on this theme and that of Soviet authors. The latter, whatever their true inclinations may be, have not been allowed to portray a generation that is as angry, bitter, and despairing as that portrayed by the Czechs and Poles. Irony and skepticism, yes, but pessimism, no. In this sense, the grip of socialist realism on Soviet writers remains much stronger. Second, although many young Soviet prose writers may dream of an "authentic" literature—and some, such as Bitov and Voinovich, come fairly close to it—the theme of fathers and sons has remained almost exclusively a social one.

Alienation and Kafka

In Polish and Czechoslovak literature, the treatment of problems of youth is closely related to the theme of alienation. The writings of the Pole, Stanislaw Stanuch, for example, focus on lonely, often amoral characters, nihilistic and obsessed by feelings of the senselessness of existence. The theme of alienation also is prominent in Czechoslovakia, in the plays of Havel and the stories of Hrabal. In both countries, it should be noted, this literary practice has strong support in the strain of revisionist philosophy, which argues that alienation is intrinsic to human life, independent of the social order, and that therefore the concept of alienation is applicable to socialist as well as capitalist society. The Soviet Union, too, has writers (one thinks of Yuri Kazakov and, to a lesser extent, of Yuri Nagibin) whose works feature alienated heroes. Such works are often severely criticized, however, and their incidence is relatively small in Soviet literature. Alienation is normally shown to be the product of error, abberation, and wrong thinking, not an organic attribute of Soviet society.

Alienation as a literary theme results to a great extent from the impact of existentialist thought on Polish and Czechoslovak writers. The attraction of negative, lonely, or amoral heroes, and concern over the absence of moral certainties and ultimate justifications for human behavior, is distinctly Western in orientation. Such concern over personal moral freedom, opposition to discipline from outside the self, and insistence on the individual's working out of his own destiny, is not found prominently in Soviet literature, for existentialist thought still represents a major ideological deviation in the USSR.

Another major influence that is shared by Czechoslovak and Polish, but not by Soviet, literature is that of Franz Kafka. After a period of Stalinist interdict, Kafka was revived in both Poland and Czechoslovakia in 1958. (An edition of 10,000 copies of The Trial was sold out in Prague on its first day.) By 1963, when the Czechs

sponsored a large international conference on Kafka, this writer had
become the most important single symbol of revisionist literary ideas
in East Europe. Kafka's vision of the defenseless, lonely individual
in a complex, anonymous, bureaucratic society has provided much of
the inspiration for the Polish theater of the absurd and is clearly
evident in the recent poetry of Mieczyslaw Jastrun. Kafka's influence
on Czechoslovak literature of the 1960s is extremely widespread—for
example, in the prose of Fuks and Hrabal.

The Soviet approach to Kafka has been gingerly and, at least in
official circles, quite evidently grudging. There is evidence (although
not detailed or conclusive) that a polemic regarding Kafka developed
at a meeting between Soviet and Czechoslovak critics and scholars
early in 1963 in Prague.[4] At a meeting of Soviet and European writers
in Leningrad in August 1963, Kafka found one Soviet defender: Ilya
Ehrenburg pleaded that the author be considered a "major historical
phenomenon" and, obviously calculating his remarks for the home
audience, attempted to justify Kafka on the grounds that he "foresaw
the terrible world of fascism."

At last Kafka began to be published in the Soviet Union in 1963.
The December issue of the Ukrainian journal Vsesvit contained translations of stories and excerpts from a number of Kafka's works together with comments by a Soviet reviewer. In the January 1964 issue
of Inostrannaia literatura there were translations of "The Metamor-
phosis" and "In the Penal Colony." (The latter may have been a genuine coup for Soviet liberals; read as allegory, it suggests both Stalin's
and Khrushchev's Russia.) A Russian translation of Parables and
Paradoxes came out in book form in 1965. Typically, however, the
Estonians led the way and were able to show the greatest daring. A
volume of stories (1965) and the only Soviet edition of The Trial (1967)
are in Estonian.

It is a sign of considerable progress, however, that Kafka has now
been published in the Soviet Union, if only minimally and after enormous delay. It would be too early to expect tangible evidence of his
influence on Soviet writers. To overtly display the influence of Kafka
would be dangerous; his vision of alienation as a natural aspect of
the human condition is still officially considered ideologically pernicious. On the other hand, Kafka's world is so relevant to the Soviet
scene that it is bound to exert a powerful attraction for writers. (One
can easily imagine, for example, how One Day in the Life of Ivan
Denisovich or Lydia Chukovskaya's The Deserted House could have
been given a Kafkaesque treatment. I see no evidence of an influence
of Kafka on Solzhenitsyn, but I would be prepared to argue, timidly,
that Chukovskaya, who is a sophisticated intellectual, may have read
Kafka in the 1930s before she wrote her novel.[5])

Closely related to Kafka's perception of the world is the theater of
the absurd, which has been developed extensively in Poland by such play-
wrights as Mrozek and Rozewicz and in Czechoslovakia by Havel and
Kundera. The Soviet authorities have discouraged such developments.
(Novyi Mir accomplished a small triumph in 1965 by merely printing
a provocatively favorable review of the New York performance of
Ionesco's The Rhinoceros.) It is possible that the Taganka Theater's
performance of Andrei Voznesenky's Antiworlds, which I have not
seen, borrows mildly from the absurd theater, since this would be
in the spirit of some of Voznesenky's poetry. Beyond this, however,
it would appear that this important trend in Western dramaturgy has
not penetrated Soviet borders. Likewise the grotesque, which has been
widely employed in the contemporary literature of Poland and Czechoslovakia, has found few practitioners in the Soviet Union. It does crop
up in the poetry of Voznesensky, Axmadulina, Evtushenko, and Sosnora,
and occasionally in the prose of Aksenov. But the best prose of this
type—that of Sinyavsky and Daniel—has never been published in the
Soviet Union.

SIMILAR LITERARY TRENDS:
INFLUENCE OR PARALLEL DEVELOPMENTS?

Thus far this essay has been almost exclusively devoted to comparing the literary life of the three countries, and little has been
offered about the possible influence of Poland and Czechoslovakia on
the Soviet Union. Let it be said, first of all, that questions of literary
influence are very much a matter of conjecture. Literary creation
is such a subjective phenomenon that even the individual writer is
hard put to explain the source of his ideas, his style, and his way of
perceiving the world, and the writer himself is a notoriously unrelia-
ble witness. Questions of literary influence are so subtle, complex,
and intangible that it is exceedingly dangerous to generalize about
them.

One can safely compare one author or one stream of ideas or
one school of stylistic conventions to another and fairly clearly define
their similarities and dissimilarities. However, similarities do not
indicate influence in themselves, for it is possible to have parallel
developments in literature that are quite independent of one another.
The problem of defining influence is increasingly fraught with danger
as one comes closer to the present. The evidence is not all in; one
lacks the perspective with which to make confident generalizations.
Trends may be ephemeral; waves that seem large may turn out to be
small. Today's literary sensation often turns out to be a bubble.

There is one other circumstance that complicates speculation in our particular case. Over the past 20 years the main trend in all three literatures has been that of Westernization. This means that similar movements in the three literatures may not be the result of their mutual interaction but, rather, parallel developments that come from the same Western source. It is probable, for example, that some Polish, Czechoslovak, and Soviet writers have adopted an ironic, colloquial method of rendering the psychology of youth not because they have read each other but because they have all read Salinger.

In all three literatures there has been an increase in the use of first-person narration and interior monologue. These practices represent a reaction against the device of the impersonal, omniscient narrator and an attempt to convey an increased sense of authenticity and emotional and moral fidelity. Czechoslovak and Polish writers, in addition, employ stream-of-consciousness techniques to this end. Soviet writers have been chary of using stream-of-consciousness because it lays them open to charges of "formalism." In recent years, however, the device has reappeared to a modest degree in the stories of Aksenov. But it is doubtful whether this is attributable to a Czechoslovak or Polish influence; there are ample models in Russian literature itself, in such early twentieth-century writers as Andrei Bely, Aleksei Remizov, and Boris Pilnyak. Likewise, first-person narration and interior monologue go back to the middle of the nineteenth century in Russian literature. The increased use of all these devices by writers of the three nations has undoubtedly been mutually reinforcing. All three literatures were motivated by the same impulse to become more human, personal, and intimate. But in this situation Soviet writers have little occasion to borrow from the technical resources of their Slavic neighbors.

The same can be said of the increased use of short prose forms— the novella and short story—and of the move toward compactness and reserve in narrative manner. The partial revolt against the large novel, in which all three literatures participated, was essentially a reaction against the didacticism of socialist realism, particularly as practiced in Stalinist fiction. Here again, the Russians had national models that were largely adequate to their purposes, of which the most useful was Chekhov.

There are certain formal devices that Czechoslovak and Polish writers used much more extensively than the Russians in this period. Andrzejewski's novel The Gates of Paradise, for example, is written as one continuous sentence; the jumbled chronology and bizarre associations of phenomena in Konwicki's A Dream Book for Our Time are indeed those of a dream. Vera Linhartova's narrative manner is so subjective as to be frequently unintelligible. If the Russians were to accept an influence from the Czechs and Poles, it might logically be in the realm of such "modernist" characteristics. But I see no evidence that this has happened.

In all three literatures there has been a great increase in documentary writing, the combination of fiction with reportage to produce works that lie somewhere between the novel and the essay, or between the short story and the sketch (the Russian ocherk). The Poles in particular have developed such hybrid genres, as in Brandys's Letters to Madame Z and Breza's The Bronze Gate. In recent years such forms also have been developed extensively by the Russians, especially by those who write about rural Russia, such as Ovechkin, Dorosh, Troepolsky, and Yashin. Here again, however, the Soviet writers may well have developed these forms independently. It has been argued, in fact, that if there has been any influence in this sphere, it has gone from east to west, and that Breza and Ladislav Mnacko may have borrowed from Ovechkin.

We have noted that the Poles have made extensive use of historical, religious, or non-Polish material for allegorical commentary on their present situation and problems. The Russians also employ historical and mythological material for the purpose of metaphorical commentary on issues of the present that cannot be discussed directly. This practice is particularly prominent among the poets, such as Martynov, Slutsky, Voznesensky, and Evtushenko, who in this respect have their counterparts in the Czech Miroslav Holub and the Pole Zbigniew Herbert. Again, this common device would seem to spring from like interests and the political pressures shared by the writers of all three countries. But surely the Soviet writers have received no instruction from the Czechs and the Poles in this matter; Russians have been evading the censors in this manner for centuries.

Although there has been only a modest amount of Soviet translation of Czechoslovak and Polish poetry, this is potentially an important source of influence. The reason is that the actual translating is done largely by established Soviet poets, such as Slutsky, Vinokurov, and David Samoilov. Criticism of contemporary Polish poetry also has been written by such prominent Soviet poets as Kirsanov and Selvinsky, in addition to Samoilov, whose extensive work as an editor and translator indicates a deep interest in Polish verse. Unfortunately, this essay can do no more than indicate that these circumstances suggest the possibility of influence from Poland on the Soviet Union.

All in all, I find little evidence to suggest that contemporary Polish and Czechoslovak literature, of and in themselves, have exerted a noticeable influence on Soviet Russian literature. The three have followed parallel paths to some extent, but they seem to have done so quite independently. Moreover, the Western Slavs seem to have gone much farther along these paths than have the Russians. In every line of literary development there seems to be a point where the Russians stop (or turn back) while the Czechs and Poles proceed.

In their battle against stale ethical abstractions and rigid notions of human nature over the past 20 years, writers have concentrated anew on individual psychology and moral problems. The effort toward a deeper understanding of the human personality and a fresh conscious-ness of personal responsibility has expanded both their esthetic and their ideological horizons. In the process, Czechoslovak and Polish writers buried an already moribund socialist realism. The Russians did not, and this fact, more than any other, explains their divergence.

One reason why the Russians have lagged behind in this respect is that they have been isolated from Western literary modernism for nearly half a century, whereas the Czechs and Poles were cut off for relatively brief periods. The most important reason, however, is not cultural but political: Soviet authorities clearly fear the ideological results of a frank admission that socialist realism is dead. As a con-sequence, they keep propping up its corpse, applying cosmetics, and shouting that it is alive.

This produces curious and somewhat pathetic results in Soviet criticism of Polish and Czechoslovak writing, particularly by critics who are evidently well disposed toward those literatures. In 1967, for example, the critics Balashov and Bernshtein commented on the fact that many foreign Communist critics assiduously avoid the term "socialist realism." Some of these critics, they reasoned, mistrust the concept of socialist realism because they themselves are ideolog-ically hostile to socialism, but others do so because of "terminologi-cal misunderstanding." The latter group, they argued, do not realize just how dynamic and flexible socialist realism can be. They have the mistaken notion that the term implies an adherence to musty principles or nineteenth-century realism, combined with a strong element of social didacticism, whereas in actuality it can indeed embrace "avant garde tendencies." Balashov and Bernshtein went on to cite a number of Czechoslovak and Polish writers whom they admire and argued that they, too, should be called socialist realists. For, they insisted (and this is the nub), the future of socialist realism lies in a union with modernist literature and, furthermore, this union is already taking place.

Laudable as this sentiment may be, it has a strong quality of wistfulness when applied to contemporary Soviet literature. Balashov and Bernshtein, I believe, were making an implicit plea for the removal from Russian literature of ideological shackles that are rusty but still quite firm. Surely a strong influence from Poland and Czechoslovakia, if permitted, would have helped to bring this about. But the elements of that influence would have been precisely those referred to by the staunchly reactionary Ivan Anisimov, at a meeting of Czech and Soviet critics and scholars in Prague in 1963, when he insisted on the impossibility of "coexistence of socialist and bourgeois ideologies." There is no evidence that the fundamental Soviet line has changed since Anisimov thus enlightened his Czech colleagues.

Since I am not a specialist on either Czechoslovak or Polish literature, I should like to emphasize that the conclusions in this essay should be regarded as tentative. Much of the background material is in secondary sources. I have been unable to compare Soviet translations with their Czechoslovak and Polish originals. Likewise, although I am confident that the general patterns in Soviet translations of the two literatures have been accurately presented here, there undoubtedly exist translations (chiefly in periodicals) of which I am unaware.

Nearly every aspect of this topic requires further investigation and analysis. Perhaps the most important of these is the informal, behind-the-scenes relationship between the three literatures. In this respect a number of questions come to mind. How many Soviet writers read Czech and Polish and therefore are not dependent on translations for an acquaintance with these literatures? How many of them travel to Czechoslovakia and Poland, and how often? Are they personally acquainted with writers in these countries and, if so, how well? In short, how extensive an exchange of ideas is there at the all-important, informal working level?

Much more information is required about the political behavior of writers in these countries. This is particularly true of the Soviet Union, where, one suspects, only a small amount of the activity that takes place is visible on the surface. It is possible, for example, that Soviet writers have more political influence, and in subtler ways, than I have indicated, and also that their political response to events in Czechoslovakia and Poland has been more pronounced than it appears.

Little has been said here about the relationship between the more conservative strains in these three literatures. Czechoslovak and Polish brands of socialist realism may have influenced Soviet literature of the more orthodox sort. A further investigation of this aspect of the subject, however dreary, would be essential.

A much closer comparison of the intrinsic aspects of the three literatures is required. I suspect, for example, that Soviet dramatists have a great awareness of the Polish theater. Although they may not be able to demonstrate their interest fully, a careful study of their work might well disclose a Polish influence. Likewise, a rigorous comparative study of contemporary Czechoslovak, Polish, and Russian poetry could quite possibly reveal an influence from west to east.

There also is the intriguing possibility that Czechoslovak and Polish literature have exerted a strong influence on the minority literatures of the Soviet Union. We have seen that the Estonians, Ukrainians, Latvians, and Lithuanians have been much more liberal than the

Russians in translating the literature of these two countries. It would follow that the writers of these nationalities may be more strongly attracted than the Russians to these Western Slavic models.

Finally, this entire subject should be considered in the larger context of the literary relationship between East and West. It has been traditional to regard Poland and Czechoslovakia as potential bridges conveying Western culture to their Slavic neighbors in the East. If, as the findings of this essay suggest, there has been little influence of Poland and Czechoslovakia in Soviet literary life, one would be forced to conclude that in this respect the bridge has been largely inoperable. The West has undoubtedly influenced Soviet literature in recent years, but it may have done this independently of East Europe.

NOTES

1. The information concerning translations is based on examination of Index Translationum for the years 1957-71; Rocznik literacki (Literary yearbook) for the years 1958-74; and the journal Novy Mir (New world) for the years 1961-74. These sources list printings of translated titles but do not indicate the size of the editions. Presumably, printings in the Russian language are larger than those in minority languages, although there may well be exceptions.

Although my conclusions are based on publications in book form, it should be mentioned that many translations appear in Inostrannaia literatura (Foreign literature), Vsesvit (The whole world, in Ukrainian), and that there are occasional translations in Novy Mir (New world), Druzhba narodov (The friendship of peoples), and other journals. It is my impression that the general pattern of publications in journals is the same as the pattern in books.

It also should be noted that a number of anthologies are mentioned in Index Translationum and Rocznik literacki without a specific listing of their contents. It is therefore possible that Czech, Slovak, or Polish authors printed therein have escaped my notice.

Finally, there is no indication in these sources of the degree of faithfulness of the translations. It is quite possible that some of them have been heavily censored, or otherwise abridged.

2. Other languages into which Polish and Czechoslovak works have been translated are Kazakh, Tadzhik, Azerbaijanian, Moldavian, Georgian, Armenian, Belorussian, Finnish, Kirghiz, Turkmen, and Tatar.

3. My impression that, on the basis of what has been translated, Soviet readers can have only a spotty and politically slanted impression of contemporary Czechoslovak literature is born out by the results of a questionnaire mailed in 1967 by the Czechoslovak Youth

League monthly publication MY 67 to universities, technical institutes, and schools of economics in Leipzig, Warsaw, Bucharest, and Moscow. To the question "Which Czechoslovak authors do you know?," the Moscow students named Hasek (122), Fucik (111), Capek (59), Hanzelka and Zikmund (writers of travelogues) (26), Mnacko, Jirasek, Majerova, and Drda (12 each). Two girls who were studying the Czech language mentioned Skvorecky, Hrabal, and Tatarka, and one student claimed to have become acquainted with the poetry of Jiri Fried from an English translation. See East Europe, October 1967, p. 28.

4. I. Bernshtein, "Plodotvornaia vstrecha " (Fruitful meeting), Inostrannaia literatura (Foreign literature), no. 5 (1963): 238.

5. In this connection, it should be noted that in Soviet criticism there is a kind of symbolic troika of Western authors who are considered inimical to socialist realism: Joyce, Proust, and Kafka. These three were a major issue at the Leningrad conference, where the Soviet line, in opposition to the majority of European writers present, was that they are the epitome of decadence.

5

THE ROLE OF THE
BALTIC REPUBLICS
IN SOVIET SOCIETY
V. Stanley Vardys

This essay examines the influence of the Baltic republics on the development of Soviet society and culture. It is commonly known that in the Soviet Union not only political but also social and cultural standards are set by Moscow, that is, by the Russian-dominated Communist Party and Soviet government agencies or public organizations. Therefore, it is much easier to speak about Moscow's impact and influence on the non-Russian republics than to discuss the reciprocal influence these republics have on either the larger Russian society or non-Russian neighbors. To consider this question, however, the term "influence" has to be used with caution. While we can, with relative ease, quantitatively examine republic share in the productive life of the Soviet state, we find it nearly impossible to accurately measure the intellectual or social effect of these contributions. As usual, Soviet sources do not offer much help. Soviet statistics show the mutuality of economic relations between Russia and the other republics, but in cultural and social affairs, Soviet writers meaningfully discuss only Moscow's influence.

Discussion of non-Russian influences has been inhibited for two reasons. The Communist Party is interested in promoting only its own model of monolithic Soviet society and its own theory that there is but a single source of Soviet culture—Marxism-Leninism as interpreted and implemented by the Russian political and cultural tradition. Different interpretations, therefore, are not welcome. In addition, the topic has been largely avoided by men of ideas in non-Russian republics both for fear of exposing their own original work and endangering it, and because of apprehension that they might be accused of deviationism, national narrowmindedness, and the like. The question of non-Russian influence on Soviet culture therefore is extremely delicate. It is, however, of great importance because it deals with a larger question; namely, whether there exists some interchange between Russian and non-Russian traditions and societies and, if there does, what kind of consequences for the future Soviet society might be expected.

In view of this complicated situation, it is preferable to examine the question of influence in terms of role. Role generally indicates a pattern of behavior assumed by an actor. We will endeavor to clarify what role has been assigned to the Baltic republics by the Kremlin, what they themselves have tried to play by their own choice, and what others expect of them. This must be done from the perspective of their own background, social evolution, and historical continuity.

THE BALTIC REPUBLICS IN HISTORICAL PERSPECTIVE

The historical fate of Estonia, Latvia, and Lithuania has been determined in great part by geography. A look at an ethnographic map shows them squeezed between the Germanic and Slavic giants and thus in the path of historic German and Russian expansionism. The area has been a meeting place as well as a battleground for these two nations that have dominated so much of Central-Eastern European history. It represented a coveted prize for both the German Drang nach Osten and the Russian search for outlets to the seas. In medieval times, the ethnic Latvian and Estonian forces could not resist the technically and materially superior Teutonic invaders, and in the long run none of the three could secure permanent conditions for free and unfettered national development. Estonia and Latvia were conquered by Russia as early as the eighteenth century, while the Grand Duchy of Lithuania, after having repelled the Teutonic knights and expanded in the direction of Moscow and Kiev, gradually succumbed to Poland, The alliance with Poland at the end of the fourteenth century was deemed necessary for resistance to the continued Teutonic menace as well as to suit the personal purposes of Grand Duke Jagiello-Jogaila (c. 1350-1434), the last strictly independent and uncommitted Lithuanian ruler.[1]

For the Baltic peoples, this early loss of freedom had two very important and far-reaching consequences. The centuries-long domination by foreign colonists or de-nationalized native nobility, as in Lithuania, severely delayed and restricted the development of culture in indigenous languages, while the fact that the ruling elites were of Western rather than Eastern Christian background laid the foundations for the extension of the Western European cultural zone to Lake Peipus and the Daugava (Zapadnaia Dvina, Duena), Nemunas (Niemen), and Neris (Wilja, Vileja) rivers. As a result, the cultures of Lithuania, Latvia, and Estonia were finally developed on Western European foundations. In the Baltic provinces (present-day Latvia and Estonia),

however, Western institutions were introduced and developed primarily
by the German colonists—the Baltic barons, as they later became
known—whereas in Lithuania the native nobles and the immigrant nobility were of Polish heritage. This left an imprint not only on Baltic
social institutions but on the national character as well. Differences
between the German and Polish cultures largely account for historical
differences between the Estonians and Latvians on the one hand and
the Lithuanians on the other. In modern times, many of these differences have disappeared, and today we are impressed not so much by
the peculiarities of the three nations but by their similarities, especially after 1918, when they briefly escaped the embrace of their
Russian rulers.

Except for this short period of independence in 1918-40, the Russians have ruled most of the Baltic region for two and a half centuries.
The medieval integration of the provinces into the world of Western
Christianity did not guarantee their incorporation into the community
of Western states. Eventually, they were absorbed into the Russian
empire. The Baltic provinces of Estonia and Livonia (in German,
Estland, Livland; in Russian, Estlandia, Livlandia) were conquered
by the Russians during the Great Northern War. Sweden formally
ceded the region to Peter the Great by the treaty of Nystadt in 1721.
Couronia (in German, Kurland; in Russian, Kurlandia; in Latvian,
Kurzeme), while a vassal of the Polish-Lithuanian crown, was dominated by Russia during the entire eighteenth century until it was formally annexed in 1795. Lithuania and Latgale (another Latvian
province) became Russian as a result of the last partition of the Polish
Rzeczpospolita (1795). In the nineteenth century (in Lithuania since
the insurrection of 1831, and in Latvia and Estonia primarily from the
1870s) the Russians began to fight actively for cultural domination
over the area as well. This led to conflicts with German and Polish
noblemen. As a result of Russian initiative, the region was considerably Russianized, linguistically as well as institutionally. However,
the ultimate winner at the beginning of the twentieth century was not
the Russian or the German or the Pole but the native Estonian, Latvian, and Lithuanian; the independent farmer, merchant, worker,
intellectual, and finally politician. After World War I, the Balts rather
than the Russians took over the cultural and political leadership and
resolutely fought off Russian and other attempts to return them to a
status of dependency.

During the two hundred years of tsarist rule, Estonia, Livonia,
and Couronia played a prominent part in the development and politics
of the Russian empire. At the same time, each maintained a unique
identity and autonomy within a very centralized Russian state.

Politically, the ruling German nobility not only retained its dominant position at home but also extended its influence to the affairs of the tsarist state. Beginning with the Couronian Count Ernst Johann Biron, a favorite of Tsarina Anna (1730-40), and Count Jacob Johann Sievers, governor of Novgorod and later of Tver', and continuing with Barclay de Tolly, a gentleman from a Riga family who commanded all Russian armies at the outset of Napoleon's invasion, many Baltic military commanders and civilian ministers held high positions in the empire and its armed forces. At first the Baltic barons were loyal to the tsars. They had welcomed and even invited Russia's rule in order to protect their economic and political privileges from the suppressed peasants and from Swedish as well as Polish-Lithuanian influences. In return for their services, the tsars guaranteed them complete autonomy at home. Until the 1870s, in an empire where the Russian language prevailed, the Baltic barons were able to keep German as the official administrative language. They kept their own court system, police, educational institutions, and the Germanic identity of the provinces. Their influence in the Court of St. Petersburg declined with the rising Russian nationalism, and as a result of quick industrialization and the emancipation of the peasantry, but regained some of its former luster after the revolution of 1905.

The Baltic provinces provided for Russia not only good, year-round salt water ports and the technical know-how that facilitated the empire's trade with England and other Western European countries but also a technologically advanced agricultural and industrial complex that contributed much of Russia's manufacturing and industrial production. In the 1890s, for example, more than half of Russia's textile workers were employed in the Baltic provinces, primarily in Estonia. In 1913, the Baltic gubernias made more industrial products per person than the gubernias of St. Petersburg and Moscow.[2] By the turn of the century, the Baltic population was already more literate and better skilled than the Russian. According to the 1897 census, the literacy rate in Estonia was 95 percent and in Latvia 92 percent. In Lithuania it was considerably lower, 54 percent, but still much higher than in other Russian provinces and close to the figures of Moscow and St. Petersburg.[3]

Russia further benefited from the scholarly and humanist activity of German scholars and clergy. The University of Dorpat (in Estonian, Tartu), first established by the Swedes and revived by the Baltic barons in the nineteenth century, had given the fledgling Russian universities about 100 professors and also 18 members of the Imperial Academy of Sciences by the middle of the century.[4] The famous Pulkovo observatory was a creation of Wilhelm Friedrich Georg Struve, a professor at Dorpat, and was started as a Dorpat university enterprise.

Humanists like Pastor Ernst Glueck, who worked in Livonia, translated the New Testament first into Latvian and then into Russian.[5]
A more strictly religious influence emanated from Lithuanian Catholic
priests, many of whom worked in parishes in Eastern Belorussia
(especially Mogilev), serving Catholic diasporas.

At this point, a discussion of Lithuania's relations with nineteenth-
century Russia is relevant. Although Lithuania's political influence
was crucial during the period when the Lithuanian Grand Duchy controlled large Russian areas, its cultural influence was always less
pronounced. Some of the first books written in Cyrillic were published
in Vilnius at Skarina's printing house (1525). After Lithuania's annexation to Russia, Polish cultural influence from the then Polish University of Wilno (Vilnius) was of some cultural consequence. Generally,
Lithuania's contribution was much more modest. Lithuania's noblemen
were politically disloyal; twice they united with the Poles in revolts
against the tsar (1830-31, 1863-64), and as a result spent their years
in exile instead of at the Court of St. Petersburg. Economically,
Lithuania remained underdeveloped and agriculture and timber
remained its primary products. Its population was kept uneducated
by Russian policies designed to destroy Polish influence. The name
of Lithuania itself was changed to that of the North Western krai.
The University at Vilnius, however, with the help of native and West
European scholars, produced scores of professors for Russian universities and specialists for Russian society. In 1831, however, it was
closed—the tsar's answer to the Polish-Lithuanian insurrection of the
same year.

After all this is said, however, it must be observed that the Balts
changed neither imperial policies nor Russia's cultural outlook. Their
participation, nevertheless, injected views, attitudes, and ideas that
were favored in Lutheran and Catholic instead of Orthodox tradition,
that were influenced by German humanist views, that helped train
Russians in Western technology, and that in turn challenged and pro-
voked Russian Orthodox traditionalists. The accusation by Alexander
III that the Baltic barons had imposed a "foreign" civilization on his
domain was partially true and, ironically, has a contemporary flavor.[6]
The Baltic region indeed served as a transmission belt of "foreign"
civilization, a relay station of Western European cultural concepts to
the then awakening Russian society, thus stimulating its development
and, one may add, its Westernization.

THE BALTS IN SOVIET POLITICS

What is the current position of the region? What role do the Balts
play in Soviet politics, economics, culture, social life? Do we find
historical continuity or a break with tradition? Have the native leaders

been able to establish their influence in Moscow and to preserve the
traditional autonomy of their lands?

In politics, the voice of the Baltic leaders at the Kremlin is weak
and only a shadow of the power their baron predecessors exercised at
the Court of St. Petersburg. While the Ukrainians and Belorussians
are already junior partners in the ruling of the Soviet Union, the Balts
so far have been held back. This conclusion can be qualified, of course,
by adding that during the revolution and the civil war, as well as after
the recognition of Baltic independence by Lenin, the Baltic Communist
colony in Moscow, although small, was quite influential and included
important government and party leaders. Among them were the famed
Latvian Riflemen to whom Lenin had entrusted his personal safety and
who played very crucial roles in the defense of the Bolsheviks. During
the early days of the revolution, the group also included the first com-
mander of the Red Army, Joachim Vacietis; the creator of Soviet law,
Peteris Stucka; revolutionary commanders and later famous Soviet
generals, the Latvian Jekabs Alksnis and the Lithuanians Vytautas
(Vitovt) Putna and Jeronimas; member of the Politburo, Latvian Jan
Rudzutak and others, again primarily of Latvian nationality. It is interesting to note that most of those leaders, including such lesser Balts
as Zigmas Aleksa Angarietis, one of the fathers of the Lithuanian
Communist Party, and his Estonian counterpart, Jaan Anvelt, were
purged by Stalin.

After the annexation of Estonia, Latvia, and Lithuania, Stalin
continued to mistreat the Balts, and until rather recently Baltic Communists could not be found in top policy-making groups of the party.
Even today the Balts do not hold important positions in the government,
the military, or the diplomatic corps. In Moscow, they merely maintain their lobbying organizations, that is, representatives of the republic council of ministers to the All-Union Council of Ministers. The
Red Army has no high-ranking Baltic officers. In foreign service, the
Balts have been noticed only in positions of second secretary, and
primarily in countries where the Estonians, Latvians, or Lithuanians
have clusters of immigrants.

After Stalin's death, Baltic Communists won symbolic recognition,
receiving for the most part appointments to ceremonial positions.
Thus, a number of Balts have chaired committees of the Supreme
Soviet and for a long time chaired the Council of Nationalities. In
1954 Vilis Lacis, a Latvian writer and winner of the Stalin Prize for
literature, became the first Baltic chairman of this council. In 1958
he was replaced by another Latvian, Janis Peive, a scientist, who
served two terms. In 1966 a Lithuanian, Justas Paleckis, took over
for one term. Like Lacis, Paleckis had been an important republic
politician, chairman of the Presidium of Soviet Lithuania's Supreme
Soviet.

The situation is somewhat different in the Communist Party, where recently Baltic Communists won recognition in the higher Party Council, the Politburo. Generally, Baltic representation in the party's Central Committee is no larger than that of any other republic of similar size. In the Central Committee elected by the Twenty-third Party Congress in 1966, there were two full and two candidate members from each republic, a ratio identical with Azerbaijan, Armenia, Moldavia, Kirghizia, Tadzhikistan, Turkmenia, but considerably smaller than that of Kazakhstan, Uzbekistan, and of course the Slavic republics.[7] The Central Committee elected in 1971 at the Twenty-fourth Party Congress counted two Latvians, two Lithuanians and one Estonian among the 155 candidate members.[8] The second secretary of the Latvian party also was chosen; however, he was ethnically Ukrainian rather than Latvian. Not only is Latvia better represented on the Central Committee than Lithuania or Estonia but also a Latvian holds the highest offices of any Balt. Arvids Pelse has been a member of the Politburo and chairman of the Committee for Party Control since 1966. In general, republic representation in the Central Committee is not assigned to persons but to positions. Recognition is given to two party (first and second secretary) and two government positions (chairman of the Council of Ministers and chairman of the Presidium of the Supreme Soviet). We have no knowledge of any Balts serving in the apparatus of the Central Committee Secretariat.

The Latvians reached the party's Politburo in 1957. In that year, Janis Kalnberzins, the Latvian Party's first secretary, was elected candidate member of the Presidium. Nine years later, Arvids Pelse, who had succeeded Kalnberzins in the position of first secretary, was elected full member of the Politburo, the first Balt so chosen after World War II. He also was given the important position of chairman of the Committee on Party Control. Comparison of careers of the two at least partially explains the continuing neglect of the Balts in the party hierarchy. Kalnberzins spent most of his life either in underground Communist work or in a Latvian prison. Pelse went to Russia only after Latvia's annexation by the Soviet Union in 1940. The degree of their assimilation into the Soviet bureaucracy and Russian society was higher than most Balts could attain. Pelse, furthermore, has some additional qualifications possessed by neither Janis Kalnberzins nor the late Lithuanian party's first secretary, Antanas Snieckus, nor his Estonian counterpart, Johannes-Ivan Kabin. In 1958 there was a Latvian "rebellion" led by a faction of "national" Communists who contradicted Moscow's orders on economic and cultural policies and whose opposition First Secretary Kalnberzins neither anticipated nor was able to suppress.[9] It was Pelse who subdued these nationalists and Khrushchev, after an inspection tour to Riga, selected him to head the Latvian party. Once in Kalnberzins's position, Pelse executed purges that lasted for three years and succeeded in sufficiently re-Stalinizing the atmosphere to stifle Latvia's intellectual and artistic development until the present time. For his negligence, the aging Kalnberzins was ousted as a candidate member of the Presidium (Politburo) and "promoted" to the largely ceremonial position of chairman of the Presidium of Latvia's Supreme Soviet. The rebellion also caused Vilis Lacis's retirement. For his services, Pelse was rewarded with a position as full member in the Politburo.

The region, it is clear, is not a chosen supplier of governmental or technocratic talent as it was in the old Russian empire, and those few Balts who are advanced in the central machinery of the party have not followed the tradition of their predecessors by using their high positions to promote the autonomy of their kinsmen.

THE BALTIC ROLE IN THE SOVIET ECONOMY

The role of the Balts in the economic life of the Soviet Union seems to be somewhat larger than in political decision making. The region's relative importance has declined in comparison to the tsarist era, but this happened primarily because the other parts of the former empire are not much better developed. The region remains the most industrialized, as it was before World War I, and today Lithuania is sufficiently advanced to be on a par with Latvia and Estonia, although its industrial production still falls considerably behind that of its sister republics. About 70 percent of the total economic product of the region is industrial; Lithuania remains below the Soviet average of 65 percent while Estonia and Latvia rise much higher above it.[10] The Balts' rate of industrial growth in the postwar period has been among the highest in the Soviet Union.

The structure of their industrial production (see Table 5.1) shows their industrial development to be similar to the non-Slavic republics. However, it compares better to Armenia and Georgia than to the rest. The table also shows that the Baltic countries have little heavy industry, a result of their lack of natural resources. They lack coal and iron and have very little oil.[11] The only important industrial resources are the oil shale—Estonia mines three fourths of the Soviet total—and construction materials for making cement. Baltic industrial development therefore has been based primarily on imported raw materials and on the availability of skilled labor.[12] The structure of industrial production (see Table 5.1) and the profile of production (see Table 5.2) suggest that Moscow has assigned the Baltic region the role of processor and technological specialist for which skills in designing, engineering, and mechanics are required. The three republics occupy

TABLE 5.1

Basic Structure of Baltic Industrial Production in Comparison
to the Soviet Total on January 1, 1968

Sector of the Economy	USSR	Estonia	Latvia	Lithuania
Black metallurgy	10.5	—	2.3	0.3
Fuel industries	13.5	13.2	2.8	3.0
Electricity	15.3	27.2	20.1	21.3
Chemical	8.9	3.0	8.6	7.3
Machine building and metal working	19.7	11.0	18.8	19.0
Forest and paper products	5.3	6.0	7.6	6.3
Construction materials	6.3	8.3	7.6	10.0
Glass and ceramics	0.5	0.7	0.9	0.5
Light industry	4.4	8.8	7.5	8.3
Food industry	8.0	19.6	22.1	21.4

Note: Figures represent percentage of total union and total republic industrial production.

Source: Narodnoe khoziaistvo SSSR v 1967 (Moscow, 1968) pp. 216-17.

0.8 percent of the total Soviet territory and have only 2.8 percent of the total population, yet their economic contribution, especially in metal working, electronics, and light manufacturing, is higher than the percentage of population and represents a considerable share of the Soviet total. In 1968, for example, Lithuania made 9.45 percent of all Soviet metal-cutting lathes; Latvia (with some Lithuanian addition) produced 23.4 percent of Soviet radios and 12.3 percent of washing machines. Estonia also manufactured almost one-third of larger transformers. In 1961 Latvia produced 47 percent of all Soviet automatic telephone exchanges while Lithuania made the small electric motors with which 80 percent of Soviet-made refrigerators and 50 percent of washing machines were equipped.[13] In addition, Baltic industrial products are exported to most republics, primarily to Soviet Russia, but also abroad, particularly to the third world. Estonia also supplies electric energy for the Leningrad region and for parts of Latvia.

TABLE 5.2

Production Profile of the Baltic Republics in 1968

	Lithuania	Latvia	Estonia	Baltic Total	USSR Total	Baltic as Percentage of USSR
Industrial resources						
Electricity (billion KwH)	6.0	2.6	9.2	17.8	638	2.8
Oil shale (1,000 tons)	—	—	16,123	16,123	21,601	74.6
Chemical industry						
Sulfuric acid (1,000 tons)	303.8	—	164.9	468.7	10,166	4.6
Mineral fertilizer (1,000 tons)	834.5	—	889.9	1724.4	43,400	3.97
Heavy industry						
Steel (1,000 tons)	—	519	—	519	107,000	0.5
Cement (1,000 tons)	851.7	814	942	2607.7	87,500	2.98
Metal-cutting lathes (1,000s)	18.9	—	—	18.9	200	9.45
Agricultural machines (million rubles)	22.9	74	5.2	102.1	1766	5.8
Buses (1,000s)	—	2.6	—	2.6	42.4	6.1

Source: Narodnoe khoziaistvo SSSR v 1967 (Moscow, 1968).

In the field of agriculture, the Baltic republics have specialized as dairy and meat farmers. This specialization, it must be added, was developed in the days of independence (1918-40). Their indexes of meat and butter production are the highest in the Soviet Union while their cost of production is the lowest. While Estonia leads the other two countries in overall efficiency of production,[14] the region as a whole is topped only by the Ukrainians and some black soil farms in grain production.[15]

Generally, the highest labor productivity in the Soviet Union is found in Latvia, Estonia, and Lithuania, in that order, followed by Russia and the Ukraine.[16] Similarly, the best return on investment in 1958-69 was found in Lithuania, Latvia, Moldavia, and then Estonia.

Of all the Union republics, Estonia and Latvia are the most industrialized. Latvia also contributes the largest share of its products to the
development of other Soviet regions. Of the taxes collected by the
central government in Moscow, Latvia's share has been the highest
for years, yet only 45.7 percent will be returned to Latvia in 1975.
Only the Russian SFSR (42.3 percent) and the Ukrainian SSR (43.3
percent) will receive a smaller portion of their taxes. Estonia will
get back 59.7 percent of its taxes, which represents the fifth lowest
return among the fifteen republics. On the other hand, Lithuania will
receive 99.7 percent, which places it behind only the Kazakh SSR and
the Uzbek SSR in proportion of taxes returned.[17] Lithuania's postwar
industrial development, in contrast to the other two republics, was
begun only in the 1950s and thus more of its income is used locally
to support a very high rate of industrialization. In 1969 this rate was
still about 11 percent.[18]

It is natural to expect that economies of such relatively developed
countries would produce a corresponding standard of living. Indeed
the Baltic republics not only produce many goods at the highest rate
per capita (for example, meat, butter, furniture in rubles, fish caught)
but Latvia's per capita income is also the highest in the USSR.[19]
Latvia is followed by Estonia. Lithuanian income, although lower, is
still the third highest. The three republics, furthermore, provide the
daily services that make life in the Baltic republics more comfortable,
neat, and pleasant.[20] To this one must add the generally high educational and cultural level of the Baltic republics, which traditionally
have been more diversified and sophisticated, especially in Estonia,
than in the rest of the USSR. All these advantages—income, better
services, a less oppressive and more colorful social and cultural
atmosphere, good climate and pleasant countryside—attract many
immigrants, especially Russians. They come to work in the expanding
industries, to seek government positions, or even to take menial jobs,
such as mining oil shale, which the Estonians themselves dislike.

The immigrants settle in urban centers, contributing considerably
to the rapid growth of cities, especially in Estonia and Latvia, and to
the creation of large Russian colonies in almost all the larger towns
of the three republics. In 1971 Estonia was the most urbanized republic, with 66 percent of its population in the cities. Latvia closely
followed with 63 percent, while Lithuania had only 51 percent. Thus,
Lithuania's average was lower than the national Soviet average of 57
percent, and closer to the Ukraine's average (55 percent). The Estonian and Latvian percentages, it must be noted, although highest among
the Soviet republics, are not highest on a regional basis. Aside from
the Northern and Far Eastern territories, and the republics whose
demographic concentration in cities is dictated by special geographic

and economic conditions, there are a number of regions in Russia and the Ukraine that are as much or more urbanized than Estonia or Latvia.

Estonia is conspicuously used as a laboratory for experiments in the application of new techniques of planning and management. The first cybernetics institute in the Soviet Union was established in Estonia in 1963.[21] Estonia, furthermore, was the first republic in which the republic computer center was joined with the regional economic council (the former sovnarkhoz).[22] In 1969, in cooperation with Estonia's economists, the Central Mathematical Economics Institute in Moscow constructed the first economic model for a republic economy—Estonia.[23]

Important experiments also have been performed in Estonian agriculture. For example, the guaranteed wage policy for kolkhozniks was tried out in Estonia (and apparently in the black soil regions as well) before it was adopted on an All-Union level in 1967. Similarly, the old age pension plan for collective farm workers was first tried out in Estonia prior to 1965.[24] In 1967 a further experiment in the management of sovkhozes was conducted, and shortly afterward all 168 Estonian state farms were given full economic accountability, that is, full autonomy.[25] This has resulted in a further increase of profitability from farm production.

Why has Estonia been preferred to Latvia as a laboratory for industrial management when Latvia's industrial development in some respects may be said to be more substantial? Why was Estonia chosen for experimentation in agriculture when production indexes in Lithuania as well as in Latvia are very similar to those of Estonia? The French Communist journal Democratie nouvelle, in a special issue on Soviet Estonia, explains that Moscow purposely chose Estonia for such experimentation because of its highly developed material, social, and humanistic culture, which makes it a "representative miniature, a 'reduced model' of the future economy of the Soviet Union."[26] The journal's conclusion is based on consultations with scholars of the Estonian Academy of Sciences, and thus may represent an "official" Estonian point of view. Moscow may have had such a plan for Estonia. If it did, however, the model was never put into operation. To be the model of the future Soviet economy, furthermore, Estonia would have to have a rather substantial heavy industry—which it does not possess. And its population is not Russian and does not adhere to Soviet ideology. It has, however, as the same journal correctly suggests, a diversified economy and a small territory and population, making it a suitable station for controlled experiments.

THE BALTS AS WESTERNIZERS IN SOVIET LIFE

If for the Moscow government Estonia serves as an experimental laboratory in the economic field, for Moscow's citizens, artists, and intellectuals, and especially for youth, the Baltic region plays quite a different role: It represents "the West." It is rare that a Soviet citizen can reach the "real" West, and the Baltics serve as a close substitute for a trip to Western Europe. The Soviet discovers "the West" in Estonia, Latvia, or Lithuania, in the gothic towers of Riga, in the Hanseatic old town of Tallinn, in the baroque churches of Vilnius, in the modern coffee shops, restaurants, music, and more fashionably dressed women.[27] Western correspondents are not the only ones who find the Baltic region to be "Western" and very different from Moscow; the Russians themselves regard the Baltic republics as sovetskaia zagranitsa,[28] russkaia zagranitsa,[29] or simply nasha zagranitsa— "our foreign country." Furthermore, Balts traveling in Russia frequently are taken for foreigners. "Coming here [the Baltic Sea region] is really like going abroad," a Moscow coed explained to a Western correspondent.[30] The same view is found in the novels of the popular Soviet writer Vasilii Aksenov. In his Zvezdnyi bilet, published in Junost' in 1961, a group of disillusioned high school graduates leave their families and travel as far west as they can, arriving in Tallinn.[31] In a later novel, Pora moi drug pora, published in another youth journal, Molodaia Gvardia, in 1964, Aksenov pictures Tallinn as full of disenchanted young Russians, all seeking new opportunities, some honestly looking for a better life, others seeking adventure, still others in search of an easy existence.[32] In this novel, Estonia's capital city is a place where Valia, Aksenov's personal hero, knows that you have to speak in English to buy liquor after hours. Tallinn emerges in the novel as a mysterious medieval place throbbing with fascination for the young Russians.

Although Estonia and Tallinn seem to represent the greatest attraction to Russian workers and intellectuals, all three republics are looked upon in a similar fashion, and an American newsmagazine has aptly dubbed the Baltic republics a "halfway house," that is, a transitional place from Russia to Western Europe.[33] Historically, the Baltic region functioned as a transmitter of Western attitudes and experiences to tsarist Russia. This role has now been revived.

As previously discussed, Western institutions and ideas were developed in the Baltic countries under the centuries-long German, Swedish, and Polish rule. These institutions and attitudes were successfully adopted and assimilated by the indigenous Estonian, Latvian, and Lithuanian intelligentsia, and Westernization was further intensified during the period of independent rule (1918-40) under the influence of German, French, and Scandinavian models. At the same time, the Baltic states became isolated from ideologically alien Soviet Russia. They not only rejected Russian revolutionary institutions but also attempted to cleanse themselves of the vestiges of Russian culture surviving from the period of Russification in the nineteenth century. They went so far as to banish the teaching of the Russian language in secondary schools. Thus after 1940 the Kremlin had to deal with a virtually foreign culture that was impregnated with strong and emotional nationalism. Stalin did not have enough time—his rule lasted only seven to eight years—to fully eradicate Baltic Westernism and nationalism, and therefore such ideas, although in somewhat adapted form, survived the forceful imposition of the Soviet system. These remain very strong, especially in the unofficial, "underground" culture of the republics,[34] but are also recognized and to some extent tolerated by the Kremlin. For example, the Balts are allowed a special eleven-year secondary education sequence that serves to preserve their ethnic and cultural tradition. Such treatment of the Balts (although it occasionally reverts to a Pelse-type suppression in order to demonstrate the limits of tolerance) is risky. But for Moscow it represents a calculated chance that political nationalism and Communist separatism will not rise to dangerous levels. So far, the party has been able to neutralize and contain the political sting inherent in this traditional Western orientation.

Thus, at least at present, the "Western" influence from the region is confined to the arts, to managerial experience, to the style of life, and is essentially nonpolitical. However, it must be stressed that we are speaking about the post-Stalinist period. During Stalin's epoch of terrorism and conformity, any appearance of "Western" style was severely suppressed and the Balts conformed completely. As a Soviet Estonian scholar recently wrote, Soviet Estonia, and the other Baltic republics, had to assimilate "the accumulated" experience of the "older" republics of the Soviet Union.[35] There could be no talk of doing anything original even in Communistic terms, not to mention spreading traditional Western ideas in their Baltic forms. The survival of these ideas—the very Baltic traditions—then was threatened. The period to 1956 was the most sterile in postwar Baltic history and creatively the most distressing, not only for the Westerners but most of all for the Balts themselves. Estonian intellectuals are reputed to refer to it as a period of "historic hole." In Lithuania, too, this period has been denounced in printed works in very similar terms.

The situation, however, changed quite considerably in the 1960s, and the Balts are now accepted as sufficiently Sovietized to be allowed to engage in the search for their old identity. Especially the Estonians and the Lithuanians are doing this with a vengeance. The Latvians are not less dedicated but more oppressed. The Baltic countries are seen as carriers of Western tradition from within the Soviet state, and known for their love of old cultural heritage, a characteristic that makes them appealing to the Soviet intelligentsia. The activity of self-renewal becomes important for the Russian who seeks to overcome the Soviet monotony and longs to rediscover his own ties with much-maligned Western Europe. In Lithuania, for example, a very non-Russian and non-Communist type of music, namely, organ music, finds its official promoters. The first and second All-Union festivals of organ music were organized in Lithuania in 1968 and 1970.[36] The largest and best Soviet organs, recently rebuilt and improved, are found in the former Catholic cathedral of Vilnius and the former Lutheran cathedral of Riga. In Vilnius it is traditional to hold Sunday morning organ music hours at the gracious cathedral, which is presently used as an art museum. In this way Johann Sebastian Bach and much religious Western music returns to the atheist country. Another example can be taken from the visual arts. At the permanent exhibit of Soviet achievements in Moscow, the guide explains that stained glass works found there come from the Baltic, primarily from Lithuania, "where they have many churches." Artists who work with stained glass now use secular themes and their art form has gained acceptance in Moscow. Displays of Lithuanian glass can be seen in Moscow's Oktiabr theater, Iakor restaurant, and in the headquarters of the Soviet Art Foundation. A huge stained glass mural adorned a Soviet exhibit building at the Montreal Expo of 1967, and another mural of even greater proportions and reasonably modern design, done by the Lithuanian artist K. Morkunas, beautified the entrance to the Soviet exhibition hall at the world Expo in Osaka, Japan.[37]

In a remarkably frank and interesting article (the only one that can be found that discusses republic influence on Soviet and Russian culture rather than vice versa) Klara Hallik, senior lecturer on scientific communism in Estonia, emphasizes that the source of Soviet culture, "however good and rich," is not a single one. By "single" she obviously means Russian. She explains that Baltic nations, too, have contributed their share, and lists as one example the "influence" that Latvian painting and Lithuanian "monumental sculpture" had on Soviet art at the end of the 1950s and beginning of the 1960s. She also discusses the influence of Estonian applied and decorative art, which "at the present time evokes great interest in the Russian republic, in the Ukraine and in other republics for its stylistic purposefulness and organic relations with ethnographic, national as well as with the figurative art."[38] Estonian craftsmen attracted the most attention at the 1969 national applied art exhibit in Moscow, which was, interestingly enough, under the artistic direction of a Lithuanian architect.[39] In the applied arts, the Estonians are closely followed by the Latvians and the Lithuanians. Most decorative art pieces, including amber jewelry and decorations made in the Baltic republics, are not available at home but shipped for sale to tourist centers like Leningrad and Moscow. The use of the "national," folkloristic element in the applied engraving arts attracted much attention in Moscow in the late 1950s and opened new artistic vistas. The government realized that there could exist a national non-Russian art (and a profitable one, in the case of decorative art) with minimal political implications. The other republics took their cue from the Balts, and in subsequent exhibits the Caucasus and even Belorussia, which usually does not demonstrate its particularity, dared to reveal the colorful beauty of their national art.

The Balts also have made an impression in other branches of art and artistic design. Modernistic composers and experimenters with twelve-tone music are found in all three republics, although it is in Estonia that they find public recognition. The Soviet Estonian encyclopedia, published in 1969, lists them by name. Estonian composers, especially Jaan Paarts, as well as Russians, Azerbeijanis, and Armenians, are in the forefront of musical Westernizers and innovators.[40] Estonian musical culture, generally, received All-Union recognition at the national competition of composers in Moscow in 1962, when Estonians won the lion's share of medals, among them three out of seven first prizes.[41] Generally, musical education in the Baltic countries has been extolled as an example for other republics to follow. In a speech at the Fourth All-Union composers' conference in 1968, Dimitri Kabalevsky, secretary of the Soviet composers' association, praised the virtues of Baltic musical education and expressed the hope "that the esthetic education in one form or another will be introduced in all classes, from the first grade to the graduating class, in the same way it is now done in Estonia, Latvia, and Lithuania."[42] Kabalevsky said that 50,000 children took part in children's choruses in Estonia, 25,000 took part in song festivals in Latvia, and 19 boys' choruses sang in Lithuania. The Lithuanians, furthermore, boast of having the only ten-year school in the Soviet Union that emphasizes musical education. The school, located in Vilnius, is named after M. K. Ciurlionis, a Lithuanian composer and modernistic painter of the beginning of the twentieth century, whose popularity the Lithuanians now promote throughout the Soviet Union. It maintains one of the 19 boys' choruses of the republic modeled after the Vienna Boys' Choir. The choir's musical director, not surprisingly, is a former Viennese, Hermanas Perelsteinas. Estonians also have some schools with music-oriented curriculums. Latvia's contribution consists of an early rehabilitation of Wagner's music. In 1956 Riga's opera house performed Lohengrin for the first time in the Soviet Union after World War II.[43]

While the Estonians have received recognition for their musical modernity and, it should be added, for their popularization of jazz, it is the Lithuanians who win prizes for architecture and suburban (microraion) planning. The Lithuanian development of Zirmunai microraion in Vilnius won first prize in the city planning competition in the Soviet Union in 1967 and again in 1968.[44] The quality of construction is poor, as it is throughout the Soviet Union, but Zirmunai is distinguished by green spaces and by the varied height of the high-rise buildings, breaking the Soviet monotony. The novostroika is pleasing to the eye and looks like any housing development in the West.[45] In 1969 Lithuanian architects won a disproportionate share of prizes at a national architectural exhibit in Moscow.[46] In 1974 they won a Lenin state prize for the development of still another microraion, Lazdynai.

These "Western" contributions to Soviet art stem from old Baltic traditions formed prior to the October Revolution and during the period of independence. Also, contemporary European ideas as well as Western style of behavior continue to be imported to the Soviet Union largely, although not exclusively, through the Baltic republics. In literature, for example, Bertolt Brecht was first produced in Estonia (1958), not in Russia.[47] Works by Albert Camus also first appeared in Estonia, in 1963 and 1966.[48] In Lithuania, Camus's The Stranger was published in 1968. Excerpts from James Joyce's Ulysses also appeared in Lithuania that same year. Generally, modern Western writers are first published in Estonia and then in Lithuania. In contemporary musical life, Estonia again has been the leader. Thus, Porgy and Bess was first produced in Estonia; although it was sung in Estonian, it was preformed by Russian artists and directed by a Russian maestro who was imported from Moscow.[49] West Side Story, too, was first produced in Estonia.[50] The first Soviet jazz festival was celebrated in Tallinn, and when Charles Lloyd, the American jazz guru, played at another such festival in 1967, he received a "fantastic eight minute and twenty-second ovation."[51]

The Balts have made a similar contribution in the field of fashion. An exhibit by the Riga, Tallinn, and Vilnius fashion houses organized at the Vilnius "university of culture of clothing" was jammed with guests from neighboring republics. In its description of the event, Pravda noted that the Baltic fashion creators use "national traditions," creatively preserving what is most valuable in the heritage of the past and adapting it to the needs of contemporary life.[52] The correspondent also was impressed by the diversity of colors and materials used. Since Baltic fashion magazines also are published in Russian-language editions, they enjoy wide circulation.

Finally, Russian and generally Soviet recreation has been diversified and brought into closer contact with its Western counterpart by the introduction into the Baltic region of certain sports that originally were American and West European. Thus, the current popularity of basketball and the prowess of Soviet basketball teams in international competition is due primarily to the Lithuanians and Latvians, who were European champions prior to World War II. Soviet basketball teams in postwar Olympics were composed almost exclusively of Lithuanians, Latvians, and Estonians. Similarly, the academic rowing competition in which the Soviets now win Olympic prizes was developed by the Lithuanians. Until recently, Soviet academic rowing boats also were manned primarily by Lithuanians. The now world famous Russian hockey teams were coached by the Balts in the early 1950s.

The list of Baltic innovations can be extended to include other activities in the arts, science, and religion. While there exists a lively scientific activity in pure and applied research, from atomic energy to the chemistry of oil shale, it is in no way specifically Western or Baltic.[53] This is not the case, however, with religion, for the dominant creeds, Lutheranism and Catholicism, represent philosophies of life different from Russian religious tradition. Furthermore, they are tied to Western religious centers and religious thought. Russians who reside in the Baltic region therefore are exposed to these religious traditions, despite the reality of a rather thorough suppression of the Western churches in the republics. Before they returned home in the late 1950s and early 1960s, Baltic clergymen, primarily Lithuanians, were privately serving not only their compatriots but also German, Polish, and other Catholic and Lutheran groups in Russia, Siberia, and Central Asia.[54]

As previously noted, most of the Western innovations that have attracted attention in the Soviet Union developed either before World War I or during the period of independence and are generally dubbed "old traditions" by the Soviets. The Baltic republics, however, still maintain rather close ties (within the Soviet context) with the West. These independent contacts were allowed only in the 1960s, after a long period if hermetic isolation that was greater than in any other European Soviet republics, and they now contribute to the preservation of these "old traditions."

Contact with the West is maintained in three ways: (1) through the regular Soviet exchange programs that are Moscow-controlled and available to all Soviet nationalities; (2) through direct or semidirect relations with Western and Eastern European neighbors; and (3) through ties with emigres, especially those in the United States and Canada, often through relationships between relatives separated by the events of World War II. All these communication links are important. Baltic scholars, writers, journalists, and also some

students recently have participated in exchange programs. A larger
number have visited neighboring countries, including the Communist
countries, primarily Poland and East Germany, and to a lesser degree
Czechoslovakia or Yugoslavia, and also neutralist Finland and Sweden.
East Germany's Ulbricht, Hungary's Kadar, Romania's Ceausescu,
and Finland's Kekkonen have paid visits to Latvia, Lithuania, or Estonia. President Kekkonen's visit was an expression of kinship to the
Estonians and a sort of a silent promise by an older brother not to
forget the younger in trouble. Indeed, Estonia, by virtue of its kinship
to the Finns, cuts a larger window to the West for the Soviets than do
the other two republics. Since 1965 ferry boats have carried passengers
daily from Estonia to Finland. In Tallinn, furthermore, the Finns have
constructed a hotel to accommodate foreign guests. The Estonians who
live on the shores of the Gulf of Finland can see Finnish TV, which
brings in both Western European and American programs. A special
antenna is apparently needed for this purpose, but many viewers consider the extra cost worthwhile and authorities have not yet objected.
Thus, a correspondent of Neue Zuercher Zeitung has reported that the
Apollo II flight to the moon could be easily watched in Estonia but
could not be seen anywhere else in the Soviet Union.[55] It might be
surmised that Estonians as well as resident Russians, and possibly
some Russians who came to Estonia specifically for the purpose, used
this opportunity to join mankind on a historic occasion. Estonia's tie
with Finland is even better appreciated by those who know that the two
languages are closely related, thus making it relatively easy for Estonians to follow Finnish programs and reports.

The Latvians are at a geographic disadvantage but have endeavored
to maintain close cultural relations with Poland and East Germany.
Through the 1960s the Lithuanians worked on renewing their old cultural relations with Germany (East), and especially with Poland. In
1969 Lithuania won first place among Soviet republics for furthering
such relations. The Lithuanian government has continued these efforts,
as indicated by the January 1975 visit to Poland by the first secretary
of the Communist Party of Lithuania, Piatras Griskiavicius.[56] Poland
is resuming its historical role as a carrier of Western influences into
Lithuania. Polish artists and scientists bring artistic diversity to
Lithuania and help keep alive ethnic feelings among Lithuania's 240,000
Poles. The Lithuanians also have an ethnic minority in Poland, and
their men of arts and sciences eagerly travel to Warsaw and Cracow.

Finally, many Balts—unlike the Russians—go to the West for
strictly private visits, especially to the United States and Canada to
visit relatives, frequently on protracted three- or even six-month
sojourns. For the most part, these visitors are middle-aged or elderly;
the young generally are not allowed on such journeys. However, many
young Balts who grew up or were born in the West now visit Estonia,

Latvia, and Lithuania and, while there, inevitably talk with members of the postwar generation. In the 1960s, furthermore, Baltic intellectuals and artists began to seek ties with their equals in the West. This has more than just personal or ethnic significance because through such ties the Soviet Balts tune in not only to professional but also to general cultural activity and expose themselves to Western ideas that in all probability serve as an antidote to their indoctrination.

It also must be stressed that the official Soviet Baltic agencies closely follow the artistic, scientific, and social developments of the emigrant Balts, who have developed a highly intense cultural life in their native languages and are becoming more and more deeply involved in American or Canadian intellectual and artistic life. Works by exile writers have been published in all three republics, although more in Estonia and Lithuania than in Latvia. Of works by exile artists, however, only those created before World War II have been exhibited in Lithuania. Before Pelse suppressed Latvian creative life, exiled artists sometimes returned for performances in Latvian concert and opera halls. In Estonia, this practice continues. Edward Tubin, an Estonian composer now in exile in Sweden, maintains close contact by frequent visits to Soviet Estonia.[57] In Lithuania, such contacts are less developed, although recorded music by exiled Lithuanians has been played not only in professional meetings but also on the Soviet Lithuanian radio. Generally, neither Western Baltic books nor records reach private citizens in the Baltic republics; Baltic exiles correctly suspect that the Soviets, by sending their own artists, writers, or sportsmen to Baltic diasporas in the West, seek to neutralize the strongly anti-Soviet attitudes of the postwar immigration. But such contacts are helpful to the Balts in keeping and renewing their "old traditions" and culture. This is a double-edged, ambiguous relationship that provides a tenuous yet real tie between the East and the West in a way not maintained by either non-Russian republics or Russia itself.

BALTIC RELATIONS WITH RUSSIAN AND
NON-RUSSIAN SOCIETIES

The final question concerns the importance of the Baltic role as Westernizer in Soviet society. A direct answer, of course, is as difficult as any appraisal of cultural penetration. However, useful responses as well as existing problems can be discovered by examining communication between groups involved with the Baltic region. They are: (1) the society of Russia; (2) the Russian minority in the Baltic region, which is a very real actor on the Baltic scene; (3) the non-

Russian nationalities beyond the Baltic borders; and (4) the Estonian, Latvian, and Lithuanian societies.

In Russia, as noted earlier, the Baltic region has the reputation of being "Western"—with a high standard of living, pleasant atmosphere, mysterious architecture, and sophisticated style of life. Some of the Baltic innovations in the arts, in economic or social life, have attracted broad attention. Since it takes time for ideas to settle in a different cultural context, we may not know for quite a while about the success of some of those we previously examined. However, we can assume that the Baltic countries are of greater attraction to Russia's liberal intellectuals than to others. An apocryphal story of the 1940s tells of Alexei Tolstoy, author of the novel on Peter I, remarking to Salomeja Neris, the talented pro-Communist Lithuanian poet who exulted in Lithuania's annexation by the Soviet Union: "If you were a large nation, you would bring us the West. Now we will bring you Asia."

Soviet intellectuals apparently follow the Baltic literary and intellectual scene, as seen in remarks by Andrei Voznesensky in Literaturnaia gazeta.[58] He said he eagerly waited to read new works of his friends Paul Erik Rummo and Vizma Belsevica. The first is an Estonian poet; the second, a Latvian poet, and her latest volume of poetry, published in 1969, was immediately taken out of circulation. Paul Erik Rummo is very popular with Estonian intellectuals and is tolerated by the authorities. However, personal contacts cannot exist on a large scale, if only because of the language barrier that separates the Russians from the Balts, a barrier that prevents the Russians from sharing the fruits of the cultural permissiveness in the Baltic. Examples of this permissiveness are the early publication of Camus and Kafka, even the contents of the new Soviet Estonian encyclopedia, which explains not only dodecaphonic music and the theater of the abstract but also include under the letter B the very unlikely combination of Father Bochenski, Brigitte Bardot, and Lavrentii Beria.[59] We may suspect that Moscow allows the Estonians and Lithuanians what it denies to others precisely because of language differences. It is a rare Russian who will want to learn Estonian or Lithuanian just to read Camus. Thus, Western ideas are confined to the boarders of individual republics, where they can be tried out on a limited scale before being allowed to enter Moscow or Leningrad.

However, there exist in the Baltic republics large and growing communities of Russian immigrants who cannot be so well separated from the currents of local intellectual life. Since the prewar years, this minority has doubled or even tripled in size. In Latvia, the percentage of Russians has climbed from 12 percent (actually a much smaller percentage after adjustment) to 29.8 percent in 1970; in Estonia from 8.5 percent to 24.7 percent; and in Lithuania from 2.7 percent to 8.6 percent. In 1959 the Russians constituted 20 percent of the total Baltic population (without the Kaliningrad region). This can be compared to the percentage for all Estonians, which is 15 percent.[60] The Russian minority has special privileges not possessed by other minorities (about 2.5 percent Belorussians; about 1.6 percent Ukrainians; 1 percent Jews; some Finns; and 3.5 percent Poles who are better treated in Lithuania). The Russians have their own dailies, newspapers for youth, specilized periodicals, schools, and theaters. For their social needs, they do not really depend on the Baltic communities; they represent a competing culture. If the larger Russian society is affected by the Balts at all, to a large degree it should be influenced through the Russian minorities in Estonia, Latvia, and Lithuania. But is it?

Relations between the non-Russian majority and the Russian minority in a republic have not been studied in either the West or the East, and little meaningful material has been published on this important relationship. However, there are some indexes that shed light on this social communication in the Baltic region. Generally, the Russians do intermingle. They live in the same housing, belong to the same sports clubs or jazz bands. In Latvia, where in 1970 only 56 percent of the population was Latvian, the schools are consolidated under the same roof; thus, one third of the school-age children, both Russian and Latvian, attend the same schools. To a degree, the indigenous population mixes with the Russians; one indicator is that in 1959 Latvia had the highest number of mixed marriages of any Soviet republic, 15.8 percent.[61] Even taking into consideration that only a percentage of these marriages were between Latvians and Russians, this is a very high number. In Estonia the figure was 10 percent; in Lithuania, 5.9 percent. Comparable figures were 3.2 percent for Armenia and 15.0 percent for the Ukraine.

A recent study by L. N. Terent'eva, a well-known Soviet anthropologist, confirms that intermarriage with Russians is more common in Estonia and Latvia than in Lithuania.[62] She conducted a study in the capitals of the three republics and found that 20 percent of all marriages in Vilnius and Riga were mixed in 1960-68. In Tallinn the figure was 11.3 percent, but as Terent'eva explained, this was because in 1959 the percentage of Estonians in Tallinn was still 60.24 percent while in Riga the Latvians constituted only 44.66 percent and in Vilnius the Lithuanians totaled 33.6 percent. Of the mixed marriages in Vilnius, only 14.3 percent were between Latvians and Russians. In Tallinn the respective percentage was 35.4 percent. These figures indicate that Estonians have more interaction with Russians than Latvians or Lithuanians. Yet at the same time, as Terent'eva shows, in mixed marriages the Estonian partner wields a greater cultural influence. According to the author, 62 percent of teenages in Estonian-Russian families chose Estonian nationality, while only 57 percent chose non-Russian nationality in Latvia, and 52 percent in Lithuania.

TABLE 5.3

Russians Fluent in the National Languages
of the Baltic Republics

	Percentage of Russians Speaking Native Tongue	Indigenous Language as Second Language
Estonian SSR		
Whole republic	1.5	12.6
Urban	1.0	11.4
Rural	5.9	22.4
Tallinn	0.9	12.2
Latvian SSR		
Whole republic	1.2	17.1
Urban	0.8	15.8
Rural	2.5	22.0
Riga	0.8	15.2
Lithuanian SSR		
Whole republic	2.0	30.8
Urban	1.8	28.7
Rural	3.2	42.3
Vilnius	0.7	20.5

Source: Itogi vsesoiuznoi perepisi naseleniia 1970 g. Vol. 6—
Natsional'nii sostav naseleniia SSSR (Moscow, 1972), Table 19, pp.
273-75; Table 21, pp. 280-83; Table 29, pp. 317-20.

Social interaction, furthermore, has a bearing on bilingualism, a
prerequisite for genuine cultural communication under Soviet conditions. Travelers to Estonia are impressed by the knowledge of Estonian displayed by young Russians. A study conducted in 1965 in Tallinn
by the History Institute of the Estonian Academy of Science showed
that, the younger and more educated the Russians, the better their
knowledge of Estonian.[63] Thus 13.2 percent of secondary school
children, 27.9 percent of special school students, 18.8 percent of
evening school students, and 28.6 percent of university students knew
Estonian rather well. Similar percentages fell in the medium bracket,
while over 50 percent of those categorized had only a weak knowledge
of Estonian. The percentages of Estonian secondary school and university students who knew Russian well, of course, were much higher,

67.5 percent and 76.6 percent respectively. The smallest percentage of Russians with good or weak knowledge of Estonian was found among construction workers, that is, the least educated group. A Russian scholar estimated that in Latvia 30 to 50 percent of Russian workers in cities "know" the Latvian language; if true, this percentage would be much higher than that of Estonia.[64] This same writer reported that on farms the figure runs between 75 and 90 percent. Table 5.3 presents the 1970 Soviet census figures for Russians speaking the national languages of the Baltic republics. It is fair to say that the knowledge of foreign languages displayed by Russians, as shown in the Baltic cases, is much better than would be found among Western Europeans or Americans. However, it is doubtful that this knowledge is sufficient for effective social communication or cultural penetration.

Furthermore, it must be stressed that Russian receptiveness to Baltic ideas or traditions is inhibited by the general dislike that the Balts display for the Russian language and nationality. Estonians frequently refuse to speak Russian, and customers who speak Russian in Estonian shops often have to wait a long time or leave without obtaining service. There still are cases reported of Latvians, and especially Lithuanians, who insist that a Russian conductor on the bus ask for the fare in the indigenous language or risk not being paid at all. While political "bourgeois" nationalism has indeed been largely destroyed, it has been replaced by cultural nationalism, now known as national communism.[65] In the postwar period the republics have been afflicted by three substantial purges, all directed against "national Communists." The Estonian purge was the earliest, in 1949-50. Pelse wielded a hatchet in Latvia in 1959-62. The Lithuanian purge of 1959 was the mildest. Currently, warnings against tendencies toward national Communism continue, and the press prints stories of opposition to Russians as marriage partners (Lithuania) and denunciation of Moscow for distorting local history in tourist brochures (Estonia). After the overthrow of Khrushchev, the Balts contributed their fair share of denunciation of the assimilationist theory, suggesting that it distorts the socialist view of national relations and that instead of assimilating languages into Russian, the government should think how better to protect the existing national languages.[66]

Unfortunately, there is no available data on cultural or social cooperation between the two communities. Although the Russians and the indigenous people work together, native authors generally are not produced in Russian theaters. A petition recently submitted to the government by two or three score Lithuanian intellectuals protesting the construction of an oil refinery on the river Nemunas, on grounds that it will pollute and destroy the environment, did not contain Russian names. A probable instance of cultural-political cooperation, however, is seen in the recent arrest of officers of the Baltic submarine fleet.

An Estonian political officer of a submarine staioned in Tallinn is said to have written a "program for the democratic movement of the USSR." Of the 31 officers and men arrested for supporting such a movement, one-fourth were reported to be Estonians.[67] The Estonians asked for equal rights for Estonia. Such cooperation with the Russians, if the story is true, would be quite unusual. However, it is possible that a memorandum signed by "representatives of the technical intelligentsia of the Estonian SSR" and smuggled out of the Soviet Union was penned by the same group of officers. The memorandum dealt with academician Sakharov's Samizdat essay, suggesting that Sakharov did not probe deeply enough into Soviet difficulties by saying that Stalinism was responsible for the inhumanity of the regime. The group from Estonia insisted that "society as a whole bears the responsibility for such phenomena."[68]

Cases of Russian cultural assimilation with the Balts are rare although individual instances doubtless could be found, given an opportunity for free research. Similarly, a partial identification of Russians with Latvian, Estonian, or Lithuanian interests and aspirations also is possible. A case in point may be the one reported in 1961 from Latvia. The Latvian literary paper Literatura un maksla reported a "strict party punishment" of three writers, two of whom were Russians. The charge against them, as far as could be deduced from Party Secretary Voss's reports, was Latvian "bourgeois nationalism," or possibly aid to "bourgeois nationalists."[69]

The third public interested in the Baltic region consists of the non-Russians of other republics. The Estonians have an added appeal for nationalities of the Finno-Ugric family with whom they are linguistically related. Thus, the Maris of the Volga Finnic group come to Estonia to write their doctoral or candidate degree dissertations in the field of linguistics.[70] So do the Karelians, with whom the Estonians maintain close cultural relations. In this respect, the Lithuanians and Latvians are less fortunate because they have no other linguistic kin. All three nations have small diaspora groups scattered throughout the Soviet Union with whom communications are maintained by private means. The Lithuanians also have a large Polish minority, which in turn has diasporas of even larger size. The only Polish newspaper in the Soviet Union, Czerwony sztandar, is published in Lithuania, but it has a circulation of only 30,000. In addition to these ties of ethnic or civic kinship, the Balts keep up relations with some other Soviet national groups, primarily the Armenians, Georgians, and Ukrainians. This is done through "days of culture," literary translations, and formal as well as informal visits.

Last but not least, we must note the reality of a Baltic public composed of the Estonians, Latvians, and Lithuanians themselves. Emergence of this public represents one of the most important social consequences of the Soviet annexation for the three nations. Baltic cultural and political cooperation, to be sure, started during the 1918-40 period of independence, but at that time the relations were rather tenuous, despite the belated political attempts at greater unity. The basic prerequisite for unity, the feeling of a community of fate, was so weak that the Latvian foreign minister, en route home from Moscow after receiving a Soviet demand to allow Soviet garrisons on Latvian soil, refused to discuss the matter with a Lithuanian diplomat who was en route to Moscow at the Kremlin's request and suspected that Stalin wanted the exact same concession from the Lithuanians.

Today the situation is different. Differences—many still remain—have given way to a feeling of solidarity and mutual confidence. After Stalin's death, the republics developed cooperative efforts in broad areas. At first, however, instead of tripartite arrangements by Estonian, Latvian, and Lithuanian groups, a four-cornered partnership including Belorussia prevailed. This approach apparently was taken to avoid any resemblance to the prewar separateness of the Baltic states.

The number of tripartite, that is, strictly Baltic exchanges began to rise after the establishment of the Baltic sovnarkhoz (1957-64), which united the three republics (and Kaliningrad oblast') economically. In 1956 a regional Communist Party school was established in Vilnius solely to serve the three republics. In 1965 the republics were treated as a unit in the All-Union reform of education. These actions by Moscow were interpreted as permission for closer Baltic cooperation, and three-cornered activities are increasing in diverse fields. Conferences on literature, music, history, fashion, and other topics become real working sessions designed for mutual help and stimulation and, it is fair to suggest, to help identify and preserve Baltic traditions. Such exchanges solidify Baltic self-consciousness and historical awareness of common fate and common needs. However, recently a clear effort has been made by the party to take Lithuania out of the Baltic orbit and to cement its partnership with Belorussia.

CONCLUSIONS

The discussion of the Baltic role in Soviet society can be summarized by concluding that the Baltic republics play a negligible role in Soviet politics, a very special role in economics, and a rather important, for Soviet conditions, cultural-social role.

Neither the Baltic Communist parties nor individual Balts have influenced the substance or style of Soviet politics. It also is clear that they are not admitted to the national apparatus of decision making.

There is, of course, the case of Pelse in the Politburo, but with other minor exceptions he is alone; furthermore, being a thoroughly socialized and Russianized leader, he has only a symbolic connection with the Baltic region. Generally, Baltic-raised and educated cadres have not been accepted as junior partners in the governing of the Soviet Union. It can be argued, of course, that the party-oriented Soviet system altogether denies an independent political role to those from non-Russian republics and that this barrier is being maintained until all vestiges of independence disappear. This argument, however, should not preoccupy us now. The fact is that the Baltic party and government authorities do not act as coparticipants in the decision-making process but only as lobbyists trying to promote their own advantage.

The Baltic role in industry is that of a processor and manufacturer politically tied down to a single source of raw materials but also assured of selling the finished product to the same customer. In other words, Baltic industrial activity supplements the Soviet industrial complex and depends on the skills of the Baltic population. In the field of agriculture, the Balts finally won Moscow's approval for the traditional Baltic specialization of production a la Denmark, that is, as dairy and meat producers. This course was not assured until the end of Khrushchev's experimentation in agriculture, but Baltic operations are very efficient, a quality highly appreciated in Moscow. This fact certainly contributes to Moscow's interest and willingness to use the region for experimentation. Estonia has been used for substantive experiments in economic management and almost was chosen for the role of "model" Soviet republic.

In the cultural and social field, the Balts act as Westernizers, that is, as promoters of Western ideas and traditions and as a substitute for Western Europe. From the Kremlin's point of view, this activity also may be regarded as a sort of social experiment. For the Balts, however, it represents a substantial cultural engagement. For the Estonians, Latvians, and Lithuanians, it means living at peace with themselves and their past. This role of Westernizer (and the relatively close relations that the Balts maintain with the West) is not dictated or artificially invented but a natural role that the Balts want to play. However, it is limited to aspects of life that involve neither politics nor philosophy. Cultural penetration also is contained by the fact that the republics are small and their languages little known. Ethno-nationalist differences with the Russians further reduce their effectiveness. Yet for the Balts the role is important in itself, not only to add diversity to the Soviet cultural outlook but also to help preserve Baltic traditions and identity against the massive demographic as well as cultural pressure of Soviet Russians.

This Western characteristic makes the Balts attractive not only to the Russians but to other national groups in the Soviet Union. Foreign Communists, too, feel more affinity for the Balts. Furthermore, they better understand the place and importance of tradition in Baltic life. The Cubans offer a good example. A delegation from Cuba went to the region to recruit more Balts as advisers, coaches and so on for Cuban basketball teams. Leaving Lithuania after a visit in February of 1970, the chairman of the Cuban delegation said that their "visit to Lithuania was not accidental. There exists a lively interest in Cuba in the Baltic Soviet republics. We are also studying in detail the experience of Lithuania, Latvia, and Estonia in economic and cultural activities. We think that we can learn much from you. For example, we saw how interestingly the life of your cities is organized and how new Socialist relations are coordinated with the traditions of the past [emphasis added]."71

This theme of coordination of contemporary life with old traditions, which in the Baltic case are Western, is frequently repeated in Moscow as well. It would indicate that the Kremlin is not interested in completely stifling these traditions. However, such a permissive attitude offers no guarantee that the traditions can survive or that such survival is considered desirable.

The question of the role the Baltic republics play has been considered in historical perspective. The region's historic role was found to be that of Westernizer. There exists a continuity between the old and the new, and therefore overlapping and parallels between the role in its old and new robes. While Baltic civilization was established on Western foundations, the region has assimilated many Russian attitudes and institutions—through centuries of struggle with Russia and then as a result of Russian rule. Thus, to a Westerner the Baltic region could give a preview of Russia. Forty-five years ago George Kennan sought a diplomatic post in Riga for the precise purpose of learning something about Russia. For the Russians themselves, however, the region has been Western. Neither the imposition of the Soviet system nor the intense demographic and institutional Russification can erase the reflection of the West in Baltic life.

NOTES

1. The ruler's Lithuanian name is Jogaila. At baptism he received the name of Wladyslaw; in Polish and European history he is known as King Wladyslaw II Jagiello.

2. A. A. Mints and M. I. Rostovtsev, eds., Sovetskaia Pribaltika (The Soviet Baltic Coast) (Moscow, 1966), p. 18.

3. Ivan M. Bogdanov, Gramotnost' i obrazovanie v dorevoliutsi-onnoi Rossii i v SSSR (Literacy and education in prerevolutionary Russia and in the USSR) (Moscow, 1964), pp. 59-61. Bogdanov gives data according to provinces. For Latvia, the more typical Couronia (in Russian, Kurliandia; in Latvian, Kurzeme) was chosen here; for Lithuania, the exquisitely Lithuanian Kovenskaia (Kaunas) gubernia.

4. Reinhard Wittram, Baltische Geschichte (Munich, 1954), pp. 177ff.

5. Heronims Tichovskis, "Provost Ernst Glueck as Educator in Livonia and Russia," Slavic Review 24, no. 2 (1965): 306-13.

6. Quoted in Alfred Bilmanis, A History of Latvia (Princeton, N. J., 1951), p. 247.

7. Sostav rukovodiashchikh organov KPSS (Composition of the leading organs of the CPSU) (Munich, 1966), vol. 1, pp. 91ff.

8. Ezhegodnik Bol'shoi Sovetskoi Entsiklopedii 1971 goda (Year-book of the great soviet encyclopedia, 1971) (Moscow, 1971). For the list of Central Committee members, see pp. 20-21. The names of officials in the republic parties and governments may be found on the following pages: Latvia, p. 142-43; Lithuania, pp. 147-48; Estonia, pp. 199-200. Brief biographies of Central Committee members are contained in pp. 577-643 passim.

9. See V. Stanley Vardys, "The Baltic Peoples," Problems of Communism, September-October 1967, pp. 62ff.

10. Mints and Rostovtsev, eds., Sovetskaia Pribaltika, p. 79.

11. Oil recently has been discovered in Latvia and Lithuania, but the known deposits are considered too small for commercial exploi-tation.

12. Mints and Rostovtsev, eds., Sovetskaia Pribaltika, p. 91.

13. Kommunist Sovetskoi Latvii (Communist of Soviet Latvia), no. 4 (April 1963): 37; A. Jablonskis, Tarybu Lietuvos ekonomika ir jos rysiai (Soviet Lithuania's economy and its economic ties) (Vilnius, 1968), p. 82.

14. E. Tonurist, first vice chairman of the Council of Ministers of Soviet Estonia, Rahva Haal (People's voice), April 16, 1969; also his article in Izvestiia, February 8, 1968, p. 2; also Jablonskis, Tarybu Lietuvos ekonomika, p. 93.

15. Narodnoe khoziaistvo SSSR v 1967 g. (National economy of the USSR in 1967) (Moscow, 1968), pp. 436-37, 472-73; Jablonskis, Tarybu Lietuvos ekonomika, p. 93.

16. Documentation for both statements in Hans-Juergen Wegener, "Regional Economic Indicators," Research Bulletin CRD 414/69, December 19, 1969, pp. 2-5.

17. Pravda, December 21, 1974, p. 1.

18. A. Ferensas, secretary of the Central Committee of the Lith-uanian Communist Party, Svyturys (The lighthouse), no. 24 (1969): 2.

19. Izvestiia, April 6, 1974, p. 5, reported that in 1970 Estonia was in the first place with 1,587 rubles, Latvia had 1,574 rubles, and Lithuania had 1,336 rubles. A German scholar had calculated similar income ratios.

20. Jablonskis, Tarybu Lietuvos ekonomika, p. 55.

21. Johannes Euchfield, president of the Estonian Academy of Sciences, in Democratie nouvelle, March 1965, p. 59.

22. Lee Kerscher, "Cybernetics: Key to the Future?", Problems of Communism, November–December 1965, p. 66

23. U. Mikhov, "Ot natsional'nykh schetov do finansovogo balansa" (From national accounting to financial balance), Kommunist Estonii (Communist of Estonia), no. 8 (1969): 26-32.

24. M. Terentyev, Ekonomicheskaia gazeta (Economic newspaper), no. 31 (1966): 29.

25. Izvestiia, February 8, 1968, p. 2.

26. Democratie nouvelle, March 1965, p. 91.

27. To learn about the management of coffee houses, the Russians go to Tallinn. See G. Iakovlev, "Chashka kofe" (Cup of coffee), Pravda, January 30, 1970, p. 3

28. The Times (London), October 5, 1964, p. 11.

29. Madeleine and Marvin Kalb, "A Visit to Tallinn," The Reporter, May 11, 1961, pp. 30ff.

30. Newsweek, August 29, 1966, p. 32.

31. Junost' (The youth), no. 6 (1961): 3-34; no. 7 (1961): 33-66.

32. Molodaia Gvardia (The young guards), no. 4 (1964): 48-93; no. 5 (1964): 53-146.

33. Newsweek, August 29, 1966, p. 32.

34. See Rein Taagepera, "Nationalism in the Estonian Communist Party," Bulletin, Institute for the Study of the USSR, no. 1 (January 1970): 3-15; Adolfs Silde, Bez Tiesibam un Brivibas (Without justice and freedom) (Copenhagen, 1965), pp. 180-91, 382-89; V. Stanley Vardys, "Soviet Nationality Policy as an Instrument of Political Social-ization," in Adolf Sprudzs and Armins Rusis, eds., Res Baltica (Leyden, 1968), pp. 119ff.

35. Karla Hallik, "Rol' kul'turnykh sviazei v ukreplenii druzhby sovetskikh narodov" (The role of cultural relations in the strengthening of the friendship of Soviet peoples), Kommunist Estonii, no. 9 (1969):29.

36. Tiesa (The truth), January 11, 1970, p. 1.

37. Tiesa, March 15, 1969, p. 3; Stasys Budrys, Lietuviu vitrazas (Lithuanian stained glass) (Vilnius, 1968). This book is written in five languages: Lithuanian, Russian, French, German, and English; Tiesa, December 28, 1969, p. 4.

38. Hallik, "Rol'," pp. 34-35. This journal frequently published unusually original and frank discussions of current ideological and political issues. It is conceivable that the inspection of this journal

by the Estonian Communist Party's Central Committee was partly caused by the publication of Hallik's deliberations. Editors of the journal, however, were only admonished, not fired. See Kommunist Estonii, no. 11 (1969): 35. This contrasts sharply with the treatment of editors of Estonian and Lithuanian weekly literary gazettes. In 1969 their liberal editors were replaced with party ideologists without investigations or formal announcements.

39. Tiesa, October 13, 1969, p. 4.

40. Boris Schwarz, "The Vicissitudes of Soviet Music," Problems of Communism, November-December 1965, pp. 80-81. In a matter-of-fact way, dodecaphonic music is explained in the Soviet Estonian encyclopedia.

41. Sirp ja vasar (Sickle and hammer), December 14, 1962; Leo Normet, "Notes sur la musique," Democratie nouvelle, March 1965, p. 96.

42. Pravda, December 18, 1968, p. 3.

43. Cf. Zhermena Genie-Vagner, "Teatr iubiliar" (A theater celebrates its anniversary), Kommunist Sovetskoi Latvii, no. 4 (1969): 55.

44. Kulturos barai (Domains of culture), no. 11 (1967): 74; also Tiesa, November 7, 1968, p. 1.

45. Neue Zuercher Zeitung, August 8, 1969, p. 3

46. Literatura ir menas (Literature and the arts), January 1, 1970, p. 15.

47. Mardi Valgemae, "Recent Developments in Soviet Estonian Drama," Bulletin, Institute for the Study of the USSR, no. 9 (September 1969): 21.

48. Hellar Grabbi, "Soviet Estonian Intellectual Scene in the Sixties," unpublished paper presented at the Conference for Baltic Studies (University of Maryland, November 1968).

49. New York Times, October 3, 1969, p. 36.

50. Grabbi, "Soviet Estonian Intellectual Scene."

51. Down Beat, July 13, 1967, p. 15.

52. Pravda, January 16, 1969, p. 6.

53. It would be tempting to speak here about developments that show Baltic science and technology at a rather highly developed level, such as Estonia hosting a UNESCO conference on the use of oil shale in 1969, or the Lithuanian conference on aspects of atomic research that was also attended by international scholars, including Americans, or research for which Latvia's atomic reactor is used, or the making of computers in Lithuania and the Kubilius school of mathematicians. It is, however, not the purpose of this paper to list the many contributions that the Baltic republics are making to Soviet science and technology.

54. "Kryziaus zygis i artimo kisene" (A crusade against the pocketbook of the fellow-man), Svyturys, no. 5 (March 1963): 18-19.

55. Neue Zuercher Zeitung, August 5, 1969, p. 3.

56. Trybuna ludu (The people's tribune), January 9, 1975, p. 1.

57. Cf. Normet, "Notes sur la musique"; Looming (Creative work) (Tallinn), no. 12, (1967), cited in Estonian Events, July-August 1968, p.5.

58. Interview with Rishina, translated in Transatlantic Review (London), nos. 33-34 (Winter 1969-70).

59. Eesti Noukogude Entsuklopeedia (Estonian Soviet encyclopedia), vol. 1 (Tallinn, 1968), pp. 325, 353, 518-19, passim. The theater of the absurd, the Beatles, Bukharin, distinguished Estonian emigre scholars-refugees from the Stalin era, and even Radio Liberty are found as entries or explained within a broader context, and this is not an exhaustive list.

60. Population totals for the Baltic region are taken from Narodnoe khoziaistvo SSSR v 1970 g. (Moscow, 1971), pp. 20-21. Prewar figures are from Royal Institute of International Affairs, The Baltic States (London, 1938), pp. 30-36. Because of border adjustments, the increase of Russians in Latvia and Estonia should be shown as somewhat greater than present figures indicate. In Lithuania, it should be somewhat smaller.

61. A. A. Isupov, Natsional'nyi sostav naseleniia SSSR (National composition of the population of the USSR) (Moscow, 1964), p. 38.

62. L. N. Terent'eva, "Opredelenie svoei natsional'noi prinadlezhnosti podrostkami v natsional'no-smeshannikh sem'iakh" (Determination of national affiliation by the teenagers in nationally mixed families), Sovetskaia etnografia (Soviet ethography), no. 3 (1969): pp. 23ff.

63. E. Piall', "O nekotorykh voprosakh razvitiia natsii i natsional'nykh iazykov Sovetskogo Soiuza" (On some questions concerning the development of nations and national languages of the Soviet Union), Eesti NSV Teaduste Akadeemia Toimetised (Izvestiia Akademii Nauk Estonskoi SSR) (News of the Academy of Sciences of the Estonian SSR), no. 17/4 (1968): 395-98.

64. A. Kholmogorov, "Sbilzhenie i ratsvet sotsialisticheskikh natsii" (The rapprochement and flourishing of socialist nations), Kommunist Sovetskoi Latvii, no. 9 (1969): 25.

65. For more information, see sources listed in notes 8 and 33; see also V. Stanley Vardys, "Recent Soviet Policy Towards Lithuanian Nationalism," Journal of Central European Affairs 23, no. 3 (1963): 313-32.

66. For example, E. Piall', "O nekotorykh voprosakh," pp. 386-401.

67. Peter Wohl in Christian Science Monitor, December 24, 1969.

68. "Harren oder Handeln?", Frankfurter Allgemeine Zeitung, December 18, 1968.

69. Literatura un maksla (Literature and science), April 8, 1961, cited in A Survey of Developments in the Captive Countries, vol. 10, (1961): 50.

70. Sirp ja vasar, January 19, 1968.

71. Tiesa, February 22, 1970.

6

THE INCORPORATION OF WESTERN UKRAINE AND ITS IMPACT ON POLITICS AND SOCIETY IN SOVIET UKRAINE

Yaroslav Bilinsky

This is a study of a problem within a question. The problem is: How successfully have Western Ukrainians—who before World War II were under Poland, Romania, and Czechoslovakia, and most of whom before World War I had been part of the Austro-Hungarian Empire— been integrated with the Eastern Ukrainians, who for centuries were under Russian rule? The broader question is: Are not all the Ukrainians, West and East, now being submerged in the so-called "Soviet people," that seem to show unmistakable traits of the Russian nation; in short, are they not being Russified? Or is this process, despite high official sponsorship, far from irreversible and even farther from attainment?

While this essay addresses primarily the first problem, the broader question cannot be completely disregarded.[1] If the Eastern Ukrainians, who are in the majority, can be shown to quickly assimilate themselves to the Russians, this is likely to make the integration of the Western Ukrainians (who possibly remain Western, that is, Europe-oriented) more difficult. On the other hand, the successful merger of Western Ukrainians in the larger Ukrainian nation is likely to delay, although probably not stop altogether, the process of building a "Soviet people" in the Ukraine.[2] The problem of subethnic integration in this case bears upon the question of ethnic identity or assimilation.

The general literature does not offer unequivocal guidance on our specialized problem. James Rosenau's conceptual framework of linkages is quite suggestive on the choice of a policy's institutions and processes, of which the interrelationship with foreign environments should be explored. But to use the term linkage in our context would be stretching his point; since the completion of its incorporation by the end of 1945, Western Ukraine has been a matter of domestic rather

than foreign policy of the USSR.[3] (R. V. Burks has successfully applied
the linkage concept to trace Soviet influence on East European Communist countries, which is somewhat different from my concern.[4])

More useful for my purposes would be an eclectic application of
the integrative factors developed by Philip E. Jacob and Henry Teune
for the analysis of both international and intranational (metropolitan-
regional) integration. In their thoughtful introduction to a series of
seminar papers, they speak of ten such factors: (1) proximity;
(2) homogeneity; (3) transactions (including communications, trade,
and mobility of persons); (4) mutual knowledge or "cognitive proximity;"
(5) functional interests (interest groups favoring or opposing integration); (6) communal "character" or "social motive;" (7) structural
frame; (8) sovereignty-dependency status; (9) governmental effectiveness; and (10) previous integrative experience.[5] In our context, factor
1 (proximity) obviously applies; whereas factors 8 and 9 do not, nor
does factor 5, on reflection. The previous integrative experience
(factor 10) has been virtually nil. Counting mail flows among regions
in the Soviet Union (part of factor 2) is impossible, although other, less
tangible communications will be taken up. Nor am I bold enough to
attempt to sketch the communal character of the West Ukrainians
versus the East Ukrainians (factor 6), at least not in David McClelland's
terms (the different mixtures of the affiliation motive, achievement
motive, and power motive). But the remaining integrative factors, to a
greater or lesser extent, can be applied to sharpen our analysis. As
far as the broader question of assimilation of the Ukrainians to the
Russians is concerned, Karl W. Deutsch's earlier six underlying
factors or balances may be quite useful.[6] I will refer to them in concluding.

Finally, the reader should be alerted to two general propositions,
which for lack of space cannot be developed here and which may therefore sound rather axiomatic. First, the essence of nationalism is
psychological, or in Walker Connor's words, "a matter of attitude
rather than of fact."[7] Second, as a major consequence, the process
of modernization (in the broad sense used by Gunnar Myrdal) does
not tend to diminish ethnic conflicts but, on the contrary, tends to
perpetuate, perhaps even to exacerbate them.[8] This view is held not
only by some American scholars but also by Soviet scholars, which is
most remarkable given the sharply assimilationist trend of Soviet
policy. Thus, for example, the Soviet ethnographer V. V. Poshishevskiy
declares: "in the USSR it is now the city, perhaps more than the
countryside, that has become the 'carrier of the ethnos.' "[9]

Now to the specific limits of this study.

By the end of 1945, approximately nine million people and 110,000
square kilometers were added to the Ukraininan SSR, which in January
1939 counted 31.8 million inhabitants and 478,000 square kilometers—

truly a significant increase.[10] The Western Ukraine comprises the
regions known as Galicia and Volhynia, which were annexed from
Poland in late September 1939 on the basis of the Molotov-Ribbentrop
Pact (now administratively organized as the provinces of Lviv, Ivano-
Frankivsk, and Ternopil; and those of Volhynia and Rovno); Northern
Bukovina (the Chernivtsi Province) and parts of Bessarabia (from
1944-54 known as the Izmail Province, then merged with the Odessa
Province), which were ceded by Romania in mid-1940; and the so-called
Transcarpathian Province, which, apart from a brief interlude of inde-
pendence in March 1939, had been held by Czechoslovakia in 1919-39,
by Hungary during the war, and was relinquished by Czechoslovakia
in mid-1945. This is not the place to describe the process of incorporation in detail.[11] Nor can I go into the various territorial claims and
counterclaims, which in ethnically mixed Eastern Europe are legion:
Some Poles regard Galicia with its capital of Lviv as ancient
Polish land while some Ukrainians are concerned with Ukrainian irre-
denta in today's Poland and Czechoslovakia.[12] My concern is to try to
evaluate the impact of the seven West Ukrainian provinces upon Eastern Ukraine and possibly the Soviet Union as a whole, in politics (both
through official Communist channels and in the literary and political
protest movement), in economics, and in education and science. Such
a vast and complicated topic inevitably leads to what some readers will
view as serious omissions: It is for lack of material rather than want
of effort that I shall have very little to say on Bessarabia, Transcarpathia, and even my own native province of Volhynia. In politics and
elsewhere, the heart of Western Ukraine is Galicia, which according
to the 1970 census contained approximately 9 million people in the
seven Western provinces and the Izmail section of Odessa Province.

POLITICAL TIES THROUGH THE COMMUNIST PARTY

Jacob and Teune advocate an analysis of the system of decision
making as one way of gauging the integration of the community (the
Ukrainian nation in our case).[13] Presumably a system that excludes
one part from effective participation in deciding important matters
in the other would be dysfunctional for integration and vice versa.
The Western Ukrainians have had a definite impact on the Ukrainian
movement of dissent, but it might be better to first study their impact
on the Eastern Ukrainians through official Soviet politics, through the
Communist Party of the Soviet Union. The particular conditions in
Western Ukraine have been partly to blame for some political fire-
works, and they also have influenced Soviet Ukrainian politics in more
humdrum but also more lasting ways.

On June 13, 1953, Moscow's _Pravda_ announced the sensational news that the first secretary of the Communist Party of the Ukraine (CPU), Leonid G. Melnikov, later confirmed to be a Russian, had been dismissed at a recent plenum of the Central Committee of the CPU. The exact date of the session was not given, nor was the name of the emissary from Moscow, although such important changes usually are made in the presence of a key central party official. Melnikov was accused of mismanaging the establishment of kolkhozes in Western Ukraine and of perverting the Leninist-Stalinist nationality policy by appointing too many comrades from the East to West Ukrainian posts and by ordering West Ukrainian colleges to change their language of instruction to Russian.[14] When formally announcing Beria's arrest on July 10, 1953, _Pravda_ linked Beria to efforts at undermining the friendship of the peoples of the USSR and encouraging "bourgeois nationalist elements in the Union republics." _Pravda Ukrainy_ on July 14, 1953, dotted the i's by saying that Beria had attempted to activate bourgeois nationalist elements in the Union republics including the Ukraine.[15]

Within those few weeks in June 1953 there occurred in Western Ukraine, in Kiev, and in Moscow an intricate powerplay that brought demotion to Melnikov and contributed to Beria's death. Despite the importance of this episode, it is completely passed over in (hopefully, embarrassed) silence by general and specialized Soviet Ukrainian historical accounts published in the 1960s.[16]

In December 1949 Melnikov had succeeded Khrushchev as first secretary of the CPU. According to circumstantial evidence, Melnikov was the protege of either Kaganovich or Malenkov, but not of Khrushchev. In the spring of 1953 Beria started fighting for more power. Among other things, he made a special trip to Western Ukraine, where he installed Menshtein as head of the Lviv police apparatus, and he put Meshik in charge of the police of the entire Ukrainian republic. It is most likely that it was Beria himself who initiated Melnikov's fall. But it is true that in June 1953 it was a loyal Khrushchev supporter, Aleksei Kirichenko, and not a Beria man, who succeeded Melnikov, as it is true that Meshik was executed together with Beria in December 1953.[17]

There is the temptation to assume that the officially specified conditions in Western Ukraine were so scandalous and so critical that Melnikov's ouster was rendered inevitable. I believe that the Ukrainian intelligentsia and the eastern cadres of the CPU had barely escaped a major purge under Kaganovich in 1947 when he temporarily replaced Khrushchev as first party secretary in the Ukraine, and that in 1953 they were strongly dissatisfied with the personnel and cultural policies of Kaganovich's deputy, Melnikov. The West Ukrainian conditions,

although real, were merely used as a more diplomatic cutting edge by
Beria, who sought to gain support from the entire Ukraine (after all,
everybody expected the unreconstructed West Ukrainians to feel strongly about Russian officials and Russian university lectures). In any case,
Khrushchev profited from Beria's pro-Ukrainian demarche in order to
reassume full control over the Ukrainian party apparatus. To sum up,
it seems that the Western Ukraine served as a sort of catalyst rather
than the basic reacting substance in the bloody and complex power
struggle of 1953. For I believe that it can be shown that the weight of
the Western Ukraine in the total Ukrainian party was relatively small.

When Soviet troops occupied the Polish-held territories in September 1939, the Communist Party had to be constructed practically
from scratch. True, in the interwar period there had been the Communist Party of Western Ukraine which, although outlawed by September 1936, had attained a membership of 4,719. But in the summer of
1938 Stalin dissolved the Communist Party of Poland or CPP (allegedly because it had been excessively infiltrated by Polish police agents).
Since the CPP was the parent party of the CP of Western Ukraine, the
latter was liquidated also.[18] By April 1940 there were 3,776 party members and candidates in Lviv Province; 2,506 Communists in Drohobych
(in 1959 merged with Lviv Province); 2,486 in Ternopil Province; or
a total of 11,280 Communists in the whole of Galicia.[19] They accounted
for a miserable 2.1 percent of the entire membership of the CPU.[20]
By June 1, 1941, however, on the eve of the Nazi invasion, CPU members in Western Ukraine numbered 36,969 already.[21]

Upon reconquest of the area—with many party members having
been drafted into the Red Army, evacuated east, or killed by the
Germans or by the Ukrainian nationalists—total membership in Western
Ukraine excluding Transcarpathia on August 1, 1944, was only 7,174
members and candidates. By the end of 1945 it had quadrupled to
28,450 members, but this was still only 9 percent of a Ukrainian SSR
total of 320,307. Curiously enough, the CP of Transcarpathia (in many
ways the most backward area) was in relatively fine shape, not having
been purged by Stalin in 1938. In November the Transcarpathians contributed to the CPU as many as 4,279 members.[22] A rough estimate
on the basis of the rather unsatisfactory data of the Sixteenth CPU
Congress gives us the following breakdown for party members in
Western Ukraine in January 1949:

Lviv and Drohobych Provinces	38,300	members and candidates
Ternopil Province	6,510	
Volhynia Province	8,310	
Rovno Province	7,410	
Stanyslaviv (Ivano-Frankivsk)	9,110	

Transcarpathia Province	13,920
Chernivitsi Province	13,920
Total	97,480 members and candidates[23]

This was about 14.2 percent of the Ukrainian SSR total of CP members, showing that the CPU was disproportionately less numerous in Western Ukraine.[24]

Comparable figures could not be obtained for the crucial year 1952. Apparently, the party simply did not publish a stenographic record of the Nineteenth Party Congress of October 1952, the last under Stalin. Table 6.1, shows the continuing disproportion of party members in Western Ukraine from 1956 to 1966. Approximately 19 percent of the total republic population lives in the Western Provinces, but the party organization in the Western Ukraine numbers closer to 10 percent of the CPU total (some 11.0 percent in 1966). The proceedings of the 1971 All-Union Congress unfortunately do not identify the congress delegates by their regional organizations, so the figures could not be brought up to date. In Table 6.2 I have tried to calculate with greater precision the estimated party membership in Western Ukraine per thousand total population in 1959, 1966, and—so far as possible—from 1968 to 1973. The figures, rough as they may be, bear out the sorry state of affairs in Western Ukraine. In 1959 in the Ukraine as a whole, the average figure was 28 party members per thousand people; in the Western Ukraine it was only 18 on the average. In 1966 the average figure for the Ukrainian SSR was 47 per thousand population; in the Western Provinces it was as low as 27 per thousand. Lviv Province and also, curiously, Volhynia Province had a more respectable party coverage. I cannot explain the Volhynia situation, but Lviv Province contains a major city that probably has acted as a magnet for ambitious party members. It has been suggested that the low number of party members in Western Ukraine may be due to the relatively low level of urbanization in that region. Table 6.3 correlates the percentage of urban population in West Ukrainian provinces with the number of party members (full and candidate) per thousand total population, then compares those figures with the average ratio of urban population to party members in the Ukraine as a whole. Table 6.3 shows an interesting fact: In all West Ukrainian provinces but two there is a surplus over the expected number of party members, as high as 48 percent in Rovno Province and 33 percent in Volhynia. Party membership in Ivano-Frankivsk Province corresponds exactly to the predicted number. The important exception, however, is in highly urbanized Lviv Province, whose main city is the unofficial capital of Western Ukraine: a deficit of 18 percent. This indicates that in Soviet Ukrainian politics the largest province of Western

TABLE 6.1

Communist Party Members in the West Ukrainian Provinces, 1956-66
(in thousands)

Province	Full Members				Candidates			
	1956	1959	1961	1966	1956	1959	1961	1966
Volhynia	5	18	20	27.5	5	6	4	2.5
Transcarpathia	15	12	14	22.5	0	0	2	2.5
Ivano-Frankivsk[a]	5	18	14	30.0	0	6	2	2.5
Lviv[b]	35	48	56	67.5	5	6	6	7.5
Rovno	0[c]	12	18	20.0	0	0	4	2.5
Ternopil	10	12	12	20.0	0	0	2	2.5
Chernivtsi	15	6	14	17.5	0	0	0	2.5
Subtotal: Western Ukraine	85	126	148	205.5	10	18	20	22.5
Total: Ukraine	955[d]	1170	1566	2117.5	?	?	-	-

Note: Figures are estimated membership at time of All-Union party congresses.

aFormerly Stanyslaviv.

bIncludes the former Drohobych Province, incorporated in Lviv Province in 1959.

cEither an error on the author's part or a small party organization that had not filled the representation quota (1:5,000) at the 1956 party congress.

dIn 1956 and 1959 the delegation from the Ukraine at the party congresses represented full members only; in 1961 and 1966 candidate members were apparently counted in the makeup of the delegation. Figures for 1956 and 1959 thus exclude candidate members; those for 1961 and 1966 apparently include them.

Sources: Author's calculations based on lists of delegates at party congresses. For 1956 see XX s'ezd KPSS: Stenograficheskii otchet (Moscow, 1956), vol. 2, pp. 507-48; Aristov in Pravda, February 17, 1956, p. 2. For 1959 see Vneocherednoi XXI s'ezd KPSS: Stenograficheskii otchet (Moscow, 1959), vol. 2, pp. 553-607, and vol. 1, pp. 258-60. For 1961 see XXII s'ezd KPSS: Stenograficheskii otchet (Moscow, 1962),vol. 1, pp. 363-584, and vol. 1, pp. 424-25. For 1966 see XXIII s'ezd KPSS: Stenograficheskii otchet (Moscow, 1966), vol. 2, pp. 389-623, and vol. 1, pp. 279-80.

TABLE 6.2

Estimated Party Membership in Western Ukraine Per 1,000 Total Population

Province	1959			1966			Circa 1970		
	Party Members	Population (1,000s)	Ratio[a]	Party Members	Population (1,000s)	Ratio[a]	Party Members	Population (1,000s)	Ratio[a]
Volhynia	24,000	890	27	30,000	964	31	35,500[b]	973	36
Transcarpathia	12,000	920	13	25,000	1,031	24	29,000[b]	1,050	28
Ivano-Frankivsk	24,000	1,095	22	32,500	1,207	27	37,452[c]	1,264	30
Lviv[d]	54,000	2,108	26	75,000	2,357	32	80,000[b]	2,408	33
Rovno	12,000	926	13	22,500	1,012	22	42,000[c]	1,060	40
Ternopil	12,000	1,086	11	22,500	1,149	20	36,000[e]	1,171	31
Chernivtsi	6,000	774	8	20,000	828	24	32,000[f]	845	38
Subtotal: Western Ukraine	126,000	7,799	18	227,500	8,548	27	not applicable		
Total: Ukraine	1,170,000	41,869	28	2,117,500	45,516	47	2,138,800[b]	46,400	46
							2,301,657[f]	47,127	49
							2,534,561[c]	47,502	53
							2,479,636[e]	48,237	51

[a]Ratio is the number of party members (full and candidate) per 1,000 total population.
[b]Data for 1968.
[c]Data for 1971.
[d]Includes former Drohobych Province.
[e]Data for 1973.
[f]Data for 1970.

Sources: For 1959 and 1966 see sources in Table 6.1. For 1968-73 see Istoriia i sil Ukrains'koi RSR, separate editions for Volyns'ka oblast' (Kiev, 1970), p. 50; Zakarpats'ka oblast' (1969), p. 74; Ivano-Frankivsk oblast' (1971), p. 74; L'vivs'ka oblast' (1968), p. 48; Chernivets'ka oblast' (1970), p. 62; Rovens'ka oblast' (1973), p. 70; Ternopil's'ka oblast' (1973), p. 62. For total membership in the Ukraine, 1968-73, see Soviet Ukraine (Kiev, 1969), p. 190a; Ezhegodnik Bol'shoi Sovetskoi Entsyklopedii 1970, p. 183b. Demographic data for 1968 in Soviet Ukraine, inset tables facing pp. 15 and 16; for 1970 and 1971 see Narodne hospodarstvo Ukrains'koi RSR v 1971 rotsi (Kiev, 1972), pp. 12ff.; for 1973 see Narodne hospodarstvo URSR v 1972 r. (Kiev, 1974), p. 9.

TABLE 6.3

Actual Versus Expected Party Membership in Western Ukraine
(in terms of all-Ukrainian urban-rural distribution)

Province	Urban Population(%) (1)	Ratio (2)	Expected Ratio (3)	Deviation (absolute figure) (4)	Deviation (%) (5)
Volhynia[a]	32	36	27	+9	+33
Transcarpathia[a][b]	30	28	26	+2	+8
Ivano-Frankivsk[b]	31	30	30	0	0
Lviv[a]	46	33	39	-6	-18
Rovno[b]	28	40	27	+13	+48
Ternopil[c]	26	31	23	+8	+35
Chernivtsi[d]	35	38	31	+7	+23
Subtotal: Western Ukraine	incomplete data				
Total: Ukraine 1968	54	46			
1970	55	49			
1971	55	53			
1973	57	51			

Notes: Ratio represents the number of party members (full and
candidate) per 1,000 total population. Expected ratio is the expected
number of party members per 1,000 based on the level of urbanization.
Expected ratio = column (1) x column (2) for the whole Ukraine/urban
percentage for the whole Ukraine. Column (4) = column (2) - column (3).
[a] Data for 1968
[b] Data for 1971.
[c] Data for 1973
[d] Data for 1970.
Sources: See Table 6.2

Ukraine does not wield proportionate weight. It also indicates that in
Lviv, and probably also in Rovno and Volhynia Provinces, the urban-
rural distribution is a poor predictor of the size of party organizations,
and that other questions must be asked.

How many indigenous people were drawn into the party? Was
the party organically connected with the western milieu or was it
superimposed? Soviet sources are rather reticent, but by splicing
several of them together a remarkable picture emerges of the western
oblasts as a whole and Lviv oblast in particular. In 1946 the West

Ukrainian party organizations accepted a total of about 4,000 candidates, of whom 1,114 were drawn from the local population.[25] The same author writes with reference to the Lviv Province party organization:

> If until July 1, 1947 there had been accepted into its ranks 452 persons from among the local population, in 1954, on the other hand, the Party organization contained 3,478 local activists.[26]

This is all very impressive until we compare these figures with the totals. In 1947 the Lviv Province party was 15,943 strong, which would leave the Galicians some 2.8 percent; on January 1, 1954, Lviv Province had as many as 26,470 Communists, allowing the indigenous people about 13.1 percent of the total party membership.[27] Not surprisingly, the social breakdown of the party was rather lopsided. In 1947 there were 4,246 workers or 26.5 percent, only 887 individual peasants or kolkhoz members (5.5 percent), and 10,810 officials and members of the intelligentsia (68 percent). In 1953 this improved to the extent that out of some 26,000 party members or less, there were 6,126 workers and 2,953 collective farmers (no percentages given in the source).[28] But the most revealing statement follows:

> Thanks to increased attention to the admission to the Party of the better people from among the local population, the national composition of the [Lviv] oblast Party organization changed markedly. If in 1948 the Ukrainians constituted in it 37.5, the Russians 49.1 and representatives of other nationalities 13.4 percent, in 1953 Ukrainians already accounted for 43.4 percent, the Russians for 42 and the representatives of other nationalities 14.6 percent.[29]

Commentaries are superfluous. The reader is merely referred to the data in Table 6.3 showing that the share of the Russians among the population was between 2.5 and 8.6 percent, the latter in Lviv Province.

I will not list in detail the organs in Kiev on which the provincial party secretaries from Western Ukraine have been represented. Analysis of the backgrounds of the 21 officials who held high provincial posts in the Western Ukraine in 1946-52 as well as the backgrounds of the seven province first secretaries elected in 1971 shows that with the possible exception of I. I. Turianytsia, the first man to hold the job of first secretary of the Transcarpathian obkom in 1945, who was quickly shunted into secondary posts, none of the secretaries was from Western Ukraine.[30] Only two Western Ukrainians are known to have risen to relatively secondary political posts. On August 13, 1953, it was announced that S. Stefanyk, one of the two sons of the well-known

West Ukrainian writer Vasyl Stefanyk, was appointed a deputy prime minister of the Ukrainian SSR. In the same period B. Dudykevych, one of the remaining former leaders of the liquidated CP of Western Ukraine, was made second secretary of the Lviv Province Party Committee.[31] But they seem to have disappeared from sight rather quickly. On the other hand, the career of an East Ukrainian who has specialized in West Ukrainian assignments shows both the difficulties and eventual rewards in terms of Ukrainian and All-Union party status.

Ivan S. Hrushets'kyi, born in 1904, held a succession of important party posts in the Western Ukraine after 1940. After the war he alternated as first secretary of the Lviv Province Party Committee (1944-48, 1950, 1961-62) and that of Volhynia (1948-49, 1951-61). These posts brought him some recognition in the All-Ukrainian and All-Union party organizations. In 1962 he was made one of the secretaries of the CPU Central Committee (dropped from this position by 1966) and candidate member of the Ukrainian Politburo. But he obtained full membership only rather late in his career, in July 1972. Shortly thereafter, in September 1972, he was chosen chairman of the Ukrainian SSR Supreme Soviet, a semihonorific, semiretirement post. At the All-Union level, Khrushchev and Brezhnev have had him elected full member of the CPSU Central Committee since 1961.[32] Hrushets'-kyi's successor as first secretary of the Lviv obkom, Vasyl S. Kutsevol (b. 1920), also an Eastern Ukrainian, was newly elected candidate member of the All-Union Central Committee in 1966 and promoted to full membership in 1971. The same recognition on the All-Union level has been accorded his colleague, the first secretary of the Ivano-Frankivsk obkom since 1969, Viktor S. Dobryk (b. 1927). But although they are both in the good graces of Brezhnev, neither has exerted direct influence on CPU policy by advancing to a position in Kiev.

At the time of writing (August 1973) the most promising West Ukrainian graduate appeared to be Valentyn Iu. Malanchuk, a doctor of historical sciences and since October 1972 a candidate member of the Ukrainian Politburo and Ukrainian party secretary in charge of ideology. Although he was not born in Western Ukraine but in a neighboring province, in the town of Khmelnyts'ky, formerly Proskuriv, in 1928, his scholarly and party career has been intimately linked to Lviv Province for over 20 years. He studied at Lviv University in 1945-50, went into Komsomol and party work, rose to ideological secretary of Lviv obkom in 1963. In 1967 he became deputy minister of higher and specialized secondary education of the Ukranian SSR, and was then promoted to his present position. Malanchuk wrote his doctoral dissertation on Soviet nationality policy in Western Ukraine, and it was published. A Western source calls his a "fighting ideologue."[33] He is reputed to be a hardliner vis-a-vis Ukrainian nationalist dissenters—his appointment to the key postion in Kiev apparently is not designed

to increase the representation of West Ukrainian interests in the
republic capital but to put in the saddle a tried expert for the struggle
with Ukrainian and particularly West Ukrainian "bourgeois nationalism."[34]

What does all this imply in terms of potential impact on Ukrainian politics? Except in an unusual situation like that in 1953, the
weight of the West Ukrainian party organization is apt to be small.
It has relatively few members and the overwhelming majority of those
members (86.9 percent of the Lviv organization in 1954) appear to be
Russians and Eastern Ukrainians. Their numerous personal ties with
the east may lead to better communications, provided the Easterners
want to listen to the proposals of the new and old West Ukrainians.
(They apparently did in authorizing the Soviet firms, of which more
later.)

Moreover, I would agree with T. H. Rigby, who states that the
weakness of the Western Ukrainian party organization (in an area
where Ukrainians strongly predominate in the total population) contri-
tutes to the weakness of the Ukrainian element in the CPU as a whole.
The other main reason for this weakness is the fact that the Ukrainians
in the east and west "still contain a far higher proportion of peasants."[35]
I would also underline Rigby's hypothesis on the reasons for relatively
low enrollments in the party in the western borderlands:

> We would do well . . . to recall the pertinence here of econo-
> mic factors. These, however, are clearly inadequate to
> explain all the differences. Latvians and Estonians, econo-
> mically among the most "advanced" peoples of the USSR,
> figured very badly in terms of party membership rates . . . .
> National attitudes and national psychology surely play a
> big part in these differences, and their influence appears
> to be most tenacious. Thus the persistence of very low
> membership levels in the Western borderlands 20 years
> after the close of World War II was presumably due in part
> to continued resentment over Russian dominance and to
> lack of identification with the Soviet system.[36]

On the surface it appears that in 1968-71 most of the Ukrainian
provinces had more total party members than could have been expected
from the urban-rural distribution—with the significant exception of
Lviv Province, the largest. But according to a private communication
there have been complaints from Ukrainian patriots in the western
provinces that in the early postwar years West Ukrainians on instructions from the nationalist underground boycotted Soviet schools and the
Communist Party, when it was relatively easy to be admitted to both.
Now the party screens applicants very carefully indeed, particularly

if they come from Western Ukraine. In other words, the relatively small number of West Ukrainians in the party may be due to the economic underdevelopment of the area plus a combination of initial boycott of the party by the Western Ukrainians followed by anti-West Ukrainian discrimination. To return to the initial hypothesis of Jacob and Teune: On the surface the Communist Party in the Western Ukraine, centralized as it is, could have been assumed to be an excellent structural framework for integration; but on closer analysis it appears that indigenous Western Ukrainians, as opposed to Eastern Ukrainians who have been delegated to serve in those provinces, have not yet assumed their full share of responsibility and power. Therefore, we must look to other means of integration.

OTHER POLITICAL TIES

It is outside the regular party channels, through informal social, literary, and political contacts that the West Ukrainians may exert their greatest political influence upon their compatriots to the east. (In more general terms, we are dealing here with a combination of Jacob and Teune's factors of communication transaction and mutual knowledge or "cognitive proximity."[37] Ultimately, we also are concerned with the compatibility of political values shared by the elites and the peoples of the different regions, west and east.) In his assessment of the strength of modern Ukrainian nationalism, John A. Armstrong weighs the impact of Western Ukrainians as follows:

> On the whole . . . one would be inclined to accept Inkeles and Bauer's forecast of the declining strength of East Ukrainian nationalism but for one factor—the injection of the fervently nationalist West Ukrainians into the social body of the Ukraine . . . . Many thousands of West Ukrainians have gone to work in the East Ukrainian mines or factories, or have been resettled on farms in thinly settled Kherson oblast. Many East Ukrainians have lived or travelled in the West Ukraine as soldiers, officials, or technicians in the numerous factories there. Recently even East Ukrainian tourist trips to the Carpathians have been fostered, while West Ukrainians go to Black Sea resorts. Probably the most important kind of interchange, from the point of view of fostering nationalist sentiments, is that of students and instructors, whether for short-term study or for enrollment in educational institutions in the other part of the country. It is by no means a one-way flow, for West

Ukrainian institutions like Lviv University enroll a major
portion of the students in higher education in the Ukraine.
For many of these contacts, the regime no doubt tries
to select ideologically reliable persons. In any case, the
West Ukrainians are watched as closely as possible, and
occasional instances which come to light indicate that they
must be exceedingly cautious in discussing nationality questions. Considering how fervently nationalist very many West
Ukrainians are, one can hardly doubt, however, that given
the protracted and extensive contact of the type described
above many will manage to convey their ideas to the East
Ukrainians. Some of the latter may, of course, be alienated
by memories of wartime excesses by the Galicians, or even
by West Ukrainian differences in custom and pronunciation.
If, however, there is some latent tendency to national distinctiveness among the East Ukrainians, it can hardly fail to be
stimulated by contact with the West Ukrainians. Given the
extreme limitations upon direct observation, no one can
really tell whether or not this stimulus will offset the factors which tend to diminish the importance of nationalism
in the East Ukraine.[38]

There have been some opportunities for the West Ukrainians to
influence the East Ukrainians, but the outcome, almost by its nature,
is less than conclusive.

During the war numerous West Ukrainina nationalist groups,
whose members belonged to the Organization of Ukrainian Nationalists
(OUN), fanned out into German- and Romanian-occupied Eastern
Ukraine. Despite some linguistic differences (in Dniepropetrovsk,
for example, the Galicians were first taken for Poles),[39] despite
some unexpected differences in educational levels[40] and, more important, in their thinking on social policies,[41] fruitful collaboration
between the OUN members from West Ukraine and indigenous Ukrainian nationalists was established in several cities, notably Kryvyi Rih
and the entire Donetsk Basin area.[42] But the situation under German
and Romanian rule was so unique and so confused that it is difficult
to draw from it any conclusions about the continued impact of the OUN
raids on the Ukrainians in Eastern Ukraine.

The armed struggle of the Ukrainian Insurgent Army (UPA),
which was connected with the OUN mostly in Galicia and the borderland
west of the Curzon line, but not in Transcarpathia,[43] from 1944 until
the early 1950s or, in isolated instances, possibly even until 1956,
also must have left a certain impact upon the Eastern Ukrainians.[44]
There is no doubt that Soviet counteraction was publicized by the
regime in both Western and Eastern Ukraine.[45] But while interviewing

Soviet Ukrainian refugees from Eastern and Western Ukraine in 1956-57, including some non-Ukrainians who had contact with both groups in the Ukraine and in Soviet forced labor camps, I have gained the distinct impression that the psychological impact of UPA's struggle on Eastern Ukrainians should not be overestimated. My respondents from the Eastern Ukraine did not, on the whole, share the categorically hostile view of everything Russian that seems characteristic of so many Western Ukrainians. The Eastern Ukrainians also took a hardheaded view of the armed struggle, acknowledging its heroism but also pointing out its costs. Perhaps we ought to view in this perspective the self-immolations of N. Didyk on Lubianskii Square in Moscow in the spring of 1966, and of O. Makukh in Khreshchatik Street in Kiev on December 5, 1968. The latter appears to have been a former member of the UPA and OUN and a former inmate of a Soviet forced labor camp.[46]

We must not think, of course, that all West Ukrainians oppose the regime. In his detailed report to the Fifth Congress of the Writers of Ukraine in November 1966, Oles Honchar, the head of the Writers' Union, mentioned prominently Iryna Vil'de, Roman Andriiashyk, and Dmytro Pavlychko.[47] Miss Vil'de (born 1907 in Chernivtsi, Bukovina) now lives in Lviv and has written several novels, including the prize-winning Sisters Richynsky. Roman Andriiashyk has been recommended as a talented young novelist from Bukovina. Pavlychko is a well-known Galicia-born poet; at the congress he was elected one of the nine secretaries of the Writers' Union.[48] One hears in private conversations and reads in letters that Lutsiv, the director of the Lviv Opera, recently was transferred to Kiev, that the Bukovinian Hnatiuk has become a well-known opera singer and his fellow Bukovinian Mykolaichuk has become a film star. All this has been going on for some 30 years and will continue. But it seems that the participation of the Western Ukrainians in the intellectual and political opposition movement is more noteworthy and perhaps more significant in the long run.

In 1959 and 1961 there were several secret political trials in the Western Ukraine, news of which leaked out only in 1966, one year after the next wave of political arrests in Western and Eastern Ukraine. Concretely, after a trial before the Provincial Court in Stanyslaviv (Ivano-Frankivsk) on March 4-10, 1959, eight Western Ukrainian skilled workers were sentenced to two to ten years imprisonment for belonging to the "United Party for the Liberation of the Ukraine." On December 16-23, 1961, eighteen Lviv factory workers were tried and sentenced to long prison terms for belonging to the "Ukrainian National Committee," whose objective reportedly was to demand the secession of the Ukraine from the USSR. In addition, two young workers were sentenced to death and executed.[49] (More recently, in 1967 and 1968, there were arrests and long prison terms for nine Western Ukrainians accused of reviving the OUN under the label "Ukrainian National

Front," complete with a publications outfit that was literally underground—in a camouflaged earth hole or bunker in the Carpathians.[50])
It's hard to know what's truth and what's fiction in these accusations—
the imaginative approach of Stalin's NKVD was well documented by
Khrushchev, and the KGB does not seem to be radically different. The
most important trial in this Galician series is the one that became
known as the "trial of the seven jurists," in Lviv in May 1961. (Several of those arrested were lawyers by education.)

The jurists were accused of conspiring in 1959 to set up a nationalist organization, the "Ukrainian Workers' and Peasants' Union"
(UWPU). Among the UWPU's goals reportedly were "the struggle
against the Soviet political and social order, against the Communist
Party and the Soviet Government, the severing of the Ukrainian SSR
from the USSR and the establishment of a so-called 'Independent
Ukraine' (samostiinoi Ukrainy)."[51]

Actually, if we are to trust one of the defendants, no such organization ever was established. The defendants admit to having discussed a brochure entitled "Program of the UWPU." They admit to
having discussed the evils of Stalinism as well as the drawbacks of
both the centralized bureaucracy under Khrushchev and the regime's
entire policy toward the Ukraine. They favored making use of the
secession clause in the Soviet Constitution, to which end the UWPU
would legally and peacefully conduct an agitation and propaganda campaign among the Ukrainian people, a right implicitly guaranteed by
the Constitution as well. Should the Ukraine secede following a general plebiscite, its political structure would remain Soviet and the
economic order would still be "socialist."[52] Armed struggle for
independence was mentioned, but only to be ruled out as inadmissable.[53]
Typical of their thinking in 1959 is the following sentence from the
draft program:

> We are fighting for such an independent Ukraine which,
> while highly satisfying the material and spiritual needs of
> her citizens on the basis of a socialized economy, would
> develop in the direction of communism, and secondly, in
> which all the citizens would really be able to use the poli-
> tical liberties and would determine the direction of the
> economic and political development of the Ukraine—such
> is the ultimate struggle of our "party."[54]

Moreover, in late 1960 the author of the tentative program,
according to his own testimony, came to the conclusion that "for an
improvement in the lives of the people there was absolutely necessary
not the independence of the UkrSSR but the liquidation of bureaucracy."[55]
This could only be achieved by expanding "socialist democracy." The

organization was to be a legal one and was to openly combat the illegal restrictions on Soviet civil rights.[56] But before the seven could write the final draft of the program, with its de-emphasis of the secession of the Ukrainian SSR, the KGB arrested them. Their leader was sentenced to death, but his sentence was later commuted to 15 years imprisonment. The others were sentenced to prison terms from 10 to 15 years. All the sentences were to be served in corrective labor camps.[57]

Who are these dangerous conspirators? Their leader and the author of the draft is Lev H. Luk'ianenko, born in 1927 in a village in Eastern Ukraine. Until his arrest he was a member of the party and a graduate of Moscow University's Faculty of Law. He worked first in Lviv Province as staff party propagandist, attached to rural party district committees, and then became a lawyer in the Lviv countryside. All the others are Western Ukrainians. Three had belonged to the party (Virun, Luts'kiv, and Borovnyts'kyi). Two were practicing lawyers (Kandyba and Borvnyts'kyi), one was a militia man (policeman) in Lviv (Kipysha), one managed a rural club (Luts'kiv), one served as a paid propagandist (Virun), the last was an agronomist (Libovych). The oldest was 38, the youngest 26 years old.[58]

The case looks very much like a classic demonstration of the impact the fervently nationalist Galicians can have upon an East Ukrainian lawyer who shows a latent tendency to national distinctiveness. The authorities have tried to interpret Luk'ianenko's behavior as a well thought-out conspiracy from beginning to end. He had always shown anti-Soviet sentiments; he knew about the existence of remnants of the Organization of Ukrainian Nationalists (OUN) in the Western Ukraine, so he arranged to obtain a job in Lviv Province. Actually— I would be more inclined to trust the defendant—the countryside was his second choice. He initially sought a job in an Eastern Ukrainian town where his wife worked, but he did not succeed. Not wanting to go outside the Ukraine, he obtained a job near Lviv.[59] He further says in self-defense, again sounding eminently plausible to me:

> I had no idea about the OUN before my arrest. Neither before 1958, nor afterwards did I meet any people who would tell me anything concrete about this party. All the nationalist struggle in the Western Ukraine was subsumed in my mind under the concept of "Bandera's affair" (banderivshchyna). I regarded as the organizing center [of the nationalist struggle] the Ukrainian Insurgent Army (UPA), not the OUN. (It is for this reason that in the draft program of the UWPU there is mention of the UPA, not the OUN.) About the OUN I received for the first time a more or less concrete idea

from the agent of state security in the cell of the investigating prison of Ukrainian KGB, Lviv Province.[60]

This influence of the Galician milieu upon Luk'ianenko cannot be discounted; after all, he worked there from 1958 until his arrest in January 1961. But it should not be regarded as the sole cause of his political initiative. It was not Galicians but respected members of the Moscow University Law Faculty who inculcated in him the belief that the law in the Soviet state was real and not fictitious.[61] A Ukrainian Candide, he seems to have taken their statements too literally. Or perhaps he wanted to put them to the test? The story has an ominous postscript. In June 1969 Luk'ianenko and two of his follow campmates (Kandyba and Michael Horyn', convicted in a later case) addressed a petition to the U.N. Commission on Human Rights complaining they were being systematically poisoned with nonlethal drugs; within 10 to 15 minutes after eating the jail food, they would get terrible headaches and suffer partial loss of memory.[62]

The inferences that we can draw from the more recent opposition movement, on the impact of the Western Ukraine on the Eastern Ukraine, are somewhat less firm. My conclusions are based on study of the major documents by Symonenko (died in 1963),[63] Dziuba (1965),[64] Chornovil (1967),[65] and Moroz (1967, 1970)[66]; 19 documents published in the 24 issues of Suchasnist' in 1968-69 (exclusive of several documents dealing with the state of religion); the 27 issues of the Russian underground newsletter Khronika tekushchikh sobytii (dated from April 30, 1968, to October 15, 1972)[67]; and a brief analysis of the names mentioned in the five available issues of Ukrains'-kyi visnyk (Ukrainian herald), the Ukrainian counterpart of the Russian Chronicle of Current Events (from January 1970 through March 1972).[68]

I conclude:

1. The phenomenon of opposition is rather widespread in the Ukraine. Symonenko, Dziuba, and Chornovil are Eastern Ukranians; Moroz is from the West (Volhynia). The arrests of the Ukrainian intelligentsia, which Chornovil documents in large part, took place in Kiev, Lviv, Lutsk (Volhynia), Ivano-Frankivsk, Feodosia (Crimea), and Zhytomyr. People demonstrated against the trials in Kiev as well as Lviv.[69]

2. On closer analysis, however, the influence of Western Ukraine does appear in some groups of those arrested, persecuted, or simply suspected. For instance, the East Ukrainian poet Vasyl Symonenko, whose untimely death no doubt spared him many an unpleasantness from the regime, wrote a very interesting poem published in Eastern Ukraine Samizdat, in which he paid tribute to the "Ukrainian

Lion," the city of Lviv, which has not surrendered its strength and
which he begs to lend him, too, a drop of strength from its courageous
lion's heart.[70] A similar tribute to the West Ukrainian poets Shashkevych and Franko, and generally to the West Ukrainians who have not
surrendered to the Germans or the Poles, is paid by poet Ivan Drach.[71]
(Drach's wife is said to be from Western Ukraine; Chornovil's second
wife also comes from Lviv.) More to the point, perhaps, is the fact
that of the 20 convicts of whom Chornovil supplies biographical sketches,
eight are from Eastern Ukraine but all but two of those eight (Kuznet-
sova and Shevchuk) show some kind of West Ukrainian influence: They
have lived, studied, or worked in Western Ukraine or otherwise come
into contact with West Ukrainians. For instance, one of the most impressive intellectuals in the group, Sviatoslav Karavans'kyi, of Odessa
(born in 1920) had developed a strong commitment to the study and use
of the Ukrainian language in 1937-39, probably without any influence
from Western Ukraine.[72] But in 1942 he apparently was predisposed
to join an OUN-affiliated student group. When the Soviet troops came
back, he was tried and sentenced as a dangerous criminal to 25 years
in labor camps. Partially amnestied in 1960, he was rearrested in
1965 and ordered to serve the original sentence in full. The evidence
from the Chornovil group thus supports Armstrong's hypothesis about
the crucial influence of the Western Ukrainians, even though the influence is by no means onesided (note Karavans'kyi).

    3. On the other hand, a survey of the other documents and news
items discloses many names of apparent East Ukrainians, residents
of Kiev, Kharkov, and Dniepropetrovsk. My own rough count of articles
and major news items on Ukrainian dissenters in the five available
issues of Ukrains'kyi visnyk shows that 34 of a total of 134 items deal
with dissent in Western Ukraine. This is a considerable but not overwhelming proportion. A more precise count of the Ukrainian dissenters,
from the same comprehensive source, by Bilinsky, shows that only 306
of a total of 414 Ukrainian dissenters can be positively identified as to
regional origin. Of those who can be so identified, Western Ukrainians
number 151, or roughly 49 percent. But we would be the first to admit
that Western scholars should be extremely careful with such counts
of Soviet dissidents: The documents, although most probably authentic,
have not been systematically arranged; frequently they reach the West
only after several year's delay.

    The more interesting Eastern Ukrainian documents include the
relatively mild explanation by Ivan Dziuba of why in July 1963 he
stuck to his original plans to celebrate in Kiev the anniversary of the
poet Ukrainka, despite hints from the authorities that they viewed the
semiofficial celebrations very coolly.[73] There is a petition to the
Supreme Soviet of the Ukrainian SSR, the Ukrainian Party Presidium,
and the Ukrainian SSR Council of Ministers by 10 residents of Kiev,

dated February 25, 1964, proposing an increased use of the Ukrainian language, including Ukrainian-language schools and other cultural institutions in the Russian and Kazakh SSRs.[74] One could say that the West Ukrainian demands (for example, those of the seven "jurists") are more politically pointed, but certainly this is also true of Dziuba's big polemical work. Moreover, Dziuba's book does not in my judgment disclose any West Ukrainian influences: It appears to be right in the tradition of the East Ukrainian Communist writings of the 1920s and early 1930s, the tradition of the temporary Ukrainization.

To return to Armstrong's hypothesis: The Soviet policy toward all Ukrainians has been so heavyhanded and so vacillating over time, and Stalin's death provided so great a release, that the Eastern Ukrainians with their greater latent nationalism could not help but become more conscious and more militant, even without any assistance from the Western Ukrainians. On the other hand, the latter may have played the role of catalyst or of an additional, perhaps even critical, stimulus in many cases. Only a systematic and very detailed study on the basis of many more documents than are presently available can disentagle the many influences and crossinfluences from West Ukraine to East Ukraine and vice versa. Short of such a monumental effort, the impact of Western Ukraine should neither be under- nor overestimated. Before concluding, I would like briefly to consider economic and social ties.

ECONOMIC TIES

At the end of World War II the Western Ukraine was essentially an agricultural region. This appears grosso modo from our table on urbanization (Table 6.4) as well as from the more precise statistics that Soveit authors have cited. According to the Polish population census of 1931, for instance, 75.6 percent of the population of Polish-held Western Ukraine lived off agriculture, and only 9.9 percent were employed in industry as artisans.[75] Polish agricultural statistics show both the overall paucity and unequal distribution of land in Galicia and Volhynia.[76] In northern Bukovina the distribution was even more lopsided.[77] A vivid picture of the Galician village may be conveyed by the following extract from a Soviet study:

> Out of the 320 households which existed in Tuchapy [Lviv Province] before 1939, 150 had less than 2 morgy [1.4 hectares] land, 100 had between 2 and 5 morgy [1.4 to 3.5 hectares], 21 possessed up to 10 morgy [7 hectares],

TABLE 6.4

Dynamics of Urbanization in Western Ukraine
(population in thousands)

Area	1939		1959		1970		Percentage of Urban Population		
	Total	Urban	Total	Urban	Total	Urban	1939	1959	1970
UkrSSR	40,469a	13,569	41,869	19,147	47,127	25,689	34	46	55
Donetsk-Dneiper Region	14,760	7,426	16,548	10,871	20,057	14,107	50	66	70
Southern Region	4,852	1,785	5,066	2,465	6,381	3,641	37	49	57
Southwestern Region I b	12,807	2,607	12,455	3,704	11,935	4,932	20	30	41
Southwestern Region II	8,049	1,751	7,799	2,107	8,755	3,009	22	27	34
(Western Ukraine)									
Provinces									
Volhynia	1,032	169	890	231	974	313	16	26	32
Transcarpathia	—	—	920	265	1,057	314	—	29	30
Ivano-Frankivsk	1,282	294	1,095	249	1,249	384	23	23	31
Lviv	2,452	779	2,108	821	2,429	1,149	32	39	47
Rovno	1,058	139	926	158	1,048	288	13	17	28
Ternopil	1,413	204	1,086	180	1,153	269	14	17	23
Chernivtsi	812	166	774	203	845	292	20	26	35

[a]Does not include Transcarpathia Province, annexed in 1946.
[b]Territory under Soviet rule since 1921.

Sources: Population figures and percentages for 1939 and 1959 from Itogi vsesoiuznoi perepisi naseleniia 1959 goda: Ukrainska SSR (Moscow, 1963), Table 5, p. 16. Absolute population figures for 1970 from Itogi vsesoiuznoi perepisi naseleniia 1970 goda (Moscow, 1972), vol. 1, pp. 16-17. Percentages calculated by the author.

and 28 families did not have either land nor houses—they
hired themselves out as laborers. On the other hand, the
21 rich peasants had on the average 50 morgy [35 hectares]
of land each, also 15 cows and 8 horses.

The poor people led a hard life. This . . . demonstrated by the fact that during a comparatively short
period 60 peasants from Tuchapy emigrated into various
countries of the world, in search of work.

There was in the village only a two-class elementary
school; there was no club, no hospital, but on the other hand
there were as many as three saloons. The path to [further]
education for the children of Tuchapy was blocked. In the
entire village there were only two college students: one
was the son of a rich peasant, the other was the priest's
son. This is what Tuchapy looked like before 1939.[78]

The Soviet approach to the hundreds of Tuchapys has been to
carry education into the villages (of which more later) and to collectivize the peasant households, a process finished by about 1951. The
collectivization helped to establish political control over the villages
and also to cut off the armed nationalist underground from its bases
of support.[79] However, there are recent indications that it failed to
solve the perennial problems of rural overpopulation and unemployment. For instance, the editors of Ekonomika Radians'koi Ukrainy
in July 1969 reported on an article received from I. Popov, a candidate of economical sciences, and N. Popova, a graduate student, both
from Lviv University. Both authors complained of rural overpopulation. In 1965 in the Ukrainian SSR there were, on the average, 64
country dwellers per 100 hectares of agricultural land, but in Western
Ukraine the proportion rose to 109 rural dwellers and to as many as
117 in Lviv Province.[80] They recommend the introduction of labor-
intensive forms of agriculture such as cattle raising and the cultiva-
tion of linen, potatoes, and fruit.[81]

In somewhat more general terms, involving urban unemployment
as well, there are revealing forecasts by M. H. Ihnatenko, a candidate
of geography at Chernivtsi University, which were published in a relatively esoteric collection of scholarly papers. Ihnatenko has estimated
that in 1970 only 72 percent of the ablebodied urban population and 88
percent of the ablebodied rural population would find jobs in Western
Ukraine, the combined average being 83.4 percent. Furthermore, as
admitted by Ihnatenko, the employed rural population includes many
people who are considerably underemployed. Refining his estimates
to exclude mothers with small children and so on, he concludes that
about 335,000 people are not likely to find employment in Western

Ukraine unless the government immediately starts building a number
of labor-intensive chemical industries in that region—which, incidentally, has already been promised. A majority of the unemployed
(65.4 percent) are in the West Ukrainian towns and cities.[82]

For our purposes, the most important question is: How many
of the unemployed do leave those provinces to seek work in Eastern
Ukraine, in Russia, and beyond? Unfortunately, I have not been able
to find any absolute figures on such outmigration in the Soviet sources
available to me, nor could I calculate those figures on the basis of
differences between the expected natural increase and the actual increase. One Soviet geographer, writing on Rovno Province, while
studiously avoiding the disclosure of any migrant totals, has nonetheless provided us with some interesting breakdowns. There is a net
outflow of youths aged 16 to 19 because there are only two colleges
in the province. (Lviv Province offers more educational opportunities,
to be sure, but it is Rovno that may be the more typical West Ukrainian province.) Most mobile in both influx and outflow are persons in
the age group 20 to 29. Most migrants move to other provinces of the
Ukrainian SSR (an average of 74.8 percent in the years 1961-64). In
the same period, 12.9 percent migrated to the Russian Republic and
7.3 percent went to Kazakhstan. The migrants go mostly into the
neighboring Ukrainian provinces, but they also move into the industrial
areas of Eastern Ukraine, notably Donetsk Province. The peasants
among the migrants are being resettled into the Crimea, the Nikolaev
and Kherson oblasts. The author also voices complaints about the
number of unemployed in the towns of Rovno Province (more than
13 percent of the labor force).[83]

Turning to industry, there is little doubt that by Soviet Ukrainian
standards (large factories, machine building, fuel extraction) the Western Ukraine was underdeveloped.[84] At the same time it should not be
forgotten that in 1938-40 consumer goods and food were much more
plentiful in formerly Polish Galicia and Volhynia than in Eastern
Ukraine. Thousands of badly clothed and ill-fed Soviet citizens then
rushed under all kinds of pretexts into Galicia, and in particular into
Lviv. To many of them, the Western Ukraine gave a taste of the European luxuries from which they had been rigidly isolated by Stalin's
policy.[85]

After the war the Soviet government decided to quickly indus-
trialize the Western Provinces.[86] The results have been quite impressive on the whole, although in the 1960s the disparity in favor of
Western Ukrainian industrial growth diminished and at least two
provinces (Chernivitsi and Transcarpathia) actually fell behind the
average Ukrainian growth rate.[87] Looking at the interpolated 1967
figures in Table 6.5, we note that from 1962 to 1967 not only did
Chernivitsi and Transcarpathian Provinces fail to keep up with the

TABLE 6.5

Economic Development in the Provinces of the Ukrainian SSR
(as percentage of All-Ukrainian levels; Ukrainian SSR = 100)

Province	Industry as Percentage of Gross Output of Industry and Agriculture, 1962	Per Capita Gross Output: Industry and Agriculture, 1962	Per Capita Gross Output: Industry		Per Capita Fixed Productive Capital in Industry		Consumption of Electric Energy 1962	Industrial Employees Per 1,000 Population	
			1962	1967	1962	1967	1962	1962	1967
Ukrainian SSR	71.5	100	100	100	100	100	100	100	100
Dnipropetrovsk	84.9	140	164	176	238	230	296	149	134
Donetsk	91.0	130	163	165	258	223	251	182	164
Zaporozhe	80.6	166	188	171	159	149	313	138	141
Voroshilovgrad	87.7	112	136	137	215	184	208	168	156
Kharkiv	83.4	143	165	140	96	97	97	160	143
Kiev	79.6	113	124	101	70	75	68	123	121
Odessa	69.8	113	109	96	65	59	53	86	83
Kherson	60.9	113	97	93	84	84	46	85	95
Crimea	69.7	96	93	96	82	89	68	82	84
Lviv	77.7	87	94	88	73	92	56	90	99
Nikolaev	58.2	108	87	80	61	63	52	85	91
Sumy	56.8	88	70	76	50	64	32	78	85
Kirovograd	44.5	93	58	60	67	65	43	58	59
Poltava	58.7	93	76	80	41	60	30	72	79
Chernivtsi	63.1	74	66	63	31	31	23	65	69
Cherkassy	48.7	79	54	59	43	52	29	52	56
Zhytomyr	55.2	66	51	58	37	43	22	62	70
Ivano-Frankivsk	59.8	48	39	47	45	77	17	54	63
Chernihiv	43.2	82	50	72	27	41	19	43	53
Transcarpathia	5.2*	51	47	44	36	33	18	63	75
Vinnytsia	465.4*	73	47	51	29	34	19	41	47
Volhynia	47.5	55	37	37	39	36	21	46	49
Rovno	46.8	56	37	48	30	34	23	47	55
Khmelnytsk	39.0	66	37	45	26	28	18	39	44
Ternopil	34.1	55	27	34	22	25	14	30	35

*Printing error; most probably should be:: Transcarpathia, 65.2; Vinnytsia, 45.4.

Sources: For 1962, see M. M. Palamarchuk, V. D. Siiusar, and S. I. Bazhan, "Rivni ekonomichnoho rozvytku raioniv Ukrains'koi RSR i osnovi napriamy ikh zblyzhennia," Materialy pershoho z'izdu Heohrafichnoho tovarystva URSR (Kiev, 1966), p. 78. For 1967, see M. M. Palamarchuk, "Sblizhenie urovnei razvitiia material'nogo proizvodstva oblastei Ukrainskoi SSR," Ukrainskai la SSR: Ekonomi- cheskie rienoy (Moscow, 1972), p. 221.

TABLE 6.6

Ethnic Composition of the Western Ukraine, 1930 and 1970
(percentages)

Province	Population (1,000s)	Ukrainian	Russian	Jewish	Polish	Hungarian	Romanian	Others
1930								
Volhynia	999.3	74.7	0.6	10.7	10.6	–	–	3.4[a,b]
Transcarpathia	725.0	62.1	–	14.1	–	17.9[a]	–	5.9[a,b]
Ivano-Frankivsk[c]	1400.8	72.7	–	12.3	13.5	–	–	1.5
Lviv	2315.0	59.3	–	12.8	26.8	–	–	2.1
Rovno	1033.6	74.7	0.6	10.7	10.6	–	–	3.4
Ternopil	1339.7	59.8	–	12.0	27.3	–	–	0.9
Chernivtsi	854.0	67.2	1.2	14.0	3.3	–	14.3[d]	–
1970								
Volhynia	974	94.9	4.1	–	–	–	–	0.9[e]
Transcarpathia	1057	76.5	3.3	1.0	–	14.4	2.2	2.6[e]
Ivano-Frankivsk	1249	95.0	3.7	–	–	–	–	1.2[f]
Lviv	2429	87.9	8.2	1.1	1.7	–	–	1.0[f]
Rovno	1048	93.5	4.3	–	–	–	–	2.2[g]
Ternopil	1153	96.0	2.3	–	1.3	–	–	0.4[h]
Chernivtsi	845	68.8	6.3	4.4	–	–	10.0	10.5[h]

Notes: (1) Percentages were calculated by the author from absolute figures obtained from sources. For simplicity's sake, former Izmail Province, a section of Bessarabia, has been omitted. In 1954 that province was united with Odessa Province, and it is difficult to present data on that area for 1930 and impossible to do so for 1959. All province boundaries are those of 1959.

a Computed on the basis of absolute figures interpolated from Kubijovyc.

b Includes 34,000 Czechs and Slovaks (4.7 percent); the remainder are Germans.

c Formerly Stanyslaviv Province.

d This is a maximum figure, which contains a number of German settlers. For both Chernivtsi Province and former Izmail Province, Kubijovic gives the following numbers: 257,000 Romanians; 97,000 Bulgarians; and 80,000 Germans. Bulgarian settlements in Bukovina are not known, while German ones are.

e Includes 10,000 (0.9 percent) Slovaks.

f Includes about 12,000 (0.5 percent) Belorussians.

g Includes about 14,000 (1.3 percent) Belorussians.

h Includes about 78,000 (9.3 percent) so-called Moldavians.

Sources: Prewar figures are from the Czechoslovak and Romanian censuses of 1930 and the Polish census of 1931, as recalculated by Lew Shankowsky, formerly of Prolog Research Associates, New York City, to fit the 1959 boundaries. Shankowsky used detailed village-by-village results and administrative maps in these adjustments. The Polish figures have been modified somewhat to adjust for apparent falsifications with respect to the number of Ukrainians. Less detailed breakdowns (by areas of political subordination, not provinces) are available in Volodymyr Kubijovyc, ed., Ukraine: A Concise Encyclopedia, vol. 1 (Toronto, 1963), pp. 212–13, "Table II: Ethnic Composition of the Population of Ukrainian Lands in 1932". I have interpolated some absolute figures from this table in order to compute the indicated entries. Figures from 1970 are from Radians'ka Ukraina, April 25, 1971, p. 2; also in Digest of the Soviet Ukrainian Press, no. 6 (1971): 20–23.

average increase in gross industrial output per capita but also that output declined in much more important Lviv Province. What little industry there is in Volhynia has been stagnating. On the other hand, industry in Ternopil, Rovno, and Ivano-Frankivsk provinces is being built up more repidly than in the Ukraine as a whole. Even more interesting is the fact that industry in Ivano-Frankivsk (petro-chemicals?) is being rapidly capitalized (note the jump from the fixed productive capital in industry, per capita, in share of the Ukrainian average, from 44 percent in 1962 to 77 percent in 1967). Commenting on the economic development of the Western Ukraine in general, Vsevolod Holubnychy wrote to me:

> A general observation can be made on the basis of these data that between 1962-1967, there took place a slight shift to the west and north in the location of industries on the whole territory of the [Ukrainian] republic. This trend is planned to continue.

For instance, while the plan for 1975 calls for a percentage increase in the gross value of output of industry and agriculture per capita of 173 for the Ukrainian SSR (1965 = 100), in the Western Ukraine the planned increment is between a low of 182 for Chernivtsi Province and a high of 259 for Ivano-Frankivsk Province.[88]

What impact will all these developments have on the Eastern Ukraine? Whether West Ukrainian industry was developing more slowly than Ukrainian industry as a whole (in the mid-1960s) or faster (as planned for the early 1970s), for a considerable number of years the Western Ukraine is apt to remain comparatively underdeveloped in the overall economic sense. Paradoxically, some Western Ukrainian assets such as natural gas and electric power have been exported to East European countries and to Russia rather than to Eastern Ukraine. However, there are some indications that in the late 1950s (the heyday of Khrushchev's economic "autonomization"?) the commercial ties with Eastern Ukraine increased while those with the Russian Republic decreased.[89] It would have been interesting to make a similar analysis for the late 1960s to see whether Western Ukraine is being strongly integrated into the rest of the Ukraine, but I have not seen any relevant data.

The rapid industrialization has provided the regime with an excellent opportunity to import, into Western Ukraine, East Ukrainian and Russian officials, managerial and technical personnel, and industrial workers whose loyalty to the government has been tested. To a certain extent this was advisable for economic reasons, too: More than half the industrial workers had been non-Ukrainians (mostly Poles),[90] and in 1944-46 a great many Poles were repatriated to Poland, creating

TABLE 6.7

Ethnic Composition of Cities and Towns in Western Ukraine, 1959
(percentages)

City	Population (1,000s)	Ukrainian	Russian	Jewish	Belorussian	Polish	Hungarian	Romanian	Slovak	Other
Lviv	410.7	60	27	6	1	4	0	0	0	2
Chernivtsi	146.1	43	22	25	0	0	0	7	0	4
Ivano-Frankivsk[b]	66.5	66	24	2	0	2	0	0	0	6
Lutsk	56.3	76	19	1	2	1	0	0	0	1
Rovno	56.2	67	26	2	2	3	0	0	0	0
Ternopil	52.2	77	17	0	0	4	0	0	0	2
Izmail	48.1	32	60	3	0	1	0	3	0	1
Uzhhorod	47.4	50	17	4	1	0	12	0	12	4
Mukachevo	46.4	57	16	5	0	0	16	0	1	5
Drohobych	42.1	70	23	3	1	3	0	0	0	1
Stryi	36.2	68	25	2	0	2	0	0	0	2
Kolomyia	31.3	72	19	3	0	4	0	0	0	2
Boryslav	28.6	80	12	0	0	4	0	0	0	4
Sambir	23.6	72	16	0	0	8	0	0	0	4
Zolochiv	10.5	76	16	0	0	4	0	0	0	4

Note: Prior to 1939, Chernivtsi and Izmail were under Romanian rule; Mukachevo and Uzhhorod were in Czechoslovakia; and the remaining cities were in Poland.

[a]Moldavians according to official Soviet statistics.

[b]Formerly Stanyslaviv.

Sources: Total population figures from Itogi vsesoiuznoi perepisi naseleniia 1959 goda: Ukrainskaia SSR (Moscow, 1973), Table 6, pp. 17ff. Nationality percentages derived from graphs in V. I. Naulko, Karta suchasnoho etnichnoho skladu naselennia Ukrains'koi RSR (Kiev, 1966), made available to the author by Prolog Research Associates, New York City. Absolute figures for population by nationality in these cities have not been published.

many vacancies.[91] The number of immigrant East Ukrainians cannot be determined accurately, while the number of Russians is relatively easy to guage: There being only an insignificant number of Russians in Western Ukraine before the war (a total of 22,400, as shown in Table 6.6) even in the cities (see Table 6.7), practically the entire Russian population in Western Ukraine in 1959 consisted of newcomers (403,-000 - 22,400 = 380,600).[92]

Very interesting data are available on the process of penetration. Among the technical industrial personnel in Lviv Province, for example, native Galicians constituted only 56 percent of the total; among the manual workers they made up 64 percent.[93] If we disregard the small share that might still be held by the remaining Poles (total Polish population in the province was 51,900 in 1959) and let ourselves be guided by the vague figure of "close to 70 percent" for Ukrainians among the industrial workers,[94] we arrive at the following rough estimate: About 56 percent of the technical industrial personnel in Lviv Province are native Galicians (mostly Ukrainians), about 14 percent are Eastern Ukrainian immigrants, and the rest (some 30 percent) are Russians with a sprinkling of Jews, Belorussians, and other Soviet nationalities. (In 1959 Lviv had 27 percent Russians, 6 percent Jews, and 1 percent Belorussians; see Table 6.7). One West Ukrainian refugee believes he has discerned a definite immigration pattern: A Russian official assigned to Lviv will first establish his family, then he will call for his parents and older relatives, who will be given jobs and apartments commensurate with their frequently lower educational qualifications (as nightwatchmen, house superintendents, and so on). Thus we obtain a simultaneous colonization process on several socioeconomic levels. Assuming that the East Ukrainian and Russian immigrants will remain in touch with their friends "back home," the Western Ukraine must exert some impact on the old pre-1939 Soviet society, but this is very difficult to measure.

But there is another economic impact, which fortunately is much more concrete than the movement of goods in 1955-59 or the personal ties maintained by East Ukrainian and Russian immigrants (some of the latter may also hail from Eastern Ukraine). Under Polish rule some of the most capable of the Ukrainian intelligentsia were kept out of government service and industry and willy-nilly went into the agricultural and consumers cooperative movement, which grew by leaps and bounds.[95] They acquired a lot of management experience that helped them in the early 1960s to develop the notion of the Soviet "firm." As Leon Smolinski has pointed out, the idea was first applied in Poland. But the first Soviet firm was set up in Lviv in September 1961,[96] and by November 1963 the concept had spread to the eastern provinces of the Ukrainian SSR, to Georgia, the Turkmenian SSR, and the Russian Republic. About 568 enterprises in the USSR had been

united in about 150 firms.[97] The first firm, called Progress, was a
union of shoe factories in various West Ukrainian towns that were
subordinated to the Lviv sovnarkhoz. They agreed to coordinate production and specialization, thus achieving significant economies.
Later, cutting across jurisdictional lines, the firm opened its own shoe
store in Kiev; it was quite popular, as was their other shop in Lviv.
Fizprylad, a Lviv firm manufacturing scientific apparatus for schools,
opened branches in Dniepropetrovsk, Lugansk, and Odessa, among
other places. The firms are now trying to integrate research and
manufacturing processes at several plants. They seem to have been
actively supported by local party functionaries and to have received
the sanction of the All-Union party under Khrushchev, but now they
appear to be running into opposition from jealous ministries.[98] In
summary, they are successful anomalies in that they function without
any clearcut legal sanction—an interesting contribution to the Soviet
economy by enterprising West Ukrainian managers.

In conclusion we may say that, despite determined efforts at
industrialization, the Western Ukraine, with the possible exception
of Lviv Province, still presents a picture of relatively low productivity per capita in both industry and agriculture, coupled with overpopulation and high unemployment and underemployment. This appears
in Table 6.5. If the Western Ukraine has exercised an impact on the
republic and All-Union economies, it has been chiefly owing to several
valuable traditional resources such as oil and natural gas (now diminishing in importance) and the enterprising spirit and organizational
ability of industrial managers (a resource that has been appreciated
only since the early 1960s). The Western Ukraine exerts some demographic influence on Eastern Ukraine, but I have not been able to
measure it. In more general terms, owing to large-scale investments
in Western Ukraine, commercial transactions, and population transfers,
a greater homogeneity is being established between Western and Eastern
Ukraine, which would favor a greater integration of the Western provinces into the Ukrainian Republic as a whole and could help the Western Ukraine in extending influence in certain areas. But those areas
are apt to remain somewhat limited, because from an overall economic
viewpoint Western Ukraine is still the weaker partner.

EDUCATIONAL AND SCIENTIFIC TIES

Within a year of the occupation of Galicia and Volhynia, the
Svoiet government strengthened the network of primary and secondary
schools. Of particular interest was the adding of 136 new full secondary ("ten-year") schools to the 157 secondary schools operating in

September 1939. For the first time, 35 secondary schools were located in West Ukrainian villages.[99] The Soviet government could similarly improve the school system in northern Bukovina and Transcarpathia.[100] It would appear that, between the two basic categories (urban and rural, the latter being as a rule inferior), the Western Ukraine has been covered with an adequate network of primary and secondary schools.

In higher education, the regime also has realized some welcome opportunities. An entirely new university was established in Uzhhorod, the capital of Transcarpathia, in 1946, and the Univeristy of Lviv was renamed in honor of West Ukrainian poet Ivan Franko and given the order of Lenin on its three hundredth anniversary in 1961.[101] Various technical institutes have been set up. In all, college enrollment in Western Ukraine rose from 10,800 in 1945-46 to 111,100 in 1965-66, with added possibilities for higher education in Kiev, Kharkov, Odessa, Moscow, Leningrad, and other cities.[102] I have not been able to determine how many students in the Western Provinces are native Western Ukrainians; 76 percent of the student body in the mid-1960s consisted of Ukrainians, but this figure obviously included arrivals from Eastern Ukraine.[103] In April 1969, in an open letter, Soviet citizen A. Koval' demanded:

> Abolish the unwritten instructions concerning the limitations on admission to higher educational institutions of emigrants (vykhidtsiv) from Western Ukraine (on the territory of Eastern Ukraine), and also of Jews.[104]

Although the evidence appears authentic, the existence of a numerus clausus against West Ukrainians at East Ukrainian universities has not been confirmed by other sources, nor is it clear how long this policy may have been in effect. It may have been instituted in the wake of the arrests of Ukrainian nationalists in 1965.

If we do not raise such questions about the composition of the student body in West Ukrainian colleges, the aggregates look rather impressive. For instance, in 1950-51 West Ukrainian higher educational institutions graduated 6,146 out of a total of about 33,900 college graduates in the Ukraine as a whole, or about 18 percent.[105] This would correspond to the share of the Western Provinces in the total population of the Ukrainian SSR in 1959 (18.6 percent). Even more interesting is a time series for the most advanced Western Province, Lviv. In 1946-50 its higher schools graduated 8,900; in 1951-55 the figure was 19,600; and in 1956-60 it was 31,900 students. The corresponding figures for the Ukrainian SSR being 126,000 and 203,100 and 190,500, we obtain the share of the Lviv oblast in the production of college-educated "specialists" as follows·

7.1 percent in 1946-50; then 9.7 percent in 1951-55; and 11.0 percent in 1956-60.[106] The population of Lviv Province numbering but 5 percent of the total population of the Ukrainian SSR (in 1959), we cannot but conclude that at least one province of Western Ukraine has grown into a major center of higher education for the entire republic. But my evidence does not show to what extent the colleges of Lviv draw on West Ukrainian students and to what extent they serve Eastern Ukraine, quite apart from Russia and other republics. Nor have I come across data showing conclusively the distribution of college graduates from Lviv. I do know that as of December 1960 Lviv Province employed only 38,000 professionals with college degrees.[107]

The deliberate staffing of West Ukrainian schools and colleges with East Ukrainian and other "old Soviet" personnel is important not only for studying the incorporation of Western Ukraine but also for gauging a possible impact on Eastern Ukraine through news sent back by the new immigrants. The situation in the schools after the war was unsatisfactory from the regime's point of view. About half of the school teachers were indigenous personnel who had obtained their education in Polish, Czech, and Romanian schools.[108] In Lviv Province, as late as 1950, things were rather scandalous. According to a Soviet author:

> Out of 6,917 teachers only 410 were Party members, and 64 percent of the teachers had remained on the occupied territory. Individual teachers would go to church and would advise their pupils not to attend school on religious holidays. As a result of such "educational work" in a number of villages of the Lviv Province not more than 20-25 percent of the pupils would go to school on religious holidays.[109]

To eradicate such shortcomings, the government in 1945 dispatched 10,358 school teachers from the Eastern Ukrainian provinces and other Soviet territories into Western Ukraine, 9,368 in 1946, then 6,100 in 1947, and 5,638 teachers in 1948.[110] Altogether, in 1946-50 some 30,000 school teachers were sent to Western Ukraine.[111]

Figures on imported university professors are rather fragmentary. According to one source, in 1945 alone some 398 college faculty administrators were sent to the Western Provinces from the eastern area[112]; another has it that in 1944-45 as many as 938 scientific and scholarly personnel were dispatched to Western Ukraine, including 69 full professors.[113] In any case, this was a considerable proportion; for as late as September 1950 the total faculty in West Ukrainian colleges numbered 2,200.[114] In the mid-1960s there were 479 Ukrainians on the faculty of Lviv University (there had been "only a few" under

Poland), of whom 259 had been born in the Western Ukraine—an indication of the continuing large share of nonindigenous personnel.[115]

In 1968 a biographical directory was published in Soviet Ukraine, including brief biographical data on 1,644 "doctors of science" and full professors who were then employed by higher education institutions of the Ukrainian SSR.[116] Unlike the biographical directories of the USSR Supreme Soviet, this book does not give nationality but it does state place of origin, which allows us to calculate the number of Western Ukrainians: 59, or 3.6 percent. Of interest may be the further breakdown according to region. In inverse order of annexation, one senior scholar came from Transcarpathia, three from Bessarabia and Bukovina, 11 from Volhynia, 33 from Galicia, ten from Ukrainian borderlands that in 1945 were included in Poland, or from Poland itself, and one had been born in Czechoslovakia. All but 12 were teaching in Western Ukraine. Who are the exceptions? One woman from Bukovina (Turkevych) has lived in the Eastern Ukraine since before the war and has continued teaching there. The same applies to five scholars from Volhynia (Katz, who has taught in Chernivtsi since 1955, and Lazarevych, Skrypchyns'ka, Sliusars'kyi, and Volyns'kyi) and two scholars from Galicia (Shkvaruk and Shtokalo). In all, only four scholars and scientists who were born in the Western Ukraine (Galicia, specifically) and started their academic career there have been able to transfer to East Ukrainian institutions: the graphic artist V. I. Kasiian, who was educated at Charles University in Prague and now occupies a chair at the Kiev Institute of Fine Arts; the mathematician I. I. Danyliuk (born in 1931), a graduate of Lviv University (1958) who worked for the Siberian Division of the USSR Academy of Sciences (1958-65) and in 1965 became a professor of newly established Donetsk Univeristy and director of the Donetsk computer center of the Ukrainian SSR Academy of Sciences; O. S. Parasiuk, of whom more later; and the medical scientist Iu. D. Iatsozhyns'kyi, a graduate of the new Ivano-Frankivsk (Stanyslaviv) medical school (1951) who taught at the Tadzhik medical school (1959-64) and since 1964 has held a chair at the Crimean medical school. To cite another criterion relevant to their potential impact, seven of the fifty-nine have been awarded Lenin prizes: surgeon Fedynets' from Transcarpathia; agricultural scientists Hzhyts'kyi and Kyiak; artist Kasiian; composer Nicholas F. Kolessa; mathematician Shtokalo, and electrical engineer Maksymovych. All except Maksymovych are from Galicia. Maksymovych was born in today's Lublin Province (Poland) but had taught at the Lviv Polytechnical Institute before becoming rector of Lviv University in 1963.

A partially overlapping biographical register is that of the full and corresponding members of the Ukrainian SSR Academy of Sciences, appended to the second volume of its official history (1967).[117] This register of the cream of Ukrainian scholarship lists both present and deceased members. Altogether 19 out of 243 full members (about 8 percent) had been elected from West Ukrainian lands along with 7 out of 181 corresponding members (about 4 percent). Seven of the full academicians had died before 1939, including the immensely influential historian Michael Hrushevsky.[118] Of the other 12 academicians, 7 died more recently: the literary historian M. S. Vozniak and his colleagues V. H. Shchurat and K. I. Studyns'kyi; international lawyer V. E. Hrabar (Transcarpathia); the folklore scholar and musicologist Filaret M. Kolessa; the mathematician M. P. Kravchuk; and the historian I. P. Krypiakevych.[119] Alive are physicist O. I. Leipuns'kyi (acutally born in Poland, he has been teaching in Eastern Ukraine and Russia); chemical engineer B. S. Lysin (Volhynia); mathematician O. S. Parasiuk; mechanical engineer H. M. Savin (born in Poland, he has held responsible academic positions in Western Ukraine); and the mathematician I. Z. Shtokalo. (The inclusion of Leipuns'kyi and Savin could be debated, since the two are not from Western Ukraine.)

If the membership of the West Ukrainians in the Ukrainian Academy of Sciences may seem small, we must not forget that some of the foremost West Ukrainian scholars have sought refuge in the West rather than risk possible mistreatment at the hands of the NKVD and KMGB. On the other hand, the ablest West Ukrainians are not barred from making a career on an all-Ukrainian scale. Take, for instance, the mathematician Ostap S. Parasiuk. Born in 1921, he graduated in 1947 from Lviv University and stayed there as a graduate student in 1947-49. While teaching at Lviv University in 1947-56, Parasiuk was invited to the Ukrainian SSR Academy of Sciences Institute of Mathematics, where in 1955 he defended a Soviet "doctorate" in mathematics. In 1956 he was offered a teaching position at Kiev University, becoming a full professor there in 1957. In addition he has held several research appointments: deputy director of the academy's Mathematics Institute, 1956-66; section head in that institute since 1957; learned secretary of the academy's Section of Physics; and division head in the academy's Institute of Theoretical Physics.[120] Parasiuk's way may have been smoothed by follow mathematician and fellow Galician Shtokalo, who has been teaching in the Eastern Ukraine since 1931, or Parasiuk may have advanced entirely on his own. In any case, among West Ukrainian scholars he stands in a class by himself, proving that very able men will have a direct impact beyond their native region.

To summarize, it would appear that traditionally, as in economics, so in education and science—the Western Ukraine has been below East Ukrainian Soviet standards. In addition, many of the most prominent West Ukrainian scholars emigrated to the West during World War II.

The Soviet government brought in tens of thousands of school teachers and hundreds of college professors from Eastern Ukraine; feedback from them must have had a certain impact on those who stayed behind, but its extent is difficult to gauge. In the 1960s Lviv became a major center of higher education serving more than the Western Ukraine, but again we lack precise data. Individual West Ukrainian scientists and scholars have made successful careers in Eastern Ukraine, but their numbers are still low when compared to all-Ukrainian totals. On the basis fo such fragmentary data, I am tempted to conclude that the impact of Western Ukraine in education and science might be greater than its impact in economics, but certainly smaller than its impact in politics. An earlier (conference) version of this essay also included a brief section on the impact of religion as practiced in Western Ukraine. For reasons of space, I am omitting it here; it is easy to demonstrate that religion, including an underground Catholic church, is alive in Western Ukraine despite all the contrary efforts of the regime. Because of religious differences (most Eastern Ukrainians are Ortho- dox, while most Western Ukrainians were Catholic until 1946), how- ever, it would be difficult to prove that the Western Ukraine has exerted any major influence upon the Eastern Ukraine in this area.

CONCLUSIONS

In this essay I have tried to summarize the possible impact of Western Ukraine on Eastern Ukraine in several fields: official party politics, the gray area of literary and political protest movements, economics, education, and science. It appears that it is in the field of dissent that the contribution of the Western Ukrainians may be the most important, although it is far from insignificant in other fields. But how great will the West Ukrainian contribution to Ukrainian nation- hood turn out to be in the long run, if the bulk of Ukrainians demon- strate a tendency to assimilate themselves to the Russians?

Karl W. Deutsch has stressed the importance of six underlying factors or balances in any analysis of assimilation: the similarity of communication habits (language and culture); the existence of facilities for learning and teaching the new language and culture; frequency of contacts between members of different nations; the distribution of material rewards and penalties; the existence of compatible or incom- patible values and desires between the nations; and the persistence or withering away of political and social symbols and barriers.[121] As I have sought to document elsewhere, in the Ukraine the first three balances would be favorable to assimilation; the last three (distribu- tion of material rewards and penalties, different values, and the

persistence of political symbols and barriers) are not. Possibly a
very gradual assimilation with the Russians will result.[122]

The advocates of the disappearance of the Ukrainian nation may
point to the fact that, whereas in the 1959 population census 93.5 percent of the Ukrainians living in the Ukraine gave Ukrainian as their
native language, in the 1970 census only 91.4 percent did.[123] But
Walker Connor has sharply questioned the proposition that linguistic
assimilation is equivalent to national assimilation, and I believe he
is right.[124] Common wisdom has it that East Ukrainian cities, as
opposed to those in Western Ukraine, have been largely Russified,
but the Soviet ethnographer Pokshishevskiy has noted the growth of
the Ukrainian component in the population of Kiev and has supposed
that "some Kievans, after some hesitation whether to consider themselves Ukrainian, later did so with absolute conviction; more children
of mixed marriages have also declared themselves Ukrainians."[125]
In short, there is a serious question among scholars both in the West
and in the Soviet Union whether the assimilation of the Ukrainians,
their disappearance in the Russian sea, is indeed as inevitable as the
Soviet government would like to assume. In any case, the vicious
persecution of Ukrainian intellectuals, the trials in 1965-66 and again
in 1972-73, and the removal of the Ukrainian Party Secretary Shelast
for nationalist deviations[126] would indicate that the attempted assimilation—whether or not it is successful in the end—is far from being a
smooth natural process that could be conveniently hidden under the wide
cloak of modernization.

What may be the ultimate contribution of the Western Ukrainians
in this process of attempted assimilation? It would seem to me that
at the very least they will help to delay it; at most, they can help to
reverse it. Consider some of the intangibles in the situation, which
by their very nature are almost impossible to document.

The West Ukrainians (most notably the Galicians) are the products of an almost totally different world. Under the relatively liberal
Austrian rule after the late eighteenth century, they had built up an
impressive network of schools and cooperatives, and they had also
benefited from the unifying authority of a firmly rooted church. Polish
rule in the interwar period was on balance too weak to stop this process of cultural, economic, and political growth. On the contrary, it
stimulated and partly overstimulated it (as in the development of the
fervently nationalistic OUN). It would seem that living side by side
with Poles over generations led to a peculiar love-hate relationship
that, perhaps unconsciously, has influenced the Galician mentality:
the aristocratic notion that the elites have a duty to serve the national
cause together with some of the aristocratic disdain of the common
masses; the insistence on discipline and unquestioning obedience from

subordinates; a somewhat romantic conception of military and political
struggle; and above all, pride in having built the infrastructure of a
small state and in having preserved native culture against inroads from
the West—these are the features that are peculiar but not exclusive to
the Galicians. Many of them also share with the Poles a total rejection
of the Russians as barbarians. In addition, the hard Galician soil has
made them quite enterprising, adept at both economic and political
organization.

The Eastern Ukrainians, on the surface, appear more individual-
istic (sometimes to the point of anarchy), easygoing, and "soft". It is
on closer acquaintance that many of them also show much common
sense and hardheadedness, together with a capacity for sustained work.
But the generations of Russian rule—the destruction of Ukrainian political autonomy and the nearly total suppression of Ukrainian cultural
institutions under the tsars, the terror and famine under Stalin—have
left deep scars on their mentality. They do not believe that individual
Russians are absolute enemies; they have lived with them side by side
too long. An innate sense of practicality may lead some of them to see
a virtue in bowing to the demands of the stronger neighbor, thus
spreading the cancer of demoralization. (There is a certain wistful
admiration in the poems of Symonenko and Drach addressed to Lviv,
"the city of lions," and to the West Ukrainian poet Shashkevych.) On
the other hand, many East Ukrainians are sufficiently proud of the
language of Shevchencko and of the Ukrainian culture to speak up in
public (as at the Congress of Writers in 1966), to write petitions, dis-
tribute leaflets, and to go to jail. Many do resent Moscow's heavyhanded rule in the Ukraine no less intensely than the West Ukrainians and
are prepared to go to forced labor camps to prove the strength of their
convictions (Luk'ianenko, Chornovil, and others).

After some preliminary, limited interchanges in the nineteenth
century as well as in the interwar period, and after the more intensive
exchange of views and men in the last 30 years, there now seems to be
a real synthesis between the two parts of the Ukraine, manifested by
the wave of widespread arrests, political trials, and demonstrations
in 1965-66. Future historians may confirm and minutely document
the West Ukrainian contribution to the political and cultural development of the Ukraine; the melding of the two parts is taking place before
our eyes.

NOTES

1. See Roman Szporluk, "Nationalities and the Russian Problem in the U.S.S.R.: An Historical Outline," Journal of International Affairs 27, no. 1 (1973): 32ff. and passim: also Szporluk, "The Nations of the USSR in 1970," Survey 81, no. 4 (1971): 90ff. and passim.

2. I owe this point to Robert S. Sullivant.

3. James N. Rosenau, "Toward the Study of National-International Linkages," in James N. Rosenau, ed., Linkage Politics: Essays on the Convergence of National and International Systems (New York, 1969), pp. 44-63.

4. R. V. Burks, "The Communist Policies of Eastern Europe," in ibid., pp. 275-303.

5. Philip E. Jacob and Henry Teune, "The Integrative Process: Guidelines for the Analysis of the Bases of Political Community," in Philip E. Jacob and James V. Toscano, eds., The Integration of Political Communities (Philadelphia, 1964), pp. 16-45.

6. Karl W. Deutsch, Nationalism and Social Communication: An Inquiry into the Foundations of Nationality (New York, 1953), pp. 130-37.

7. Walker Connor, "Nation-Building or Nation-Destroying?," World Politics 24, no. 3 (1972): 337. See also Hermann Weilenmann, "The Interlocking of Nation and Personality Structure," in Karl W. Deutsch and William J. Foltz, eds., Nation-Building (New York, 1963), p. 46; Isaiah Berlin, "The Bent Twig: A Note on Nationalism," Foreign Affairs 51, no. 1 (1972): 22,27.

8. Gunnar Myrdal, Asian Drama: An Inquiry into the Poverty of Nations (New York, 1968), vol. 1, pp. 57-69.

9. V. V. Pokshishevskiy, "Urbanization and Ethnogeographic Processes," Problemy urbanizatsii v SSSR (Problems of urbanization in the USSR) (Moscow, 1971), pp. 53ff., as translated in Soviet Geography: Review and Translation 13, no. 2 (1972): 116. See also Szporluk, "Nationalities and the Russian Problem," pp. 38, 38n for other references to Pokshishevskiy and to Iu. V. Arutiunian.

10. Calculated from Itogi vsesoiuznoi perepisi naseleniia 1959 goda: Ukrainskaia SSR (Results of the All-Union census of 1959: Ukrainian SSR) (Moscow, 1963), p. 11, Table 1. The Crimea has been counted as part of the Ukrainian SSR in January 1939 although it was not annexed until 1954. Source hereinafter cited as Itogi perepisi UkrSSR.

11. See Jaroslav Bilinsky, The Second Soviet Republic: The Ukraine After World War II (New Brunswick, N. J., 1964), pp. 84-89, 415-17.

12. Not to mention the more important ones in the Russian SFSR. See, for example, Volodymyr Kubijovych, ed., Ukraine: A Concise Encyclopedia (Toronto, 1963), vol. 1, Table 1, pp. 210-11.

13. Jacob and Teune, "The Integrative Process," pp. 35ff.

14. See Pravda, June 13, 1953, p. 2.

15. Cited issues, editorials on page 1 of each.

16. See, for example Narysy istorii Kommunistychnoi Partii Ukrainy (Outline history of the Communist Party of Ukraine) (2nd rev. ed.; Kiev, 1964), hereinafter cited as Narysy ist. KPU. Also V. Iu. Malanchuk et al., L'vivs'ka oblasna partiina orhanizatsiia: Korotkyi narys (The Lviv provincial party organization: a brief outline) (Lviv, 1961), hereinafter cited as Lviv obl. part. orh.

17. For more details, see John A. Armstrong, The Politics of Totalitarianism: The Communist Party from 1934 to the Present (New York, 1961), pp. 245-47; Bilinsky, The Second Soviet Republic, pp. 233-41; Borys Lewytzkyj, Die Sowjetukraine 1944-1963 (Cologne, 1964), pp. 66, 87-89. According to the 1971 letter of seventeen Latvian Communists, on June 12, 1953 the Politburo of the Communist Party of the Soviet Union in a secret session decided to reverse Stalin's nationality policy. See "Obrashchenie 17 kommunistov Latvii k rudo-voditeliam riada kompartii, a takzhe k Aragonu i Garodi po povodu provodimoi pravitel'stvom SSSR politiki assimiliatsii i iskoreneniia vsego natsional'nogo v Latvii, iiul'-avgust 1971 g." (Appeal of 17 communists of Latvia to the leaders of a number of communist parties as well as to Aragon and Garaudy concerning the policy of assimilation and rooting out of everything national in Latvia which is being carried out by the USSR government, July-August, 1971), Arkhiv Samizdata (Samizdat Archives), AS no. 1042 (Munich), p. 3.

18. The authors of Ukrain'ska Radians'ka Entsyklopediia (Ukrainian Soviet encyclopedia) (Kiev, 1965), vol. 17, pp. 151a, 197a, call this a blunder. Membership figure from Narysy ist. KPU, p. 451.

19. V. L. Varets'kyi, Sotsialistychni peretvorennia u zakhidnykh oblastiakh URSR (v dovoiennyi period) (Socialist transformations in the Western Provinces of the UkrSSR, in the prewar period) (Kiev, 1960), p. 152.

20. According to Khrushchev's speech at the Sixteenth Congress of the CPU, there were 521,078 CPU members "up to" the Fifteenth Congress in May 1940. See XVI z'izd Kommunistychnoi Partii (bil'-shovykiv) Ukrainy 25-28 sichnia 1949 r.: Materialy Z'izdu (Sixteenth Congress of the Communist Party, Bolshevik, of Ukraine, 25-28 January, 1949: Materials of the congress) (Kiev, 1949), p. 46; hereinafter cited as XVI z'izd KP(B)U.

21. Narysy ist. KPU, p. 456.

22. See ibid., p. 528, for UkrSSR total as of January 1, 1946. Other figures from O. A. Kirsanova, Torzhestvo istorychnoi spraved-

lyvosty: Zakonomirnist' vozz'iednannia zakhidno-ukrains'kykh zemel'
v iedynii Ukrains'kii radians'kii derzhavi (Triumph of historical justice: A law of history fulfilled in the reunification of Western Ukrainian lands in a single Ukrainian Soviet state) (Lviv, 1968), pp. 663-64;
hereinafter cited as Torzhestvo (1968).
 23. Based on delegate count in XVI z'izd KP(B)U, pp. 237-52.
No key for representation has been given in the report of the mandate
commission (ibid., pp. 109ff.); I have calculated it by dividing the total
of full members by the total of voting delegates (572,950 / 657 = 870),
repeating the procedure for candidate members and nonvoting delegates (111,325/85 = 1,310). Aggregate figures by Khrushchev, ibid.,
pp. 46. The delegates also represent troops, police and so on stationed
in the Ukrainian SSR. Another source gives the total regular CPU
membership as 78,837 for July 1, 1948. See V. P. Stoliarenko and Kh.
Sas, "Diial'nist' partorhanizatsii v period kolektyvizatsii zakhidnou-
krains'koho sela (1947-1950 rr.)" (Activity of the party organization
during the collectivization of the West Ukrainian village, 1947-50),
Ukrain'skyi istorychnyi zhurnal (Ukrainian historical journal), no. 5
(1963): 72; hereinafter cited as Ukr. ist. zh.
 24. The republican total was 684,275; see note 12 above (572,950
+111,315).
 25. Torzhestvo (1968), p. 663.
 26. Ibid., p. 666.
 27. The 1947 figure was obtained by addition of the social categories in Lviv obl. part. orh., p. 191; 1954 figure given directly in
ibid., p. 190.
 28. Torzhestvo (1968), p. 191.
 29. Ibid., p. 192.
 30. The former 21 emerged from a lengthy study of Soviet Ukrainian newspapers, the latter seven have been conveniently assembled
in Digest of the Soviet Ukrainian Press (hereinafter DSUP), no. 3 (1971):
1-2. Their careers have been checked against Lewytzkyj, op. cit., pp.
299-371; Deputaty Verkhovnogo Soveta SSSR: Sed'moi sozyv (Deputies
of the USSR Supreme Soviet; Seventh convocation) (Moscow, 1966); and
Deputaty Verkhovnogo Soveta SSSR: Vos'moi sozyv (Deputies of the
USSR Supreme Soviet: Eighth convocation) (Moscow, 1970).
 31. Lewytzkyj, Die Sowjetukraine, p. 89; Stefanyk's other son
is living in Canada.
 32. See especially Radians'ka Ukraina (Soviet Ukraine), July
29, 1972, p. 1, as translated in DSUP, no. 9, (1972): 8-10. Also sources
cited in note 30 above.
 33. See Radio Liberty, Issledovatel'skii biulleten' (Researchers'
bulletin) 16, no. 41, TsIO 278/72 (1972): 2. The full title of his 696-
page dissertation, translated into Russian, is "Torzhestvo leninskoi
natsional'noi politiki (Kommunisticheskaia partiia-organizator

razresheniia natsional'nogo voprosa v zapadnykh oblastiakh UkrSSR)''
(The triumph of the Leninist nationality policy: the Communist Party
as the organizer of the solution of the nationality problem in the Western Provinces of the UkrSSR)(Lviv, 1963). See also official announce-
ment and biography in Radians'ka Ukraina, October 11, 1972, p. 1.

34. The Ukrainian-American newspaper Svoboda (Liberty) on
August 9, 1973, p. 1, reported the arrest of nine dissident Ukrainian
Lviv University students by the KGB. Reportedly, a commission
headed by Malanchuk recommended that they be tried, whereas a
parallel commission from Moscow recommended their release and
their professors' dismissal from the university, but no trials.

35. T. H. Rigby, Communist Party Membership in the U.S.S.R.,
1917-1967 (Princeton, N.J., 1968), pp. 389-90; the quotation is on p. 389.

36. Ibid., p. 390.

37. Jacob and Tuene, "The Integrative Process," pp. 23-29.
Possibly their factor of homogeneity also could be applied (ibid., pp.
18-23) since they tend to give it a considerable attitudinal component.
But they choose a social rather than a political connotation for the
term homogeneity.

38. John A. Armstrong, Ukrainian Nationalism (2nd rev. ed.;
New York, 1963), pp. 309-10.

39. Lew Shankowsky, Pokhidni hrupy OUN: Prychynky do istorii
pokhidnykh hrup OUN na tsentral'nykh i skhidnikh zemliakh Ukrainy v
1941-43 rr. (Raiding groups of the Organization of Ukrainian Nationalists: Contributions to the history of the OUN raiding groups in the
central and eastern lands of Ukraine in 1941-43) (Munich, 1958), p. 35.

40. Ibid., pp. 71-72.

41. Ibid., pp. 71-74, 106-07, 116-17.

42. Ibid., pp. 55, 104, 164-67. See also Armstrong, Ukrainian
Nationalism, passim.

43. The significance of this particular point has been discussed
in ibid., pp. 294-95.

44. The struggle has been analyzed in ibid., pp. 291-304 and in
Bilinsky, The Second Soviet Republic, pp. 111-40, 417-22.

45. A very interesting source is the semifictional account of
Vladimir Beliaev and Illarion Podolianyn, Ekho Chernogo Lesa (Echo
from the Black Forest) (Moscow, 1963: 365,000 copies). The authors
apparently are concerned about the persistence of the echo; UPA's
success in sending men underground into various cities of the Eastern
Ukraine and even Russia. More recent but much more limited in circulation is the incidental analysis by Leonid A. Leshchenko, Ukraina
na mizhnarodnii areni, 1945-1949 (The Ukraine in the international
arena, 1945-49) (Kiev, 1969; 1,200 copies), pp. 145-49, 187-209,
which represents the most explicit and scholarly Soviet treatment so

far. In somewhat veiled but truly artistic form, the UPA appears in
the short story by Lviv writer Iaroslav Stupak, "Hordynia" (Pride),
Vitchyzna (Fatherland) (Kiev), no. 12 (1966); 18-24.

46. See Posev (Sown land) (Frankfurt/Main), no. 4, (1969): 10.
Suchasnist' (The present times), no. 3 (1969): 105, identifies Makukh
as an OUN member but dates his suicide to May 11, 1968. Both sources
agree that he died shouting "Long live a free Ukraine!"

47. Literatura Ukraina (Literary Ukraine)(Kiev), November 17,
1966, pp. 3, 5.

48. Ibid., November 20, 1966, p. 1 and DSUP, no. 1, (1967): 20.
See, however, Miss Vil'de's complaints about lack of progress in
cultural matters in Lviv in the same editions: Lit. Ukraina, p. 2.
DSUP, pp. 10-11.

49. See the documents forwarded from the Mordovian labor
camps reprinted as Ukrains'ki iurysty pid sudom KGB (Ukrainian
jurists tried by KGB courts) (Munich, 1968), pp. 46-47; hereinafter
cited as Ukr. iurysty (1968). Other trials on which fewer details are
available are the Protsiv trial involving six persons in Lviv in 1962,
which ended with the execution of Protsiv; the Mykola Apostol trial
in Ternopil in 1961 (five persons; Hohus' was sentenced to death).
See ibid., p. 75. The materials have been translated in Michael Browne,
ed., Ferment in the Ukraine (London, 1971), pp. 29-93. See pp. 69-70,
80 for translation of references.

50. See the document reproduced in Suchasnist', no. 3 (1969):
101-2.

51. Quotation from the court decision in Kandyba's petition,
Ukr. iurysty (1968), pp. 27-28. See also Browne, Ferment in the
Ukraine, p. 56.

52. Ukr. iurysty (1968), pp. 31-33; Browne, Ferment in the
Ukraine, pp. 59-60.

53. According to Luk'ianenko, Ukr. iurysty (1968), pp. 59-60;
Brown, Ferment in the Ukraine, p. 35.

54. Program, p. 3 as quoted by Kandyba, Ukr. iurysty (1968),
p. 33; Browne, Ferment in the Ukraine, p. 60.

55. Luk'ianenko, Ukr. iurysty (1968), p. 62; Browne, Ferment
in the Ukraine, p. 37.

56. Ukr. iurysty (1968), pp. 62-63; Browne, Ferment in the
Ukraine, p. 37.

57. Ukr. iurysty (1968), pp. 29-30; Browne, Ferment in the
Ukraine, p. 58.

58. Ukr. iurysty (1968), pp. 25-27; extract from court decision.
See also Browne, Ferment in the Ukraine, pp. 55-56.

59. Ukr. iurysty (1968), pp. 60-61 (Luk'ianenko). See also
Browne, Ferment in the Ukraine, pp. 35-36.

60. Ukr. iurysty (1968), p. 60; KGB agent had been planted in Luk'ianenko's cell. See Browne, Ferment in the Ukraine, pp. 35-36.

61. Ukr. iurysty (1968), p. 62; Browne, Ferment in the Ukraine, pp. 36-37.

62. See Stephen Constant, Sunday Telegraph (London), September 14, 1969. For text of petition see Browne, Ferment in the Ukraine, p. 216.

63. See Vasyl Symonenko, Bereh Chekan' (The shore of expectation), ed. Ivan Koshelivets, (New York, 1965); this is his diary and a selection of his poems, including works that have not been published in the USSR. I have briefly analyzed Symonenko's impact in my article, "Assimilation and Ethnic Assertiveness Among Ukrainians of the Soviet Union," in Erich Goldhagen, ed., Ethnic Minorities in the Soviet Union (New York, 1968), pp. 166-69.

64. Ivan Dziuba, Iternatsioalizm chy rusyfikatsiia? (Internationalism or Russification?) (Munich, 1968). Published in English as Ivan Dzyuba, Internationalism or Russification?, preface by Peter Archer, barrister-at-law, M.P., (London, 1968). The work was written in 1965.

65. Viacheslav Chornovil, Lykho z rozmu: Portrety dvadsiaty "zlochntsiv" (Woe from wit: Portraits of twenty "criminals") (Paris, 1967). Partially translated into English along with his May 22, 1966, petition in Chornovil Papers, preface by Zbigniew Brzezinski and introduction by Frederick C. Baarghoorn (New York, 1968).

66. Valentyn Moroz, "Reportazh iz zapovidnyka Berii" (Report from Beria's reservation), in Suchasnist', no. 3 (1968): 58-64; no. 4 (1968): 78-86; no. 5 (1968); 75-84; no. 6 (1968): 77-82; translated in Browne, Ferment in the Ukraine, pp. 119-53. Moroz, "Khronika soprotivleniia" (Chronicle of resistance), January 1970, in Arkhiv Samizdata, Sobranie dokumentov samizdata (Collected samizdat documents), vol. 6 (Munich, n.d.), AS no. 411. Moroz, "Sered snihiv" (Among the snows), in Suchasnist' no. 3 (1971): 64-81; or Sobranie dokumentov samizdata, vol. 11, AS no. 596. Moroz, "Zamist' ostann'oho slova" (In lieu of the final word) (n.d.—November 1970), in Ukrains'kyi visnyk (Ukrainian herald) (Paris-Baltimore), no. 6 (1972): 93-97.

67. Sobranie dokumentov samizdata, vol. 10, contains the first 24; the last three are separately available under the code numbers AS no. 1130, AS no. 1155, and AS no. 1200.

68. Ukrains'kyi visnyk, nos. 1, 2 (January and May, 1970; Paris-Baltimore, 1971), 246 pp.; no. 3 (October 1970; Paris, 1971), 118 pp.; no. 4 (January 1971; Paris, 1971), 191 pp.; no. 6 (March 1972; Paris, 1972), 183 pp.; no. 5 is not available.

69. Anatol' Kamins'kyi, "Z pryvodu spravy iurystiv" (Concerning the jurists' case), Suchasnist', no. 3 (1968): 78. The trials of June-September 1972, which took place in Kiev and Lviv, have been well

described in Khronika tekushchikh sobytii (Chronicle of current events), no. 27 (October 15, 1972), AS no. 1200, pp. 1-5.

70. This is the title of the poem. See Symonenko, Bereh Chekan', p. 167; or Ukrains'kyi visnyk, no. 4, p. 78.

71. The poem was presented as "Ia tak iak bachu kosmonavta . . ." (It is as if I saw the cosmonaut . . .) in Ivan Drach, Protuberantsi sertsia (Protuberances of the heart), pp. 19-20, and in distorted form as as "Druhovi" (To a friend) in Vitchyzna (Kiev), no. 8 (1964): 89, where an entire stanza and the reference to the Poles have been omitted.

72. See the excerpts from his diary in Chornovil, Lykho z rozmu (Ukrainian edition), p. 87; not translated into English.

73. Reprinted in Suchasnist', no. 8 (1968): 87-94.

74. Suchasnist', no. 9 (1968): 73-75. See also the discussion by George Luckyj in "Turmoil in the Ukraine," Problems of Communism, July-August 1968, pp. 14-20.

75. I. Ia. Kosharnyi, "Pidnesennia kul'turno-tekhnichnoho rivnia robitnykhiv zakhidnykh oblastei URSR" (Increase in the cultural and technological level of the workers in the western provinces of the UkrSSR), Ukr. ist. zh., no. 4 (1964): 39, citing Maly rocznik statysty- czny (Small statistical yearbook) (Warsaw, 1937), p. 32.

76. In 1931 a total of 36.4 percent of the households had less than two hectares (4.9 acres) each; 36.1 percent had between two and five hectares (under 12.4 acres); 13.9 percent between five and ten hectares (up to 24.7 acres); the rest up to 100 hectares (247 acres). See Varets' kyi, Sotsialistychni peretvorennia, p. 47, citing Maly rocznik statysty- czny (Warsaw, 1938), p. 63.

77. The average landlord in 1921 owned 751.1 hectares, the average small peasant 1.06 hectares. Cf. V. K. Lytvynov, "Revoliut- siinyi rukh na Bukovnyi v period svitovoi ekonomichnoi kryzy (1929- 1933 rr.)" (The revolutionary movement in Bukovina during the world's economic crisis of 1929-1933), Ukr. ist zh., no. 4 (1959): 71.

78. I. Hrynovets', "Sotsialistychni peretvorennia u seli Tuchapy" (Socialist transformations in the village of Tuchapy) in U borot'bi za radians'ku vladu i sotsializm (In the struggle for Soviet government and socialism) (Lviv, 1960), p. 182, hereinafter cited as U borot'bi (1960). The Austrian morgen approximates 0.7 hectares (1.95 acres).

79. See M. K. Ivasiuta, "Sotsialistychna perebudova sil'skoho hospodarstva v zakhidnykh oblastiakh Ukrains'koi RSR" (Sovialist reconstruction of agriculture in the western provinces of the Ukrain- ian SSR), Ukr. ist. zh., no. 4 (1959): 7-8.

80. "Pro vykorystannia trudovykh resursiv u kolhospakh: Ohliad redaktsiinoi poshty" (Concerning the use of labor resources on collec- tive farms: Review of the mail to the editor), Ekonomika radians'koi Ukrainy (Economy of Soviet Ukraine), no. 7 (1969): 65. Excerpts trans- lated in DSUP, no. 10 (1969); 6-9.

81. Ibid., p. 66

82. M. H. Ihnatenko, "Stvorennia trudomistkykh khimichnykh vyrobnytstv" (Creation of labor-intensive chemical production), Ekonomichna heohrafiia: Mizhvidomchyi naukovyi zbirnyk (Economic geography: An interdepartmental collection of scientific papters), no. 3 (Kiev, 1968; 700 copies), pp. 57, 57n, 58, 61.

83. M. O.Kovtoniuk, "Mihratsii naselennia ta ikh vplyv na liudnist' sil's'kykh naselenykh punktiv Rovens'koi oblasti" (Migrations of the populations and their influence on the population of the settled rural localities of Rovno Province), Ekonomichna heohrafiia, pp. 12-15.

84. See the brief study by V. N. Bandera, "Zachidnia Ukraina v ramkakh ekonomicy mizhvoiennoi Pol'shchi" (Western Ukraine in the framework of the economy of interwar Poland), reprint from Ukrainskyi Samostijnyk (Fighter for an independent Ukraine) (Munich), nos. 119-20 (1967), 11 pp.

85. See the anonymous but apparently authentic sketches in Milena Rudnycka, ed., Western Ukraine under the Bolsheviks: September, 1939-June, 1941 (New York, 1958), pp. 28-33 (by a Western Ukrainian) and pp. 34-52, esp. pp. 41, 43, 47-48 (by a journalist from Kiev). On the other hand, it may be that not all of the Galician workers had been able to buy expensive clothes, shoes, and so on. See V. K. Zadorozhnyi, Sotsialistychni peretvorennia i zrostannia dobrobutu trudiashchikh zakhidnych oblastei URSR (Socialist transformations and the increase in the living standard of the toilers in the western provinces of the UkrSSR) (Kiev, 1959). p. 6.

86. See H. I. Koval'chak, Rozvytok promyslovosti v zakhidnykh oblastiakh Ukrainy za 20 rokiv radians'koi vlady (1939-1958 rr.): Istoryko-ekonomychnyi narys (Development of industry in the western provinces of Ukraine during 20 years of Soviet rule, 1939-1958: A historico-economic outline) (Kiev, 1965), pp. 39-40, 40n.

87. The reader may be interested in comparing Table 2 in T. Telishevs'kyi and Il Kuhukalo, "30 rokiv u sim'i bratnikh radians'kykh narodiv" (30 years in the family of fraternal Soviet peoples), Ekonomika radians'koi Ukrainy, no. 10 (1969): 5, giving the relative growth rates,1940-68, with the figures for 1960-67 in Narodne hospodarstvo URSR v 1967 r.: Statystychnyi shchorichnyk (National economy of the UkrSSR in 1967: Statistical yearbook) (Kiev, 1968), p. 77; For the latter period the average Ukrainian growth rate is 181 (1960 = 100). Northern Bukovina is 167; Transcarpathia's growth rate was 169.

88. See M. M. Palamarchuk, "Sblizhenie urovnei razvitiia material'nogo proizvodstva oblastei Ukrainskoi SSR" (Rapprochement of the development levels of material production of the UkrSSR provinces) in Ukrainskaia SSR: Ekonomicheskie raiony (Ukrainian SSR: Economic regions) (Moscow, 1972), p. 225; as cited by Holubnychy.

89. Holubnychy communicated the following:

> In 1955 the Lviv economic administrative region
> received from the UkrSSR 71.6 percent of the total ship-
> ments and 28.4 percent from the rest of the USSR. In 1959
> the distribution changed as follows: 77.4 percent from the
> Ukrainian SSR and only 22.6 percent from the USSR.
>   From the Lviv economic administrative region were
> shipped to the UkrSSR in 1955, 59.9 percent, and to the USSR
> 40.1 percent of the total exports. In 1959 this changed as
> follows: shipped out to the UkrSSR 75.4 percent, to the USSR
> only 24.6 percent.
>   In 1955 the Stanyslaviv Ivano-Frankivsk economic
> administrative region received from the UkrSSR 51.3
> percent of its imports, and 48.7 percent from the USSR.
> In 1958 this changed to 59.3 percent of the total imports
> from the UkrSSR and 40.7 percent from the USSR.
>   From Stanyslaviv region were shipped to the UkrSSR
> 72.4 percent and to the USSR 27.6 percent of the total exports
> in 1955. The corresponding figures for 1959 were 74.5 per-
> cent and 25.5 percent.

The source is M. K. Rozdobud'ko, "Transport i mizhraionni zv'iazky
zakhidnykh ekonomichnykh raioniv Ukrains'koi RSR" (Transportation
and interregional contact of the western economic regions of the
Ukrainian SSR), in Pytannia rozvytku produktyvnykh syl L'vivs'koho
i Stanislavs'koho ekonomichnykh administratyvnykh raioniv (Problems
of the development of the productive resources of the Lviv and Stanyslaviv economic administrative regions), Vypusk 2 (Kiev, 1961), pp. 143-46.

90. Koval'chak, Rozvytok, pp. 23, 46.

91. About 810,000 Poles from Western Ukraine were then ex-
changed for approximately 480,000 Ukrainians from the borderlands
assigned to Poland. See M. D. Drak and V. P. Ohonovs'kyi in Torzhestvo
(1968), p. 659. Kosharnyi, "Pidnesennia," p. 42, writes that between
1946 and 1950 some 13,800 highly skilled workers and almost 2,000
engineers were imported to Galicia from Eastern Ukraine and the
USSR to help fill the vacancies.

92. I have deliberately used the 1959 rather than the 1970
census figures to minimize the factor of the natural increase of the
Russian colony in Western Ukraine.

93. Koval'chak, Rozvytok, p. 46n, also provides less precise
figures for the other western provinces.

94. Ibid., p. 46.

95. See on this the massive study by Illia Vytanovych, Istoriia Ukrains'koho kooperatyvnoho rukhu (History of the Ukrainian cooperative movement)(New York, 1964), pp. 315-496.

96. Koval'chak, Rozvytok, p. 177, and a lecture by Bohdan W. Czajkowskyj, of Prolog Research Associates, "Industry of the Ukraine as a Basis for Further Economic Experiments in the USSR," November 1963, used with his permission. Czajkowskyj is a prewar graduate of the Lviv Academy for International Trade. See also the following Soviet sources: I. S. Hrushets'kyi (first secretary of the Lviv obkum of the CPU) "Pershi radians'ki firmy" (The first Soviet firms), Ukr. ist. zh., no. 1 (1963): 3-12; I. Braniuk', "Firma: ee dela i nuzhdy" (The firm: its activity and needs), Partiinaia zhizn' (Moscow), no. 12 (1964): 13-18.

97. Czajkowskyj, "Industry of the Ukraine," p. 3.

98. Pyzhyk in Radians'ka Ukraina (Soviet Ukraine), October 11, 1969, p. 2, translated in DSUP, no. 11 (1969): 5-7. See also V. Petrushko and I. Politov, "Ways to Improve Management of Local Industry," Radians'ke pravo (Soviet Law), no. 8 (1969): 24-28; excerpts translated in DSUP, no. 11 (1969): 7ff.

99. T. Sokolovs'ka and I. Tolkachov, "Pershi kroky sotsialisty-chnoho budivnytstva v zakhidnykh oblastiakh URSR (1939-1941)" (The first steps of socialist construction in the western provinces of the UkrSSR), U borot'bi (1960), p. 14, a solid piece of research.

100. See the less precise figure by M. Hryshchenko, "Rozvytok narodnoi osvity v zakhidnykh oblastiakh URSR" (Development of public education in the western provinces of the UkrSSR), U borot'bi (1960), p. 201.

101. See Ukr. ist. zh., no. 6, (1961): 155-57, for data on the university. On Uzhhorod University, see Kommunist Ukrainy (Communist of Ukraine), no. 7 (1965): 35.

102. I. Ia Kosharnyi in Torzhestvo (1968), p. 739.

103. Ibid., p. 740. In 1939-41 some political activists from Eastern Ukraine who were relatively weak students were deliberately enrolled at West Ukrainian institutions; see Rudnycka, ed., Western Ukraine p. 201.

104. Anton Koval', "Vidkrytyi lyst" (Open letter), Suchasnist', no. 10 (1969): 102.

105. Former figure from P. P. Hudzenko, et al., eds., Rozvytok Ukrains'koi kul'tury za roky radians'koi vlady (Development of Ukrainian culture during the years of Soviet government) (Kiev, 1967), p. 240, hereinafter cited as Rozvytok Ukr. kul'tury (1967); latter figure for 1950, from Narodne hospodarstvo Ukrains'koi RSR v 1963 rotsi: Statystychnyi shchorichnyk (National economy of the UkrSSR in 1963: Statistical yearbook) (Kiev, 1964), p. 568, hereinafter cited as Nar. hosp. URSR (1963). No figure for 1951 is given.

106. Percentages calculated by author from absolute figures in Rozvytok Ukr.kul'tury (1967), p. 239; Narodne hospodarstvo Ukrains'koi RSR: Statystychnyi zbirnyk (National economy of the UkrSSR: A statistical handbook) (Kiev, 1957), p. 449; Nar. Hosp. URSR (1963), p. 568 for UkrSSR. For Lviv figures, see Narodne hospodarstvo L'vivs'koi oblasti v 1965 r.: Statystychnyi zbirnyk (National economy of Lviv Province in 1965: A statistical handbook) (Lviv, 1966), p. 246, hereinafter cited as Nar. hosp. Lviv (1965).

107. Nar hosp. Lviv (1965), p. 10.

108. A. D. Bondar, Rovytok suspil'noho vykhovannia v Ukrains'kii RSR (1917-1967) (Development of public education in the Ukrainian SSR, 1917-1967) (Kiev, 1968), p. 83.

109. Ibid., p. 122. Most likely, all but a few of those 64 percent were native Galicians, as were the religious teachers.

110. Ibid., p. 84. In 1945-46 there were in Western Ukraine, minus Transcarpathia Province, a total of 22,600 school teachers; see Kosharnyi in Torzhestvo (1968), p. 736.

111. Rozvytok Ukr. kul'tury (1967), p. 237.

112. Ibid., p. 240.

113. Kosharnyi, Torzhestvo (1968), p. 740.

114. Rozvytok Ukr. kultury (1967), p. 240.

115. Torzhestvo (1968), p. 741.

116. V. M Popov, et al., Ucheni vuziv Ukrains'koi RSR (Scholars at institutions of higher education of the Ukrainian SSR) (Kiev, 1968), p. 6.

117. Ie. Paton, ed., Istoriia Akademii Nauk Ukrains'koi RSR (History of the Academy of Sciences of the Ukrainian SSR) (Kiev, 1967), vol. 2.

118. The six others are Hnatiuk (Galicia), Lyps'kyi (Volhynia), Loboda (actually born in Lithuania), Pysarzhevs'kyi (Bessarabia), Symins'kyi (Grodno region), and Tarasevych (today's Moldavian SSR).

119. Unless specifically indicated, they are all from Galicia.

120. Ie. Paton, Istoriia, vol. 2., pp. 369-70.

121. Deutsch, Nationalism and Social Communication, pp. 130-37.

122. Yaroslav Bilinsky, "The Background of Contemporary Politics in the Baltic Republics and the Ukraine: Comparisons and Contrasts," in Arvids Ziedonis, Jr., Rein Taagepera, and Mardi Valgemae, eds., Problems of Mininations: Baltic Perspectives (San Jose, Calif., 1973), p. 112 and passim.

123. Radians'ka Ukraina, April 25, 1971, p. 2; or DSUP, no. 6 (1971): 20.

124. Connor, "Nation-Building or Nation-Destroying?", pp. 336-39.

125. Pokshishevskiy, "Urbanization and Ethnogeographic Processes," p. 118.

126. In late May 1972, Shelest was "transferred" to a deputy prime minister's post in Moscow. On April 27, 1973 he was dismissed from the All-Union Politburo "in connection with retirement." See Pravda, April 28, 1973, p. 1. Earlier, however, a Soviet Ukrainian party journal had attacked Shelest's 1970 book "O Ukraine, Our Soviet Land" for Ukrainian nationalism. See editorial, "Pro ser'iozni nedoliky ta pomylky odniiei knyhy" (Serious deficiencies and mistakes contained in one book), Kommunist Ukrainy, no. 4 (1973): 77-88.

**THE MOLDAVIAN SOVIET
REPUBLIC IN SOVIET
DOMESTIC AND
FOREIGN POLICY**
Stephen Fischer-Galati

On October 12, 1924, the Autonomous Moldavian Socialist Soviet Republic was established by the All-Ukrainian Executive Committee as part of the Ukrainian Soviet Socialist Republic.[1] The foundation of the Moldavian Republic was dictated by considerations of Soviet foreign policy; it was unrelated to any internal needs of the Soviet Union. The express purpose of the Kremlin was to formalize its opposition to the incorporation of Bessarabia into Romania at the end of World War I and to provide a political nucleus for the eventual reunification of all "Moldavians." Thus, from its inception the Moldavian Republic was a Soviet instrument for political action against Romania.

Artificial as it may have been in the 1920s and 1930s, the Moldavian Republic was by no means insignificant in terms of its political value to the Soviet Union. The republic was intelligently conceived and delineated. The boundaries were drawn to include a substantial segment of the Romanian population west of the Dniester but by no means all of the Romanian-speaking inhabitants of that area. The apportionment was designed to provide demographic proof of the relative proportion of Moldavians to other nationalities in the area stretching from Romanian Moldavia to Odessa. In the Moldavian Republic, the Romanian element amounted to approximately 30 percent of all inhabitants; the largest percentage, 48.5, consisted of Ukrainians. Statistically, the republic differed little from Bessarabia as a whole, where the Romanian population was a minority, often as small as 23 percent.[2]

The demographic configuration was emphasized in the establishment of the republic since the rationale for its establishment was the alleged illegality of the Romanian "seizure" of Bessarabia and the acceptance of the Romanian action by the European powers at the end of World War I. Demography alone, however, was insufficient as a

basis for legitimizing the Soviet case against the "rape of Bessarabia."
Historic arguments were therefore introduced to bolster the inalien-
able right of Moldavians to live in Soviet Moldavia. The Soviet Union
paid lip service to such standard propaganda themes as the revolutionary mission to liberate the working peasantry and working class from
the Romanian bourgeois-landlord regime and the hateful Moldavian
"boyars." It ultimately based its case on two distinct issues: the
legitimacy of Russia's historic claims to possession of Bessarabia
and the illegal dismemberment by anti-Soviet forces of the Democratic
Moldavian Republic, the self-governing unit of the Federative Democratic Russian Republic, first established in December 1917.[3]

Of the two historic claims, the former was less persuasive than
tha latter. The incorporation into Russia of Eastern Moldavia—or
Bessarabia—in 1812 was prompted by strategic and political considerations unrelated to the official justification for that action: reincorporation of a Russian province into mother Russia. The need for a safe
border and territorial base for the pursuit of the anti-Ottoman policies
of tsarist Russia outweighed all other considerations. In fact, the resti-
tution of certain segments of Bessarabia to Moldavia was first forced
upon Russia by the European powers concerned with Russia's proximity
to the Danube at the Congress of Paris in 1856 and then rescinded, for
reasons of European diplomacy, at the Congress of Berlin in 1878. No
matter what the rationale for incorporation, during the century from
1812 to the revolution the tsarist regime pursued a policy of Russification in Bessarabia directed primarily against the Romanian-speaking
inhabitants of the province. At the same time, the regime encouraged
Russians and Ukrainians to settle in Bessarabia. As a consequence of
the regime's anti-Semitic measures, Jews also were encouraged to
settle there.

Whether the Russian "melting pot" was nearing the boiling point
in 1917 is uncertain. But national and social antagonisms generated
by Romanian nationalist propaganda, anti-Semitism, and peasant pressures for agrarian reform were of utmost importance in the province.
As far as the Romanians of Bessarabia were concerned, opposition to
Romanian and Russian landlords and to Jewish merchants and money-
lenders appeared to take precedence over any clear program of political action aimed at reincorporation into a Greater Romania.[4] The
moment of crisis occurred in the spring of 1917 immediately after the
establishment of the provisional government. Indeed, the events
recorded between April 1917 and April 1918 are basic to Romanian
actions and Russian reactions to the "Moldavian" question discussed
in this essay.

THE BESSARABIAN PROBLEM AND THE
SOVIET MOLDAVIAN REPUBLIC TO 1940

The various claims and counterclaims regarding the accuracy of the records and the very sequence of events in the Moldavian crisis of 1917-18 have never been fully resolved.[5] It is, however, possible to piece together the fragments and summarize the relevant problems as follows. Immediately after the February Revolution, two currents developed in Bessarabia: a nationalist-Moldavian, favoring first autonomy and later union with the Old Romanian Kingdom, and an agrarian-revolutionary one, opposing union with "reactionary" Romania and demanding immediate expropriation of nonpeasant lands on behalf of the peasantry.

The relative strength of the two currents is difficult to ascertain inasmuch as the nationalists agreed with the agrarian-revolutionaries on the necessity of expropriation. In all probability, the Romanian peasantry was more concerned with acquisition of land than with union. By July 1917 the Romanian peasants, like the Ukrainians and the Russians, were seizing land indiscriminately, a process that resulted in the acquisition of over two-thirds of the large holdings in Bessarabia. In many instances the actions of the peasantry were spontaneous. In some cases, however, revolutionary agitators, mostly non-Romanian and frequently Jewish, were fanning the peasants' land hunger with a view toward denationalizing the Bessarabian problems. It is incontestable that the nationalist leaders, largely pro-unionist intellectuals, school teachers, and "liberal" landowners, decided to salvage the situation by maintaining the territorial and geopolitical integrity of Bessarabia proper. Therefore, immediately after the October Revolution, the Moldavian nationalist leadership convoked a national assembly (Sfatul Tarii) to safeguard the "historical and political autonomy" of Bessarabia. The express purpose of this action was to prevent peasant alienation stimulated by lavish Soviet promises, and to forestall the Ukrainian dissidents, who had broken with the Bolsheviks, from seizing Bessarabia by force. The failure of Romanian peasants to respond to nationalist propaganda, and the threat of destruction of the Sfatul Tarii by Ukrainians or Bolsheviks, ultimately forced the Romanian leadership in Bessarabia to announce in December 1917 the formation of a Democratic Romanian Republic as a self-governing unit in the Federative Democratic Russian Republic.[6] That action was expressly designed to prevent the seizure of power by the Bolshevik Soviets and provide a basis for Romanian military intervention on behalf of the republic. Indeed, in January 1918 Romanian troops marched into Bessarabia at

the invitation of the Sfat and ousted the Bolshevik Soviets. The Romanians then guaranteed the integrity of the "independent Moldavian
Republic," which the Sfat set up immediately after the Romanian army
had completed its mopping-up operations. In April 1918 the Sfat, by
an 86-3 vote (with 36 abstentions), legislated a union of Bessarabia
and Romania with the provisos that land secured by the peasants prior
to union would be guaranteed and that adminstrative autonomy would
be granted to the province by the rulers of Greater Romania.[7]

The validity of this union was immediately challenged by the
Bolsheviks, who regarded the vote as fraudulent and not representative
of the wishes of the majority of Bessarabia's population. The essential
argument was that the Sfat was improperly constituted, its membership
packed with pre-unionists, and, even under those circumstances, a
substantial number of the voters abstained from ratifying a decision
dictated by Romanian and German imperialists and Bessarabian collaborators.[8] There was more than a modicum of truth in those contentions, since many Bessarabian peasants and non-Romanian intellectuals
were opposed to union with "reactionary" Romania. The peasantry was
particularly suspicious of the Romanian ciocoi (landlords), whose
record with respect to agrarian servitude was anything but enviable.
It also is true that the union was railroaded by the nationalist Romanian leadership and that the demand for guarantees incorporated in the
resolution of April 1918 reflected the peasantry's fears rather than
the leadership's sense of social and political justice. However, the
Bolsheviks' claim that the Independent Moldavian Republic favored
Bolshevik control to secession and union with Romania was unfounded.
The number of militant Bolsheviks among the Romanian population—
even by the most conservative counts nearly 70 percent of Bessarabia's
inhabitants in 1918—was negligible. It was significant only within the
Jewish community and among Bulgarian, Russian, and Ukrainian intellectuals. Thus, it seems fair to say that in April 1918 union with
Romania was not a political prerequisite for safeguarding the independence of the Moldavian Republic but was preferable to the alternative
of Bolshevik control. In fact, the absentions recorded in April reflected
the desire of the non-Romanian members to maintain political independence as long as possible.[9]

It may be argued that the precipitous action of the Bessarabian
leadership and the Romanian government in establishing the union
played directly into the hands of the Bolsheviks. Had the Romanians
exerted more patience, the residual resistance to union would have
vanished in the face of the Russian reality and thus have reduced the
effectiveness of Bolshevik propaganda and subversion in Bessarabia
in later years. After 1918 the Bolsheviks not only challenged the legality of the union but also incited revolutionary action in Bessarabia,
which they represented as spontaneous manifestations of the population—

regardless of nationality—against Romanian oppression and in favor of restoration of the Democratic Romanian Republic of December 1917. Thus, the Autonomous Moldavian Socialist Soviet Republic created in October 1924 was, at least theoretically, the reincarnation of the Democratic Republic of 1917.

The Bolsheviks' claims to continuity and legitimacy were at best questionable; in fact, the transparency of their motives for establishing the Moldavian Republic negates the proffered reasons for that action. The Kremlin's ostensible concern for the well-being and future of the "Moldavian" population of Romanian Bessarabia and of the USSR itself was as baseless as the doctrine of deprivation resulting from the illegal seizure of Russian territory by the Romanians. Whereas it is true that the Romanian regime abided by the terms of the union stipulated by the Sfat in 1918 only until it secured ratification of the incorporation by the great powers, the fact is that the incorporation was ratified in the Bessarabian treaty of October 28, 1920.[10] And it was the legalizing of the union by Great Britain, France, Japan, and Italy that accelerated Moscow's decision to prevent the consolidation of Romanian power in the province.

From as early as April 1918 the Bolsheviks of Kishinev organized an armed political action committee that was to stage uprisings among the non-Romanian population, chiefly in the predominantly Ukrainian counties of Izmail and Hotin. The "Izmail plot" found no supporters in 1918; in Hotin, the number of conspirators was too small to insure anything but token action against superior Romanian police forces. The repression of the abortive rebellion in Hotin in January 1919 merely persuaded the Kishinev Bolsheviks to plan another uprising, this time to avenge the brutality of the Romanian regime and to rally all those who opposed the union to the Bolshevik cause. The new uprising, scheduled for March 1919, was postponed until July because of the Kishinev group's inability to coordinate its efforts with the Ukrainian forces and those of Bela Kun, who were to intervene simultaneously and "liberate" Bessarabia from Romania. The Bessarabian revolution, planned for July, was an abortive one because the Romanian secret service apprehended the Bessarabian Communist contingent prior to the uprising and thus discouraged intervention by would-be Ukrainian and Hungarian participants.[11]

By optimizing the "Bolshevik threat"—which in fact was negligible in terms of the actual support secured by the Bolsheviks in Bessarabia—the Romanians precipitated the ratification of the annexation of the province by the great powers. They also stiffened the Bolsheviks' determination to recoup Bessarabia. Thus, the Soviet government rejected the validity of the treaty of 1920 and continued to enlist supporters, primarily among Jewish intellectuals and students, for revolutionary purposes. With headquarters in Kishinev, several organizations such as the Jewish Bund of Kishinev and the MOPR (Mezhdunarodnoye Obschchestvo Pomoshchi Revolutsioneram—International Society for the Aid to Revolutionaries) coordinated efforts with terrorist organizations elsewhere in the USSR, primarily in Odessa, for the purpose of sabotaging the transportation system, terrorizing Romanian officials, and, above all, exploiting the growing disenchantment of the non-Romanian inhabitants of Bessarabia with the antiminority policies of the Romanian authorities. In 1923 the Bessarabian Revolutionary Committee was actually established in Odessa in preparation for both revolutionary and political action designed to frustrate the Romanization of Bessarabia and advance the Soviet Union's position of nonrecognition of the Bessarabian treaty.[12]

The confrontation between the Soviet and Romanian regimes on the status of Bessarabia assumed a critical turn in 1924 when formal negotiations between Russia and Romania over the establishment of a firm frontier broke down.[13] Moscow then decided to set up the Moldavian Republic as soon as the preliminary internal propaganda work was completed. Concurrently, the Soviets supported plans devised by various revolutionary organizations inside the Soviet Union and in Bessarabia proper to reunite Bessarabia with Russia. The dual thrust, the first successful and the second disastrous, ended in October with the establishment of the Moldavian Republic.

The Russian actions in 1924 were designed to force the Romanians to accept Russia's terms for a settlement of the Bessarabian question at a time of growing popular disaffection with Romanian policies in Bessarabia. The Romanian regime had reneged on many of the promises made in 1918, particularly with respect to Bessarabian autonomy and repartition of land to the peasantry, ostensibly because of the Bolshevik threat to the province and to Romania itself. It also chose to make nationalism the unifying force in Bessarabia and to question the loyalty of the non-Romanian inhabitants. The primary victims of Romanian discrimination were the Jews, branded as agents of the "Judaeo-Communist" conspiracy. The Bolsheviks countered the Romanian actions by stressing the advantages of life in the Soviet Union for all "Moldavians," regardless of national origin.

The creation in the Ukraine in June 1924 of a Department of Education for the purpose of promoting Moldavian culture was accompanied by the establishment of newspapers and the printing of readers and books in Romanian and by the gradual adoption of that language in official matters affecting the predominantly Romanian sections of the Ukraine.[14] It is difficult to assess the impact of these progressive measures in Bessarabia or, for that matter, among the Romanian-speaking population of the Soviet Union, but evidently they were insufficient to undermine the Romanian regime in Bessarabia proper. The

corollary revolutionary uprising planned by the Bolsheviks in Hotin
and Izmail failed when the incipient revolt in the Tatar-Ukrainian-
Russian village of Tatar Bunar was easily suppressed in September
1924 by superior Romanian forces. It was then that the decision
was made to minimize the failure in Tatar Bunar and to maximize the
Romanians' ostensible support for Soviet nationality by establishing
the Autonomous Moldavian Socialist Soviet Republic.[15]

The effectiveness of the Moldavian Republic in rallying the
forces of discontent outside its frontiers was minimal in the interwar
years. After 1924 the work of agitation and propaganda in Bessarabia
was conducted by members of the Bessarabian contingent of the Romanian Communist Party residing in Bessarabia proper or in Bucharest,
or through representatives of the so-called Moscow Bureau of the
Romanian Party who traversed the Russo-Romanian border as
required by the Kremlin. In general, revolutionary agitation and
action against the Romanian regime in Bessarabia declined after 1924,
partly because of the outlawing of the Romanian Communist Party in
that year but primarily because of the shift in Soviet policy whereby
a temporary accommodation with Romania was sought pending the
eventual settlement of the Bessarabian question on Soviet terms.

In the absence of membership information for the outlawed
Romanian Party in the interwar years, it is almost impossible to
determine the size and relative power of the "Bessarabian wing" of
the organization. It has been assumed that the Bessarabian contingent
was influential throughout the interwar years and it is known that men
like Petre Borila, Iosif Chisinevski and Leonte Rautu—all leading
figures in the party—were active in the Bessarabian movement from
as early as the Tatar Bunar rebellion. It also is known that they were
aware of Russia's plans to seize Bessarabia in 1940, as were many
members of the Romanian party who found themselves in Bessarabia
at the time of the reannexation of that province by the USSR. But
beyond that, no conclusive data is available to present a detailed
account of Moscow's campaign in Bessarabia after 1924 or of the
Kremlin's relations with its Bessarabian subordinates within the
province proper or the Romanian party in general.[16]

Meaningful information regarding Soviet Moldavia also is difficult to secure. As the Kremlin gradually abandoned the policy of revolutionary unification of Bessarabia with Soviet Moldavia, at least
through actions generated in the Moldavian Republic, the history of
the republic became virtually indistinguishable from that of the Soviet
Ukraine. Communism did not flourish in predominantly agrarian
Moldavia; in fact, the number of party members was infinitessimal
prior to World War II.[17] The Romanian population was particularly
inactive in political life. Romanian representation in the upper

echelons of the party and government was negligible; the principal
posts were invariably held by Russians and Ukrainians. The Moldavian Republic survived as part of the Ukraine and faced the same political and economic problems as the master republic until 1940, when
its political mission could again be justified by the Kremlin.

THE "REUNIFICATION" OF BESSARABIA
WITH THE MOLDAVIAN REPUBLIC, 1940-47

On August 2, 1940, following the seizure of Bessarabia and
northern Bukovina by the USSR, Stalin ordered the redrawing of the
boundaries of the Autonomous Republic and its elevation to the rank
of full-fledged Soviet republic—the Moldavian Soviet Socialist Republic.
The new republic had to face problems quite different from those of
its predecessors.

First, the boundaries of the republic were changed to improve
its "Moldavian" image. Northern and central Bessarabia were united
with less than half of the old autonomous republic to constitute a predominantly Romanian-speaking province. The greater part of the previous Moldavian Republic—over 1,900 out of 3,300 square miles—was
reunited with the Ukraine. The attempt to justify Soviet territorial
claims to Bessarabia and propaganda claims that "Moldavians" every-
where had at all times sought reunification within a Soviet Socialist
Moldavian Republic proved disastrous within a year of unification.
In June 1941 Romania joined Germany in a "holy war" for the reconquest of the territories seized by the Soviet Union in 1940, and within
less than a month Bessarabia and northern Bukovina were reoccupied.
A few weeks later the entire Moldavian Republic was occupied by the
Romanian armed forces; on August 19 the region between the Dneiper
and the Bug—an area corresponding to Podolia of earlier times and
exceeding even the most optimistic "Moldavian" boundaries ever
envisaged by either Russia or Romania—was renamed Transnistria
and placed under Romanian administration.[18]

Little is known about the reaction of the "Moldavian" population
to Romanian rule in Transnistria prior to the withdrawal of the Romanian forces in 1944 other than the fact that the Romanian armies and
regime were welcomed by the Romanian population in Bessarabia.
Evidence made available by Romania and Russia both during and after
the war tends to corroborate the Romanian claim that the Romanian-
speaking population of the Soviet Moldavian Republic was sympathetic
to the Romanian cause.[19] Presumably, this sympathy also was recognized by Great Britain at an early date. In November 1941 the British

government was prepared to recognize the legitimacy of Romania's claims to Bessarabia at least by requesting the withdrawal of the Romanian armed forces active in Russia only as far as the left bank of the Dniestr. In fact, the Romanians' refusal to limit their gains to Bessarabia alone resulted in the British declaration of war on Romania in December 1941.

The British position of 1941 had not been totally reversed by 1944 and found support in both the United States and Romania. It is precisely because of the positive reaction of the Romanians in Bessarabia and Romania proper, and the equivocation of the Western allies, that the Kremlin sought reconfirmation of the legality of the seizure of Bessarabia and northern Bukovina at a time when the allies were seeking the realignment of Romania on the side of the anti-German forces in April 1944. Russia's apprehensions regarding the intentions of its allies and possible contestation of its rights to Bessarabia were officially laid to rest on September 12, 1944, in the Armistice Convention with Romania when the "cobelligerent" Romanian regime acknowledged the legality of the Soviet annexation of Bessarabia and northern Bukovina in 1940. By the time the Romanian peace treaty was signed in February 1947, the very names of Bessarabia and northern Bukovina were expunged from all official maps and documents. And there were good reasons for not mentioning Bessarabia by name.[20]

Opposition to the cession of the provinces was still rampant in 1947 among anti-Communist political groups, in Romania as well as in exile, and the Russians seemed particularly anxious to consolidate their western frontier with all European neighbors at that time. In fact, Russia's plans for empire envisaged the rectification of prewar frontiers long before 1947; in the case of the Romanian border, at least from as early as 1943. The so-called Tudor Vladimirescu division organized that year under the leadership of the "Bessarabian" members of the Romanian Party was to be the vanguard of the "forces of liberation" from fascism for the occupied Moldavian Republic and later for Romania itself. In April 1944 the Russians reaffirmed their formal claims to Bessarabia with the tacit consent of their Western allies and supporters in Romania. Russia was to retain Bessarabia after the war and in return Stalin would repudiate the validity of the Vienna Diktat of 1940 whereby part of Romanian Transylvania was incorporated into Hungary on Hitler's orders. Recognition of the validity of Romania's claims to northern Transylvania and of Russia's claims to Bessarabia and northern Bukovina became explicit in March 1945 when Moscow consented to the reincorporation of northern Transylvania into Romania, while Bucharest reaffirmed the validity of the provisions of the Armistice Convention with respect to the provinces annexed by Russia in 1940. On a bilateral basis the Bessarabian question was resolved in 1945; the treaty of 1947 merely ratified the Russo-Romanian understanding. Unofficially, however, the Western allies, as well as a segment of the Romanian Communist leadership, had second thoughts about Bessarabia at the time of the signing of the peace treaty with Romania. In 1947 the Bessarabian question was closed de jure but not de facto. And it is in this context that the problems of the Moldavian Soviet Socialist Republic have to be examined.

SOVIET RULE IN THE MOLDAVIAN REPUBLIC AFTER 1947

A major unknown in any analysis of the problems related to the Moldavian Republic is the interrelationship between Russo-Romanian relations (at both the party and state levels) and the specific policies pursued by Moscow in Moldavia. This interrelationship is particularly obscure during the period antedating the Romanization of the leadership of the Romanian party and the corollary degrading of the Bessarabian contingent of the party between 1952 and 1956. It is, however, reasonable to assume that the Kremlin was at all time concerned over any Romanian action that would in any way allude to Bessarabia or to Russian "imperialism" in any form. The summary purging of Lucretiu Patrascanu in 1948 was to a significant extent caused by his questioning the fraternal intentions of the Kremlin toward the Romanian party and state, particularly with respect to Bessarabia and northern Bukovina.[21] And it also is clear that Titoism, incipient as it was in Patrascanu's case, and in its pure Yugoslav form, was regarded as a deadly and contagious disease by Stalin. The Kremlin's apprehensions also extended to contacts between Romanians on both sides of the Russo-Romanian frontier from at least as early as 1949 and were of more than passing concern by 1952.

The first detailed postwar account of developments in the Moldavian Republic is contained in the proceedings of the Second Congress of the Communist Party of Moldavia held in February 1949.[22] The speakers' principal purpose was to emphasize the economic gains attained by the republic following the reunification of Bessarabia. But the secondary theme, the inadequacy of political education, focused on the "idealization" of feudal Moldavia in literary and historical works and the prevalent "bourgeois-nationalist" distortions regarding the history of Moldavia. The same theme, with gradually growing emphasis on ideological deviations, was reiterated with vigor on the occasion of the twenty-fifth anniversary of the establishment of Soviet Moldavia in October 1949.[23] At that time the historic link between Bessarabia and Russia was explicitly delineated in terms of the century-long identity of interests, the rape of Bessarabia by "foreign

imperialists'' in 1918, and, above all, the mass murders committed
by the Nazi and Romanian forces during the three years of occupation
of Soviet Moldavia during World War II. No attempt was made to differentiate between Romanian ''fascists'' and Romanians in general.
In the historic context, the term Moldavian was made synonymous
with the Romanian-speaking population of the Soviet province. The
largesse of the Soviet Union toward the Moldavians, both before and
after ''liberation'' from the ''foreign'' occupation, singled out the
Romanian element. That emphasis apparently reflected the Kremlin's
concern over the political attitude of the Bessarabian peasantry, which
at that time was subject to the pressures of collectivization. It represented a deliberate policy of reorienting the national allegiance of the
Romanian population of the province away from Romania. Thus, Moscow's concern with Moldavia was politically rather than economically
motivated. Indeed, the statistical data provided at that time reveal the
fundamental economic insignificance of Soviet Moldavia to the Soviet
Union. Agricultural production in Soviet Moldavia represented less
than 1 percent of the total for the Soviet Union; industrial production
less than 0.5 percent.[24]

The doctrine of historic identification of the Romanian population
of Soviet Moldavia with Russia was restated and underlined on every
significant occasion. At the time of the tenth anniversary of the establishment of the republic, in 1950, the chairman of the Moldavian Council of Ministers, G. Rud, reaffirmed the Moldavians' faith in the ''Great
Russian people'' since the days of Yaroslav the Wise and the Russians'
historic struggle for self-determination.[25] In 1951, at the Third Congress of the Moldavian party, Leonid Brezhnev—then the party's secretary—reiterated the same doctrine while castigating the ideological
deficiencies of the Moldavians.[26] In September 1952 the plenum of the
party's Central Committee was devoted to reaffirmation of Soviet
historical doctrines relative to Moldavia and denunciation of improper
interpretations of that history. Brezhnev himself attacked the interpretations of the ''reunification'' of 1940 as erroneous, saying it was an
event that, in his view, represented ''an achievement of the Communist
Party's Leninist-Stalinist national policies.''[27] His criticisms were
echoed by other plenum participants, who roundly condemned the
idealization of the Moldavian historic past in poetry and literature and
the improper treatment by Moldavian historians of the ''seizure of
Bessarabia'' by Romania in 1918 and of the Romanian occupation of the
Moldavian Republic during World War II. The criticism singled out the
deliberate misconstructing of the degree of identification of the historic interests of Moldavians on both sides of the Russo-Romanian
frontier—which, according to the attackers, was not determined by
national considerations but by class hatred and common opposition
to imperialist aggression.

The scope and directness of the 1952 attacks reflected at the least
the prevalence of far-reaching "bourgeois-nationalist" heresies among
the Romanian population of Soviet Moldavia. A clue to the reasons for
this disaffection is provided by the repeated criticism voiced by Brezhnev's predecessor, N. G. Koval, by Brezhnev himself, and by other
members of the party and government from as early as 1950 regarding
the political education and unsocialist attitudes toward collectivization
displayed by Moldavians of Romanian origin. The rapid pace of collectivization in Bessarabia, which recorded a fourfold jump between 1949
and 1951, was not, at least to the peasants, the source of joy reported
by Brezhnev at the Third Congress of the party.[28] In fact, the disaffection of the Romanian population was recognized by Brezhnev himself in September 1951 when he attributed the unhealthy attitudes of the
collectivized peasantry to improper implementation of the provisions
of the collective farm statutes by overzealous officials and to shortcomings in the political education of the masses. Inasmuch as the
spread of "bourgeois-nationalist" and romantic heresies was mentioned at the same time, it is safe to assume that all was not well in
1951. By 1952 Romanian nationalism had to be reckoned with in practical political terms. On March 22 the proportion of the Romanian to
the non-Romanian population of Soviet Moldavia was altered through
an administrative reorganization that diminished the concentration of
Romanians in certain sections of the republic.[29] To compensate for
these changes, which in effect increased the political power of the
non-Romanian minority over the Romanian majority, the Kremlin began
to promote the development of publications in "Moldavian," ostensibly
as a reflection of Stalin's concern for the well-being of the Moldavians.
But that gesture was inconsequential in altering the essential subordination of the Romanian majority to the Russian and Ukrainian minorities that wielded power in Soviet Moldavia.[30]

The Russian concern with Moldavian culture, primarily in the
areas of education and linguistics, may very well have been prompted
by factors transcending domestic political considerations. It should
be noted that it was in the late spring of 1952 that Gheorghiu-Dej
scored a major victory over the Muscovite segment of the Romanian
party and enunciated the doctrine of the Romanian party's concern for
the well-being of and socialist progress for all Romanians.[31] The
possible reverberations in Bessarabia of the news of the degrading
of Ana Pauker and her "Bessarabian" supporters and the emergence
of a Romanian leadership in Romania cannot be discounted, particularly
since Stalin himself was at that time condemning "cosmopolitanism"
and encouraging "nationalist" anti-Semitic reactions in East Europe.

Be this as it may, it is evident that at the Fourth Congress of
the Moldavian Communist Party, held in September 1952, a policy

of economic progress and massive political education was formulated
by the Kremlin and by the Moldavian leadership.[32] At that congress,
as well as at the Nineteenth Congress of the CPSU, which followed
immediately, Brezhnev summarized the tremendous economic gains
achieved by the Moldavian Republic since the reunification of Bessarabia and provided statistical data that indicated a 21-fold increase
in the production of canned goods since World War II and a sevenfold
increase in the production of grapes. The prognosis for the following
five years was even rosier in view of the vast commitments of the
CPSU and the Moldavian party to the optimum exploitation and development of the Moldavian economy. Brezhnev also recited the achievements in education since reunification, particularly among the Romanian
population in the territories annexed in 1940. The pointed attack against
pre-World War II Romania was directed as much against the obscur-
antism of the old regime and its imperialist allies as against Moldavian intellectuals and, by inference, those who distorted the reality of
the past and failed to recognize the achievements of the present.[33]

Impressive as the statistical information may have been in the
educational-cultural field (elimination of illiteracy, existence of 46
institutions of higher learning and 26 research institutes) and, for that
matter, in the economic field, those achievements, as well as the plans
for future development, represented the fruition of narrow political
considerations. The Moldavian Republic in 1952, and also five and even
ten years later, remained a marginally viable political creation of the
Kremlin maintained, in the last analysis, as a justification for the
"reunification" of Bessarabia.

This basic contention is not invalidated by the fact that economic
progress was indeed achieved in the Moldavian Republic during the
Khrushchev era. The economic commitment to Moldavia was substantial in those years. Emphasis was placed on the development of agricultural products, particularly cereals, sunflowers, sugar beets, and
grapes, and the results were rewarding even to the perennial party
critics concerned with shortcomings in agriculture. Industrial growth,
mostly in such agriculture-related industries as canning and wine
making but also in machine building, also was impressive. According
to Soviet statistics, industrial production tripled between 1950 and
1958 and virtually doubled again between 1958 and 1964. Nevertheless,
inasmuch as the economic growth of the Moldavian Republic was pro-
portionately only slightly above that attained in other Soviet republics,
the increases in agricultural and industrial production recorded in
Moldavia remained insignificant in relation to those recorded for the
Soviet Union as a whole. In 1964 they still represented less than 1 and
0.5 percent respectively for agriculture and industry.[34] More significant for the purposes of this essay are the demographic and cultural-

political statistics related to the Romanian population of the Moldavian Republic.

The census figures for 1959 indicated that virtually no change had occurred in the demographic composition of the Moldavian Republic since 1941.[35] "Moldavians" (Romanians) represented slightly over 65 percent of the total population in both years. The percentage of Ukrainians had declined by approximately 2 percent between 1941 and 1959 (from 16.4 to 14.6) while that of Russians increased from 6.0 to 10.2 percent. Only minor fluctuations were registered with respect to the other "coinhabiting nationalities." Significantly, representation in the Moldavian Communist Party was in inverse proportion to the national configuration of the republic. Thus, only 1.3 percent of the Moldavian population belonged to the party in contrast to 7.3 percent of the Russian, 3.8 percent of the Ukrainian, 13.3 percent for the Belorussians, and 4.5 percent of the Jews. With the exception of the Gagauzy—1 percent of whom were members of the party—the Moldavian percentage was the lowest. An analysis of the composition of the party's Central Committee between 1952 and 1954 also reveals the preponderance of Russians and Ukrainians, who represented over 70 percent of the total membership.[36]

The lack of significant Romanian representation in the party may be ascribed in part to the predominantly agrarian nature of the Moldavian population of the republic. However, such an explanation would be inadequate since the percentage of Romanian industrial workers in Moldavia was larger than that of other nationalities, and that of technocrats was reputedly numerically equal to that of the Russians and nearly twice as large as the Ukrainians. In fact, it would appear that even prior to 1964, when the Russo-Romanian conflict became a matter of public record, the Russian political leadership was pursuing a policy of political containment of the Romanian population of Moldavia, if not one of actual de-Romanization.

In the absence of hard facts that would permit one to determine the evolution of Soviet internal policies directed against the Romanian majority in Moldavia, it is necessary to rely on such statistical data as have been provided by the Moldavian regime. In the area of cultural activities, for instance, the percentage of books published in "Moldavian" decreased from 75 percent to 49 percent between 1950 and 1964, that of periodicals from 60 percent to 52 percent, and that of newspapers from 65 percent to 48 percent. In education the decline in the number of schools that use Moldavian as the language of primary instruction has been comparable.[37] The official rationale for the decline of cultural and educational activities in the Moldavian language was provided by the first secretary of the Moldavian party, I. I. Bodyul, at

the Twenty-second Congress of the CPSU in 1961, when he ascribed
to the Moldavians a desire for amalgamation with the coinhabiting
nationalities at the expense of the maintenance of a Romanian identity.
To what extent Bodyul's contentions that "since olden time the Moldavian people have gravitated toward Russia and the Russian people" and
that "despite long isolation of a large part of the population from its
motherland, the Moldavian people did not forget the Russian language
and lovingly preserved common traditions" had any validity in fact
does not deserve serious consideration.[38] But his claims are significant in terms of the policy of denationalization of the Moldavians
and the reasons for it.

THE MOLDAVIAN REPUBLIC AND
SOVIET-ROMANIAN TENSIONS IN THE 1960s

In part, Bodyul's statements reflect continuing official apprehension over the low level of political education and bourgeois nationalistic
manifestations of the Moldaviasn. Constant criticism of the improper
ideological orientation of the Romanian-speaking peasantry and intellectuals has been a recurrent feature of all congresses, plenary sessions, and lesser meetings of the Moldavian party since 1949. But a
new dimenstion became apparent at the Twenty-second Congress: the
fear of divisive nationalist manifestations within the Soviet bloc, the
socialist camp, and the Soviet Union proper. Bodyul's remarks on the
Moldavians' historic aspirations were prefaced by a lengthy attack on
Albanian nationalism and deviationism and a covert one on the Romanians and Chinese. The omission of Romania from the list of "fraternal
socialist countries" condemning the Albanian heresies was in all likelihood not inadvertent. Nor did Bodyul invoke Lenin's view "that under
socialism nations would draw together and their friendship would grow
stronger" (with which he prefaced his remarks on the pro-Russian
sentiments of the Moldavians) for oratorical effect alone.[39] At the
least, his statements, when read in conjunction with Khrushchev's and
those of other Soviet leaders, were indicative of the Kremlin's determination to avert, if not actually correct, nationalist deviations in the
Soviet Union and prevent the possible internationalization of such tendencies by parties (and states) fraternal not only to the CPSR but also
to coinhabiting nationalities of the USSR.

Whether one agrees with the view that the Romanian party's
opposition to Khrushchev's internationalism and its effects on the
"Romanian road to socialism" may be traced to 1954 or somewhat
later, it is evident that a visible breach between the Russian and

Romanian views on socialist unity and the relationship between the
Kremlin and Bucharest occurred at the Romanian party's Third Congress in 1960.[40] By 1961 the Romanian leaders, headed by Gheorghiu-
Dej, had challenged the Kremlin's claims to supremacy in the socialist
camp and had tacitly endorsed the validity of the basic Chinese and
Albanian positions regarding the rights of individual members of the
camp. The Twenty-second Congress of the CPSU crystallized the
Romanian stand in defense of individual parties' rights to chart their
own countries' road to socialism. The doctrine of Romanian national
communism was de facto formulated in October 1961 at the time of
Bodyul's statements on the Moldavian population.[41]

Nevertheless, it is impossible to draw more than inferences
from the debates, speeches, and other materials published in the USSR
and Romania at that time regarding an organic relationship between
Russian policies in Moldavia and Romanian policies in Romania and
vis-a-vis the Soviet Union. Isolated instances of actions that became
more evident after 1961, and particularly after the explicit formulation
of a Romanian doctrine toward the USSR and Moldavia in 1964, were
observed as early as 1955. Thus, in 1955 the official Moldavian radio
and press announced plans for the relocation of Moldavian peasants
in the "virgin lands" of Kazakhstan. Small numbers of "young Moldavian volunteers" were reported to have actually left for these lands.[42]
Similar announcements were made in 1957 and again in 1960. It is
possible that these moves were motivated by factors immediately
related to Khrushchev's agricultural utopia and were in fact unrelated
to any specific nationality policies affecting the Moldavians as such.
By the same token, the reported mobility of Moldavians after the
Twenty-second Congress also may be related to policies of homogenization affecting all coinhabiting nationalities.[43] However, by 1964
the interrelationship between Soviet internal and foreign policies and
Moldavian and Romanian factors had become a matter of record.

In 1964 the Romanian Communist Party overtly challenged Soviet
supremacy in the camp and defended the right of individual Communist
parties and states to complete sovereignty. These concepts, spelled
out in detail in the celebrated Statement of April 1964, were evoked
in response to Russian pressures directed against the Romanian party
and the Romanian state.[44] The principal leverage used by Moscow to
force Gheorghiu-Dej and his associates into compliance with Soviet
policies vis-a-vis members of the camp, particularly China, was to
reopen the territorial questions related to Transylvania and Bessarabia.
It is not certain whether the Kremlin's actions were in response to
Mao Tse'tung's statement of July 10, which specifically included
Bessarabia among the territories illegally seized by the Soviet Union,
or whether they were prompted by Romania's disloyal "neutrality" in

the Sino-Soviet conflict. But it is known that Khrushchev stated to a top-level Romanian delegation present in Moscow at the time of Mao's statement that the Soviet Union was willing to conduct a plebiscite in Moldavia if Bucharest was prepared to permit similar action in Transylvania.[45] Khrushchev's confidence was apparently based on evidence of total Moldavian commitment to the Soviet Union as submitted by Moldavian officials and the Moldavian press. The immediate Romanian reply is unknown, but data released a few months after the July confrontation would indicate that the Romanians were indeed interested in reopening the Bessarabian question either because of the Kremlin's position with respect to Transylvania or because of the change of rulers in Moscow following Khrushchev's political demise. In December 1964, only two months after the reiteration of what were then standard Soviet theses regarding the history and aspirations of the Moldavians, a highly inflammatory tract entitled "Karl Marx—Notes on the Romanians" was published under the imprimatur of the Romanian Academy of Sciences. The seizures of Bessarabia in 1812 and 1878 were condemned and the legitimacy of the historical theses regarding the Romanian character of Bessarabia were defended—all in Marx's own words.[46]

The Soviet reaction to this thinly disguised "provocation" reflected Moscow's concern with the Romanian challenge and its impact in the Moldavian Republic. In the summer of 1965 Brezhnev demanded and secured from Gheorghiu-Dej's successor, Nicolae Ceausescu, formal reiteration of Romania's acceptance of the frontiers established at the end of World War II.[47] Apparently unconvinced of the sincerity of Ceausescu's guarantees, the Kremlin and the leadership of the Moldavian party next engaged in a systematic campaign of denunciation of nationalist phenomena in Moldavia and of further revision of the doctrine of voluntary association with Russia by Moldavians past and present. The Russian positions were most explicitly stated by Bodyul in an article published in November 1965. Aside from reiterating the Moldavians' specific desire to become part of Russia, and the Moldavians' further aspiration to become "just one of the Soviet peoples," Bodyul makes a claim for Russian and Moldavian unity based on a common Cyrillic alphabet and a common rejection of the "distortions voiced by those who utter lies about the ancient ties between the Moldavian and Russian peoples."[48]

At the Twelfth Congress of the Moldavian Communist Party held in March 1966, Bodyul went a step further in accusing Romania of seeking revision of the results of World War II and of conducting nationalist propaganda through radio and television programs beamed into the Moldavian Republic.[49]

The Romanians' reaction was as direct as the Russians' action. In May 1966 Ceausescu denounced the Ribbentrop-Molotov agreement with respect to Bessarabia and northern Bukovina and, by obvious implication, the Russian theses with respect to the history and aspirations of the Moldavians.[50] The Russian riposte was not long in coming. A series of articles published in the Moldavian press restated the fundamental Russian theses, and the Kremlin's reaction assumed other forms as well.

At the plenum of the Central Committee of the CPSU held in September 1965 it was decided to accelerate the industrialization of the Moldavian Republic at the expense of agricultural production.[51] Although it is possible that the decision was motivated by purely economic considerations, in all likelihood this was not the case. It is noteworthy that as early as March 1965 the agrarian policies of the Kremlin were distinctly discriminatory with respect to Moldavia. At the March Plenum of the CPSU the Moldavian Republic alone of all Union republics was denied the benefit of securing increased purchase prices for grain crops. Inasmuch as the overwhelming majority of the Romanian population of the republic was engaged in agriculture, it may be assumed that one of the purposes of the decision was to drive Romanian peasants into other forms of economic activity or to induce their relocation elsewhere in the Soviet Union.[52] In the absence of statistical data, it is difficult to confirm rumors and heresay evidence that a substantial part of the Romanian peasantry was indeed forced out of Moldavia. Statistical information, however, is available to prove that the number of Romanians in industrial production in the Moldavian Republic has remained virtually unchanged since the decision to speed up industrialization while the influx of non-Romanian specialists in industry and corollary economic activities from other republics has gained momentum since September 1965. Concurrent migration of Romanian industrial workers and technocrats to newly developed centers in Siberia has been reported by foreign observers, but no hard evidence to that effect has been supplied by official Soviet sources.[53]

The process of homogenization of the coinhabiting nationalities in Moldavia and the relocation of workers and technocrats in industry and agriculture on a Unionwide basis has been acknowledged by Bodyul on several occasions and, in fact, has become a standard political argument against "nationalist" manifestations in the Moldavian Republic. It provided the basis for the first secretary's request that "the colloquial Moldavian language" be made closer to the literary Moldavian language taught in schools. The literary language, according to Bodyul, revealed the similarities between Moldavian and Russian more clearly.[54] The Russification of the language of the republic in general was given further legitimacy by Bodyul on the occasion of the plenum

of the Moldavian party, held in February 1967 preparatory to the
fiftieth anniversary of the October Revolution. At that time, he repeated
all previous contentions in matters historical and political and introduced a new rationale for Soviet policies in Moldavia—the knowledge
of the present and "future generations" of Romanians that "their
fathers did not conceive a life for themselves outside of Russia."[55]

The effect of various measures adopted in 1965 and the ensuing
years with respect to the Moldavian Republic cannot be fully assessed
at this time. The lack of statistical data, demographic, economic, and
cultural, precludes positive statements. So does the lull in Russo-
Romanian polemics on Bessarabia that followed the Czechoslovak
crisis of August 1968. However, in view of the continuing pressure
exerted by the Soviet Union on Romania since August 1968, including
the massing of troops at the Moldavian border and the possibility of
military action by way of the Moldavian Republic, at least a modicum
of credence must be given to reports in the non-Russian and non-
Romanian press. These reports emphasize the economic gains recorded in Moldavia and the de-Romanization of the republic in line with
the Soviet policy of redistribution of the population throughout the
USSR on the basis of occupational skills rather than nationality. To
what extent the Soviet policy toward Moldavia is motivated by conflict
with the Romanian Socialist Republic or by fear of disloyalty on the
part of the Romanian inhabitants of Moldavia is a matter of conjecture.
Reports in the foreign press immediately after the military crisis of
the summer of 1968 make no mention of the attitude of the Romanian
inhabitants of Moldavia when Soviet tanks and troops were moving
toward the Romanian frontier. It may thus only be assumed that at
least part of the population may have been apprehensive about the fate
of relatives in Romanian Moldavia.

It would be exaggerated to presume that the relationship between
Soviet Moldavia and Romanian Moldavia is comparable with that
between East and West Germany, for instance, or, for that matter,
that Soviet policy in the Moldavian Republic is comparable to Soviet
policy in East Germany. The Soviet Union does not fear the possibility
of reunification of Soviet and Romanian Moldavia into a Greater Socialist Romania; nor is it too concerned by the threat of subversion of
Soviet Moldavia by Romanian propaganda emanating from Bucharest or
Iasi. But the Kremlin and the leaders of Soviet Moldavia seem anxious
to solidify their control over the Moldavian Republic and provide at
the same time a historic rationale for the existence of a marginally
viable political entity. Consolidation and rationalization are to a considerable extent a function of Soviet-Romanian relations. In that
respect, Soviet policy differs little from the tsarist policy of prerevolutionary days. Russian imperialism and Romanian nationalism also
differ in form more than in substance from earlier prototypes. So do

Russian policies toward the historic regions comprising the Moldavian Soviet Socialist Republic. All told, Soviet Moldavia may not be the weakest link in the Soviet chain but it is probably the most artificial, considering the historical circumstances of its formation and its questionable claim to a separate ethnic identity.

NOTES

1. The most comprehensive, if not necessarily objective, study on the Moldavian Republic is Istoriia Moldavskoi SSR (History of the Moldavian SSR) (Kishinev: Historical Institute of the Moldavian Academy of Sciences, 1968), vol. 2. The best analysis of factors leading to the establishment of the republic in 1924, although also lacking in objectivity, is Charles Upton Clark, Bessarabia (New York, 1927), pp. 239ff.

2. The most reliable statistical data for that period are provided in Antony Babel, La Bessarabie: Etude Historique, Ethnographique et Economique (Paris, 1926), pp. 198-233.

3. For the Soviet position, see J. Okhotnikov and N. Batchinsky, La Bessarabie et la Paix Europeenne (Paris, 1927), which comprises a substantial collection of Russian documents made available to the so-called "Association des Emigres Bessarabiens," which sponsored publication of the volume.

4. A comprehensive discussion of this problem will be found in R. W. Seton-Watson, History of the Roumanians (Cambridge, 1934), pp. 346ff. See also Stephen Fischer-Galati, "Roumanian Nationalism," in Peter F. Sugar and Ivo J. Lederer, eds., Nationalism in Eastern Europe (Seattle, 1969), pp. 390ff.

5. Although very brief, the clearest statement is by Henry L. Roberts, Romania: Political Problems of an Agrarian State (New Haven, 1951), pp. 32ff.

6. See Andrei Popovici, The Political Status of Bessarabia (Washington, D. C., 1931), pp. 121ff.; Clark, Bessarabia, pp. 158ff.

7. Clark, Bessarabia, pp. 151-57.

8. Okhotnikov and Batchinsky, La Bessarabie, pp. 44ff.

9. Clark, Bessarabia, pp. 155-57.

10. For the text of the treaty, see Popovici, The Political Status, pp. 251-55.

11. Clark, Bessarabia, pp. 239ff. provides a standard account of these events. For the Russian version, see Okhotnikov and Batchinsky, La Bessarabie, pp. 133ff.

12. Clark, Bessarabia, pp. 249ff.

13. Ibid., pp. 277ff.

14. Ibid., pp. 279ff.

15. Contradictory views are expressed in ibid., pp. 261-76, and Okhotnikov and Batchinsky, La Bessarabie, pp. 70ff., 149-53.

16. The most detailed account of the history and problems of the Romanian Communist Party during that period is Ghita Ionescu, Communism in Romania, 1944-1962 (London, 1964).

17. For a brief account, see Walter Kolarz, Russia and Her Colonies (London, 1956), pp. 149-52.

18. A detailed factual statement will be found in the informative, if not always impartial, study by C. Cioranescu, et al., Aspects des Relations Russo-Roumaines (Paris, 1967), pp. 165ff.

19. Ibid., p. 168.

20. Ionescu, Communism, pp. 71ff., 126ff.

21. Stephen Fischer-Galati, The New Romania: From People's Democracy to Socialist Republic (Cambridge, Mass., 1967), pp. 17ff.; consult in conjunction with Ionescu, Communism, pp. 151-56.

22. Pravda, February 11, 1949, contains a detailed summary of the proceedings.

23. Pravda, October 11 and 12, 1949.

24. Pravda, October 12, 1949.

25. See article by G. Rud, chairman of the Moldavian Council of Ministers, in Izvestiia, September 3, 1950.

26. Pravda, April 4, 1950.

27. Pravda, September 7, 1952.

28. Ibid.

29. Four new regions were created within the framework of the Moldavian Republic (Beltsy, Kagul, Tirasopol, and Kishinev), ostensibly to "secure better operational supervision over the life of the districts of the republic." Pravda, March 22, 1952.

30. Statistical data will be found in Merle Fainsod, How Russia is Ruled (Cambridge, Mass., 1953), p. 234; for comparative purposes, see T. H. Rigby, Communist Party Membership in the U.S.S.R., 1917-1967 (Princeton, N. J., 1968), p. 381.

31. Fischer-Galati, The New Romania, pp. 38-43.

32. Pravda, September 23, 1952.

33. Pravda, October 8, 1952.

34. For detailed statistical data, see Cioranescu, et al., Aspects, Tables A and B following p. 256.

35. Ibid., table following p. 246.

36. Rigby, Communist Party Membership, p. 381.

37. See Cioranescu, et al., Aspects, Table F following p. 254.

38. Pravda, October 27, 1961.

39. Ibid.

40. Fischer-Galati, The New Romania, pp. 57ff., 78-81.

41. Ibid., pp. 81ff.

42. Sovetskaia Moldaviia (Soviet Moldavia), March 31, 1955.

43. Cioranescu, et al., Aspects, pp. 196ff.

44. The text of the statement in English is available in William E. Griffith, Sino-Soviet Relations, 1964-1965 (Cambridge, Mass., 1967), pp. 269-96.

45. Fischer-Galati, The New Romania, pp. 99ff.

46. Karl Marx, Insemnari despre Romani (Notes on the Romanians) (Bucharest, 1964). For an accurate summary of the Romanian arguments, see Cioranescu, et al., Aspects, pp. 220ff.

47. Scinteia (The spark), September 12, 1965.

48. I. I. Bodyul, "May the Friendship of Soviet Peoples Grow Stronger and Flourish," Sovetskaia Moldaviia, November 23 and 24, 1965.

49. Sovetskaia Moldaviia, March 2, 1966.

50. Scinteia, May 7, 1966.

51. A detailed summary of these decisions as they affected the Moldavian Republic was published in Sovetskaia Moldaviia, February 20, 1966.

52. Pravda, March 27, 1965.

53. Cioranescu, et al., Aspects, pp. 211ff.

54. Sovetskaia Moldaviia, November 28, 1965.

55. Sovetskaia Moldaviia, February 16, 1967.

ZYGMUNT BAUMAN is Professor of Sociology and head of the Department of Sociology at the University of Leeds. Until 1968 he held the chair of general sociology at the University of Warsaw and from 1968 to 1971 was Professor of Sociology at Tel Aviv. His works in English include Between Class and Elite, Culture as Praxis, Socialism: The Active Utopia, and Toward Critical Sociology.

YAROSLAV BILINSKY is Professor of Political Science at the University of Delaware. He earned his B.A. at Harvard College and his Ph.D. at Princeton University. He is the author of The Second Soviet Republic: The Ukraine After World War II and many other monographs and articles on Soviet nationality policies and Ukrainian nationalism.

DEMING BROWN is Professor of Slavic Languages and Literature at the University of Michigan and was Chairman of the department from 1957 to 1961. He received his B.A. and M.A. from the University of Washington and earned his Ph.D. at Columbia Univeristy. He is the author of Soviet Attitudes Toward American Writing and numerous articles on contemporary Russian prose and poetry.

STEPHEN FISCHER-GALATI is Professor of History and Director of the Center for Slavic and East European Studies at the University of Colorado. He received his A.B., M.A., and Ph.D. from Harvard University. He is the author of numerous books and articles on Romania and Eastern Europe including Twentieth Century Romania, Man, State and Society in East European History, and The New Rumania: From People's Democracy to Socialist Republic.

ZVI Y. GITELMAN is Associate Professor of Political Science at the University of Michigan. He received his A.B., M.A., and Ph.D. from Columbia University. He is the author of Jewish Nationality and Soviet Politics, as well as many articles on political change and political power in East Europe.

LEON SMOLINSKI is Professor of Economics at Boston College and an Associate of the Russian Research Center, Harvard University. He received his M.A. from the University of Cincinnati and his Ph.D. from Columbia University.

ROMAN SZPORLUK is Professor of History at the University of Michigan. He holds a Master of Jurisprudence degree from Maria Curie-Sklodowska University in Lublin, Poland, a Bachelor of Letters from Nuffield College, Oxford, and a Ph.D. from Stanford University. He is the editor and cotranslator of Russia in World History: Selected

Essays by M. N. Pokrovskii, and author of a number of articles on Soviet nationality problems.

V. STANLEY VARDYS is Professor of Political Science and Chairman of the Russian Studies Committee at the University of Oklahoma. He received his B.A. from Carroll College, Helena, Montana, and his M.A. and Ph.D. from the University of Wisconsin. He is the editor and coauthor of _Lithuania Under the Soviets_, editor of _Karl Marx: Scientist? Revolutionary? Humanist?_, and author of numerous articles on Soviet nationality policies and the Baltic peoples.

ENVIRONMENTAL DETERIORATION IN THE
SOVIET UNION AND EASTERN EUROPE
edited by Ivan Volgyes

MODERNIZATION IN ROMANIA SINCE WORLD
WAR II
Trond Gilberg

MULTINATIONAL CORPORATIONS AND EAST
EUROPEAN SOCIALIST ECONOMIES
Geza P. Lauter and
Paul M. Dickie

PERSONAL AND SOCIAL CONSUMPTION IN
EASTERN EUROPE: Poland, Czechoslovakia,
Hungary, and East Germany
Bogdan Mieczkowski

POLITICAL SOCIALIZATION IN EASTERN EUROPE:
A Comparative Framework
edited by Ivan Volgyes

POLITICS IN THE GERMAN DEMOCRATIC
REPUBLIC
John M. Starrels and
Anita M. Mallinckrodt

THE POLITICS OF MODERNIZATION IN EASTERN
EUROPE: Testing the Soviet Model
edited by Charles Gati,
with introductory essays by
Vernon V. Aspaturian and
Cyril E. Black

SOCIAL CHANGE AND STRATIFICATION IN
EASTERN EUROPE: An Interpretive Analysis
of Poland and Her Neighbors

Alexander Matejko
foreword by Seymour Lipset